Dutch Civilisation in the Seventeenth Century

AND OTHER ESSAYS

J. H. HUIZINGA

Dutch Civilisation
in the
Seventeenth
Century

and other essays

SELECTED BY
PIETER GEYL AND
F. W. N. HUGENHOLTZ
TRANSLATED BY
ARNOLD J. POMERANS

FREDERICK UNGAR PUBLISHING CO.
NEW YORK

Printed in the United States of America
Library of Congress Catalog Card No. 68-22778

Foreword

A few years ago the late Professor Geyl asked me to join him in selecting some of Johan Huizinga's essays for translation into English. The centrepiece of the collection was to be *Dutch Civilisation in the Seventeenth Century*, a work which reveals a profound insight into the special character of the Golden Age of the United Provinces, so different from cultural achievements elsewhere on the continent. This work, and his essays on the *Spirit of the Netherlands* and on the position of the Netherlands between Western and Central European cultural influences, represent the best and most typical of Huizinga's writings on his own country.

Huizinga's approach to historical theory is most brilliantly revealed in his piece on Spengler and H. G. Wells—*Two Wrestlers with the Angel*—an essay which is important both for its theme and for what it reveals of Huizinga's intellectual stature.

Similarly, how Huizinga developed into the eminent author of *The Waning of the Middle Ages* and of the many important studies on Renaissance problems is shown by the autobiographical essay *My Path to History* and by his inaugural lecture, in which he made clear his basic ideas about history.

The death of Professor Geyl, himself both an admirer and a severe critic of Huizinga, is the sad cause of my signing this Foreword alone.

F. W. N. Hugenholtz

Contents

Dutch Civilisation in the Seventeenth Century[1]

I

Were we to test the average Dutchman's knowledge of life in the Netherlands during the seventeenth century, we should probably find that it is largely confined to odd stray notions gleaned from paintings. True, one or two will have read Vondel or Hooft, or even Spinoza, and few will have forgotten all they were taught at school about our great leaders, sailors and the servants of the East India Company, but their recollections of political and historical events are likely to be hazy. Moreover, what they lack in general knowledge they but rarely make good with any real appreciation of the work of our great masters, let alone of those twin treasure-houses of art and history combined: drawing and engraving.

Had we applied the same test a century ago, in the age of Potgieter and Jacob van Lennep, the results would have been quite different: in 1840, knowledge of history, in the ordinary political sense of the word, was far greater than it is today. Literature, too, was much better known, if only by its greatest works. Art, on the other hand, played a far less important part in nineteenth-century man's historical vista than it does in ours. Here we come up against an intellectual transformation that was not confined to our country alone: as more and more visual material for the appreciation of the past became quite generally available, so thinking and writing about the past fell into increasing

[1]First published by H. Tjeenk Willink & Zoon, Haarlem, 1941.

neglect. In what follows, we shall try to eschew the one-sided aesthetic view of today as much as the one-sided political approach of the last century, and look at civilisation in the widest possible context.

Though Dutch civilisation in the seventeenth century is a thing of the past, and hence intangible, it was so full of life that we can hardly think of it as an abstraction. In order to grasp it more fully, we cannot do better than start from that mainspring of all historical knowledge: our perpetual astonishment that the past was once a living reality. In the case of the Netherlands, this amazement is particularly great. How was it possible, we ask, that so small and relatively remote a country as the young Republic should nevertheless have been so advanced politically, economically and culturally? We can see why Athens and Florence, Rome and Paris should, in their time, have all been centres of culture, but it seems incredible that their mantle should have fallen, for however brief a time, on a small water-logged country between the Ems and Vlie and the Maas and Scheldt.

Nor does this peculiar phenomenon exhaust our wonder. For it leads us directly to another marvel: where else was there a civilisation that reached its greatest peak so soon after state and nation came into being? It must be remembered that a hundred, indeed only fifty years before Rembrandt's birth, there was no Dutch nation in the sense in which we here speak of it. Even while the passionate strains of national unity were being sounded by the Sea Beggars, Prince William of Orange was still trying diligently, and without much hope of success, to discover the form best suited to the Dutch state. He did not live to see it born, and no one in the anxious years of 1584-1588 could have told what lay in store for the Netherlands. And then, there it suddenly was, a new state, built on the shaky foundations of the Union of Utrecht, a torso of the rich Low Countries

which Burgundy had joined together and which Charles V
had possessed.

The young commonwealth still faced the urgent and seem-
ingly hopeless task of armed liberation. For many years
its chances of survival were to hinge on the capture of such
small towns as Breda, Delfzijl, Geertruidenberg, Nijmegen,
Zutfen, and Groningen. And all that while our sailors were
venturing further and further into polar regions and into
India, with the result that the trade of Amsterdam and the
volume of shipping in the towns round the Zuiderzee grew
daily, while state and nation gradually took shape. Far too
narrow a shape, you might say, if you are the kind who
disagrees with history. However, it remains a fact that
glorious Brabant and fierce Flanders could contribute little
more to the Republic than the national fervour of the refugees and later, much later, the fragments of land that the
Republic conquered by force of arms—a fact we may deplore, but one that we can never alter. The Republic became a separate state and its people a nation apart. And
onto its small stage there now crowded, within less than a
century of its birth, a pageant of great deeds and distinguished figures: statesmen, generals, sailors, painters, poets
and scholars, and founders of commercial empires. Can you
point to another nation that reached its cultural peak so
soon after its creation?

Our astonishment would be somewhat tempered were we
to find that, in the seventeenth century, Dutch culture was
merely the most perfect and clearest expression of European
culture in general. But such was not the case. On the contrary, lying though it did between France, Germany and
England, our country differed so greatly from them and in
so many respects, that it proved the exception and not the
rule.

It has become quite the thing to stamp the kind of civilisation Europe enjoyed in the seventeenth century with the
title of 'Baroque'. Stamp is the right word, and the unfor-

tunate thing is that such impressions so rarely rub off. This applies equally well to 'Renaissance', 'Gothic' (which, of course, has very little to do with the Goths), and 'Romantic'—all of them devices for hiding our incomprehension under a veil of sonorous words. They help us to sustain the illusion that we can survey a historical period as a whole, grasp the nexus between isolated events, while, at best, we can have no more than the vaguest suspicion that this unity, this nexus really exists. However, the terms have become common coin and can no longer be withdrawn from circulation—the only question is what are they really worth? The use of the word 'Baroque' in its modern, very general sense is actually a sign of failure, and if we nevertheless use it here it is because we believe that, vague though it may be, it is better than nothing at all.

Now, what pictures are conjured up by the word 'Baroque', as it is applied to the style and essence of the seventeenth century, depends on whether we are thinking of early or of late Baroque. For while early Baroque went hand in hand with a generous wealth of forms and ideas, with the colourful vitality of a Goltzius engraving or a play by Bredero or Ben Jonson—in short the very qualities linking it to the Renaissance, from which it followed without any sharp break—the term 'Baroque' only becomes meaningful when we contrast it with the Renaissance. Now if we do that, we shall find a revival of rigid and exclusive formulae, of the subordination of detail to the needs of the whole. The urge to conform was one of the strongest impulses of the seventeenth century, be it in doctrine, manners, painting or prosody. Pomp and circumstance, theatrical gestures, strict rules and a closed system were the aims, obedient reverence for church and state the ideal. While acknowledging the monarchy as the divinely chosen form of government, each region subscribed to the principle of unrestricted autonomy and self-interest. Grandiloquence went hand in hand with etiquette. Ostentation was the order of the day. The renewed faith found its expression in the canvases of Rubens, the Spanish painters, and Bernini.

This conception of the Baroque, imperfect though it is, fits in fairly well with our general picture of Papal and Venetian Italy, of the England of William Laud and the Cavaliers, and of France at the beginning of its *grand siècle*. But does it also fit our picture of Dutch culture in the seventeenth century? Indeed, there is one figure whom it fits almost perfectly, namely Vondel; but for the rest it does not apply in the least. A landscape by Ruisdael or Van Goyen, a genre piece by Jan Steen, a Civic Guard by Frans Hals or Van der Helst, and the most characteristic work of Rembrandt—all of them breathe a completely different spirit, sound an entirely different note. In fact, in its essentials, the Netherlands of the seventeenth century bore only the slightest resemblance to contemporary France, Italy or Germany. Neither their rigid style and pretentious gestures nor their great pomp is characteristic of our country.

This brings us to the heart of our purpose: the nature of Dutch culture in the seventeenth century. If our civilisation was, indeed, distinct, then the distinction must have sprung from the material, social and ethical conditions, under which it matured. However, these factors alone will never suffice to explain the differences—historical phenomena cannot be resolved in the same way as natural processes; at best we may grasp them more or less vaguely as such. The most essential aspects of an historical phenomenon will forever elude all our attempts to derive them from social, economic, political or intellectual causes. The historian, in the final analysis, rarely knows causes, and must base his opinions or conclusions on the known effects and circumstances. Now it is these we intend to examine in this brief essay.

The most fundamental circumstance, quite literally speaking, is, of course, the geographical situation, and the structure and nature of our country. Once again we meet an astonishing fact—that so small an area, and one, moreover, that did not even constitute a geographical unit, an area made up of moors, grass-land, watery reaches and fields, should not only have turned state and nation in so brief a space of time, but should also have developed a unique culture—one that radiated across much of Europe and constitutes a highlight in the spirit of the age.

In order to realise how extremely small a geographical area was, in fact, involved in this cultural advance, we must remember that not all regions of the Republic contributed to it in equal measure. The share of the Generality-Lands, of Brabant, Zealand-Flanders, Maastricht and the Overmaas district, for instance, was very small indeed. As provinces without a voice in the Union, governed from The Hague and cut off from the centre by religious differences, they pursued their rural life in increasing isolation. Although they remained closer than the North to the Spanish South, this proximity profited them little; though they spoke the same tongue, they played as good as no part in the flourishing cultural and political life of the Republic, nor did they share in the advantages of trade or industry.

Moreover, not even the Seven Provinces of the Union made equal contributions, for can any province other than Holland, Zeeland and Utrecht really be said to have furthered the culture, greatness and glory of the Netherlands as a whole? Though we, who are attached by ties of memory, kinship and love to all parts of our country, cannot forget the beauty and goodness of incomparable Friesland, noble Guelders, the prosperous and pious medieval towns on the Ijsel, we must remember that, seen from Holland itself, the Republic looked like a flimsy embroidery round a strong and colourful central pattern. The Hollander and Zeelander knew little of their eastern and northern cousins. The Frisians were probably the closest to them, for in Friesland lay the Stadholder's Court as a visible token of the glory of the House of Orange. Groningen with its lush and boggy surroundings seemed a remote and backward region, and this despite its university. To the south of Groningen lay the vast moors of Drente barely touched by the centuries, then lonely and humble Overijsel, the Veluwe and finally Het Gooi, a long strip dividing the rest from the heart of the country. Again even Utrecht and Zeeland failed to make a contribution in any way comparable to that of rich and mighty Holland. Truly, Dutch civilisation ← in Rembrandt's day was concentrated in a region not much more than sixty miles square. That this cultural concentration occurred just there and just then remains a most remarkable fact.

We are used to mentioning shipping and the proximity of the sea as the first and foremost factors in this extraordinary development. And rightly so. From the time that this region first appeared in historical records, there has also comm. been mention of a race of seafaring men. Even earlier than the Frisians, the Caninefates, whom most of us will remember from our schooldays, were renowned sailors; by the fourteenth century, Holland and Zeeland had become maritime powers, whose ships rendered the King of England excellent service. A century later, the commercial influence of the towns of Holland and Zeeland had grown to considerable proportions; at the same time their naval power could be underpinned with the political might of the Dukes of Burgundy, so much so that they became serious rivals to the Hanseatic League. It is unnecessary to examine the rise of navigation more closely; it follows from the very position of the two provinces: across the sea from England and neighbouring on Northern Germany and France. However, it should be remembered that in the late Middle Ages, the Zuiderzee certainly contributed as much as the North Sea to the development of Dutch shipping: the water-way from North Germany to Flanders followed a regular network of inland channels.

It may even be argued that these inland waters played a

more important part in the rise of our country than the sea. Where else could you have found a similar system of natural communications, a complete network of veins and arteries, as it were? On rivers and canals large and small, all inter-communicating by means of countless branches, you could cross the length and breadth of the country under sail, or with oars and tow-ropes, safely, comfortably and—at a time when the horse represented the utmost in pulling power and roads were bad or non-existent—with comparative speed. This hydrographic structure of our country was partly re-flected in the democratic structure of our people. A country divided by watercourses such as ours must needs have a considerable measure of regional autonomy, and it was no mere chance that, while such ancient offices as alderman, bailiff, etc., were transformed or disappeared with time, that of dike-reeve was preserved unchanged. The poorest peasant or fisherman, no less than the greatest gentleman, could travel about our country in his own boat, albeit he often chose roundabout routes so as to avoid the tollman or other obstacles to his progress. Though our moors resounded with the hooves of hunters, noble carriages played no great part in our daily traffic, and the social importance of the nobility was, for that very reason, much smaller here than abroad. Because the Netherlands bordered on three large expanses of water—the Wadden, Zuider and North Seas—and constituted the delta of three rivers—the Rhine, the Maas and the Scheldt—it was destined to become and re-main a country of sailors, fishermen, traders, and farmers. Now the life of sailors and traders is largely an urban one; and the Netherlands could, in fact, boast important trading centres even before the emergence of medieval towns: Dorestad under the Carolingians, and Tiel in about A.D. 1000. However, their heyday was long past by the time the great developments occurred that gave Flanders its Bruges, Ghent and Ypres, and Germany its flourishing and famous towns in the Rhineland and Westphalia—some, for instance

Cologne (which contained a colony of Roman veterans as early as A.D. 51) built on earlier foundations; others on insignificant, later beginnings. In the twelfth century, when Bruges, Ghent, Louvain and Liége were already mighty towns, urban development in the Northern Netherlands hardly went beyond Utrecht, the only bishopric in the area— not until the thirteenth century did Dordrecht, Middelburg, Haarlem and Leyden become towns of any importance. All of them lay close together, but because each had its own system of waterways and its own hinterland, and also because continuous rivalry between medieval cities was the rule, each succeeded in preserving its special character. When at the end of the Middle Ages, Amsterdam, the youngest of them all, outstripped the rest, it did so under economic conditions that were no longer those of the thirteenth century. And even then, Amsterdam's pre-eminence did not cause any of the others to decline; on the contrary, a group of the very smallest towns, especially in North Holland, could still look forward to their finest hour. By the fifteenth century, Holland was predominently urban and so, to a lesser degree, were Zeeland and Utrecht, and as trade and industry gradually became the main sources of wealth, so culture, too, assumed an increasingly urban aspect. The economy of our leading region was thus based on a multiplicity of small towns crowded together in a small space and leaving by far the largest portion of the land covered by water, heath, fields, and pastures.

Not only did the very lie of the land thus restrict the inordinate expansion of the towns, it also helped to save our country from the evils of extensive landlordism. Even in the rural provinces, where fairly large estates were quite common, they were incomparably smaller than their counterparts in France and Germany. It is a well-known fact that, outside of Guelders and Overijsel, the last vestiges of serfdom had practically disappeared from the Netherlands by the end of the Middle Ages. The predominant system governing the relationship between landlord and peasant was free tenure; indeed, in Groningen and Friesland, many peasants were the 'well-born' possessors of their own patrimony, their own land. In these two provinces the peasants were, moreover, represented as an Estate, thanks largely to the absence of feudal lords who elsewhere wrested the land from them and thus barred them from effective participation in public life. But even in other parts of the country, where the peasantry had lost their vote, they were not necessarily subjected to economic oppression. Where the soil was rich and new territory could be opened up or reclaimed, there were ample opportunities of leasing land on reasonable conditions. Was Ostade very far wrong when he represented the Dutch peasant as a happy-go-lucky and well-fed fellow?

The old landed nobility was, and for the most part remained, simple and patriarchal in outlook, and remarkably lean of purse. Like the old German nobility, it was untitled: you were simply *heer van*, master of, but even the *van* was not a necessary adjunct of landownership, as witness the Schimmelpennincks, Torcks, De Cocqs and so many other families. Though *Jonkheer* and Baron were occasionally used as forms of address, they never became official designations of rank, nor, with one exception, was the title of *Graaf*, Count, bestowed on a Dutch family before 1700—by the Emperor in Vienna. Holland's most important and ancient families had a chequered career. The Arkels died out early on; one branch of the Egmonts produced the Dukes of Guelders, only to disappear again when the Duchy itself lost its independence during the reign of Charles V. Another branch, serving Burgundy in the south, earned the highest honours there, while yet others stayed at home to merge with the nobility of Holland or to lose even that distinction. The Brederodes continued as Holland's leading family until 1653, when their coat of arms was broken over the grave of Johan Wolfert, the last of the line, at Vianen.

The Wassenaars, finally, also remained at home and can be found there to this day. In Zeeland, the Borselens were well on the way to becoming great lords under Burgundy, when their line died out before 1500; other, less prominent, Zeeland familes survived until about 1600.

Thus the power of the nobility in the Republic remained slight, at least as far as Holland and Zeeland were concerned. The clergy, as an Estate, had ceased to exist with the victory of the new faith; in fact, Calvinism could not have spread so quickly had the clerical Estate been more firmly rooted in the first instance. Late in adopting Christianity, and far from the centres of government and the hierarchy, the Northern Netherlands, unlike Liége, Brabant, Flanders and Hainault in the South, never proved fertile ground for a rich and influential class of prelates. From Friesland in the North to the Maas and Scheldt in the South, there was but one diocese, that of Utrecht. The numerous Frisian monasteries attained great spiritual and economic power, as witness the historiographers Emo and Menco in the thirteenth century or the learned cloister Aduard in the fifteenth, yet for all their famous abbots, they were unable to produce any really great men. The diocese of Utrecht could boast only two important monasteries: Egmond and Middelburg, of which only the latter came to play a political part towards the end of the Middle Ages. In time, a host of convents rose up in various towns; the towns on the river Ijsel also built homes for the Brothers of the Common Life and the Windesheim cloister of regular canons, but all these institutions emerged in the late Middle Ages—too late to gain the clergy political power. Had it been otherwise, even the mighty Charles V could not have taken the almost unprecedented step of forcing the bishop of Utrecht to surrender his temporal rule in 1528. Thus in the Netherlands, neither the Reformation nor the later Revolt had to contend with a very strong church, with a host of rich abbeys and powerful prelates: moreover, the Church

19

as a spiritual force had lost too much of its hold on the people to stem the rising tide of the new faith, be it Lutheran, Baptist, Spiritualist or Calvinist.

As a result, the merchants were left as the only economically viable and articulate group at the top. They were not yet rich, but were evenly spread over a large number of towns, especially in Holland and Zeeland. As the power of the nobility waned and that of the old Church collapsed, so the economic predominance of the merchant class was necessarily transformed into political and social predominance as well—the leading merchants became magistrates without, however, severing their connection with trade completely. It is not easy to form a clear picture of this transformation, for we know very little about those magistrates of Dordrecht, Haarlem and Leyden who, in the early fifteenth century, administered the law *consilio et animis*. Only in the course of the sixteenth century do their outlines become less nebulous, and we meet them as highly cultured products of the Chambers of Rhetoric and those cradles of humanism, the Schools of the Modern Devotion. You may call the class to which Pompejus Occo, the later Spieghel and Roemer Visscher belonged and from which the magistrates were recruited, patrician, but not yet a regent class, for it remained an easy matter to enter the charmed circle of those whom Leicester's men mockingly called the 'Sovereign Lords Miller and Cheeseman', even at a time when rich burghers had begun to acquire a kind of quasi-nobility by the purchase of estates. It would be interesting to discover what percentage of the existing manors was acquired by leading citizens in a given province during a given period of the seventeenth century. Such possession did not by itself bestow nobility, although the 'top ten' would often substitute the name of their manor for their own. In the long run, however, the family name won out, even when, in the nineteenth century, its members were ennobled by royal decree. Thus the Zuidpolsbroeks re-

verted to the old family name of De Graeff, and the Hille-
goms or Vromades to the name of Six.

It may seem strange that the Netherlands should have become so prosperous and have paved the way for so great a
civilisation, while engaged in a long and bitter struggle for
freedom. Yet the roots went back many centuries—sea links
with Norway and the Baltic countries and trade with France
and Spain had already brought prosperity to the Netherlands in the late Middle Ages and, towards the end of the
sixteenth century, trade with the Levant and India, and
soon afterwards with Persia and the East Indies, added
further to the country's wealth. Moreover, hostilities did not
altogether disrupt trade and industry. There were many lulls
in the fighting, and the wars were restricted to a small
arena. Nor did the weapons, destructive though they were,
cause devastation on a large scale. In fact, commerce was
never completely disrupted or even seriously disturbed, particularly after 1575, when the Province of Holland rarely
saw the enemy on its own soil. Even the Spanish and
Portuguese threat to Dutch shipping probably produced as
many trading benefits as it brought dangers. Thus by 1596,
when the Republic had only been in existence for some eight
years and Prince Maurice was still busy consolidating the
borders by fortification and battle, Amsterdam was able to
inform the States-General that the volume of Dutch trade
and shipping was far greater than that of England and
France. And yet the commercial might of the Republic was
then only in its infancy.

It might be thought that Dutch economic predominance
was due to the precocious emergence of a sound economic
theory and hence to superior economic planning. This was
certainly not the case. The Netherlands prospered under an
antiquated economic system, one, moreover, that most
neighbouring countries were trying to discard for a more
efficient one. In fact, the Netherlands achieved greatness

under a system of premercantilism and medieval 'liberty'—the kind of freedom that worked to the advantage of a small minority at the expense of everyone else.

When mercantilism proper first made its tentative début in the powerful monarchies of France and England during the late Middle Ages, it was so hedged in fiscal restrictions as to bring few real advantages to trade. But along the remote North Sea coast, where the central authority of the German Emperor had grown extremely slender, an entirely different situation prevailed. Here shipping and trade advanced as opportunity allowed, and opportunity proved consistently favourable, not least because the Hundred Years' War (1338-1453) stunted the economic growth of England and France.

When the various regions of the Netherlands fell into the hands of the Dukes of Burgundy from 1384 to 1428 and came under a central authority for the first time, the new rulers wisely refrained from interfering with a system that had engendered so much prosperity. Only the Austrian emperors, who had far more decided views on economic policy, felt impelled to enforce fiscal measures at the expense of economic freedom, or rather of local independence, even in the Netherlands. Thus Brussels attempted to levy a tax on the Dutch grain trade in 1505. Amsterdam, however, depended for its rapid growth on unrestricted grain trading, and, insisting on its ancient privileges, forced Brussels to revise the taxation proposals time and again and ultimately to abandon them. We need not speculate on the extent to which the Duke of Alva's taxation plans contributed to the outbreak of the Revolt—free trade had by then become so much a part of the Dutch tradition that the country retained the old system of economic decentralisation even after the great struggle against the foreign invader was won. Thus the rich Republic of the Seven Provinces, whose trading empire was the envy of all the other nations, had no laws for controlling the explosive growth of commerce and industry. The States-General had no authority to interfere with economic life although, as the highest public body in the land, it granted charters and trading rights to the East and West Indian companies.

Clearly, therefore, it was not by progressive commercial ideas or superior economic theories that the Dutch became masters of world trade; that they did so was due far more to the absence of state interference. No doubt, the East India Company played a leading role in the rise of joint stock companies but, generally speaking, the Netherlands achieved greatness not by organisation but by the lack of restriction or rather by keeping organisation down to the minimum. This was called 'freedom' in the Middle Ages and, by virtue of it, each region enjoyed autonomy, passed laws for its own benefit, and sought to impose restrictions on outsiders. It was this view of freedom which turned the closure of the Scheldt into a cornerstone of Dutch National policy in 1648. In 1585, the closure had been justified as a desperate war measure against Spanish Antwerp, and Amsterdam grew rich as a result. Even in 1609, when the truce was signed, the closure could still be defended on the grounds that, but for this, the enemy might have had twelve years in which to regain the upper hand. However, after 1635, when Antwerp had grown so weak that she would have fallen like a ripe plum to any invader—that she did not was largely due to the insistence of Amsterdam (the French alliance played strange tricks with the Union) —the closure of the Scheldt ceased to make good sense. But by then, and particularly by 1648, it had become so much a dogma that rescinding it seemed unthinkable.

The absence of competitors was a prime cause of the vast commercial expansion of the Republic—Dutch prosperity went hand in hand with exceptional economic passivity in most other European countries. Clearly, Amsterdam, whose commercial heart was the grain trade, could never have reached the heights it did had Poland, Sweden and

23

Denmark ruled the Baltic with all the power and means at their disposal. Amsterdam chose free trade, not for theoretical reasons—for no such theory existed at the time—but simply because its most immediate interests were best served by continuing along the accustomed paths. Only when the rise of banking in the wake of commerce opened Dutch eyes to the disadvantages of mercantilism, did Amsterdam indeed become the cradle of progressive economic thought, though not yet of scientific economic theories. The Republic may thus be said to have by-passed mercantilism.

Like trade, industry, too, benefited greatly from the absence of central restrictions. In the towns, industrial life was able to develop smoothly within the framework of the old—and in many ways antiquated—guild system, so that crippling restrictions imposed by one town could not seriously hamper the welfare of the rest; outside the towns, industry could grow up in even greater freedom. Now, it was precisely the industries most closely tied to commerce and shipping, namely the manufacture of vinegar, spirits, madder, salt, soap, tar, tow, sugar and tobacco, herring-fishing and the working of wood, stone, iron and other materials that were least affected by municipal and guild restrictions. Moreover, there was no one to interfere with profits or the free movement of labour, or yet with the increasing agricultural prosperity that came with diking and draining and, to a lesser extent, with the cultivation of virgin soil. Even the climate contributed to Dutch prosperity, for without the prevailing west wind the Netherlands would never have become the country of windmills—windmills that pumped more water than they ground grain, and that until recently were so typical of the Dutch landscape. Without windmills, Holland would not be the country of the polders, nor would she have had enough motive power for pursuing her old crafts and many of her newer industries.

There is really no need to add to the obvious reasons for Dutch prosperity in the seventeenth century such hypothetical influences as a capitalistic outlook or a Calvinistic spirit of enterprise—as so many historians did only thirty years ago. Prosperity flowed quite naturally from the medieval system and there was never a point where the old was deliberately shaken off and the new warmly embraced.

Everyone knows how predominant a role the old Province of Holland played in the development of trade, industry and transport. Even Zeeland failed to keep up with her sister maritime province, and the rest of the country lagged far behind—it was less populous, less urban in character, and the soil generally far less fertile. Looked at geographically, the Republic presented a strange pattern: because of the presence of the Zuiderzee and the Frisian Islands in the North, and the mouths of the rivers Maas and Scheldt in the South, the Seven Provinces lacked a continuous shape, let alone a centre and periphery. Even in union, they remained a conglomerate and one, moreover, that became still less cohesive with the subsequent conquest of the so-called Generality-Lands. If one examines the map of the Netherlands with fresh eyes, it looks like a fantasy, a mere whim of history, and shows far better than the map of any other country that the Old, unlike the New World of the American Far West, did not draw its boundaries with compass and ruler.

What is true of the economic structure of the Republic applies equally well to the political system. The State, too, was thoroughly conservative, holding fast to old traditions and established laws. A love of liberty was kept alive, but the concept of political freedom was again that of the Middle Ages: a chain of limited privileges that worked to the disadvantage of all but the few. In short, freedom was no more than exemption from the general law. Only at the time of the Revolt, when the ideas of *patria* and fatherland and even the word 'Netherlands', acquired a halo of glory, did the narrow medieval concept of freedom widen into

25

the idea of common striving and common suffering. This view of freedom may have been far narrower than that which prevailed in the eighteenth century, but it was no less strong and cohesive, for all that.

There is little point in discussing the political structure of the United Provinces in terms of centralisation or decentralisation. For while political power was certainly not centralised, the kind of system formed by the provinces, each claiming full sway over its own affairs, and each with its own social sub-divisions and classes, was in no way typical of decentralisation either. And indeed, what was there to decentralise when there was no centre to begin with? Thus, if a name must needs be given to the political system of the Republic, separatism, or if you like, particularism (as a fact rather than a creed) applies far better than either centralisation or decentralisation.

The division of the country into a host of legal and administrative districts was bound to go hand in hand with a conservative attitude. Indeed, apart from the radical or visionary excesses of such groups as the Anabaptists in Munster and the Levellers in Cromwell's England, most Europeans, in the sixteenth and seventeenth centuries, if they had any attitude to the state, were anxious to preserve and maintain it. The rebellion against the Spanish authorities was a conservative revolution and could not have been otherwise—in those days, it was not the rebels but the lawful governments who were the reformers and innovators. The new political forces, which appeared at that time in the Netherlands as elsewhere, originated in the kind of princely centralism and absolutism that had already triumphed—or else was in the process of triumphing—over the system of medieval Estates in France, Spain and England. In about 1400, when the Dukes of Burgundy became masters of the Netherlands, an insistent striving for unification and absolute political power was only just beginning to make itself felt. In fact, the Dukes, from Philip the Bold to Charles the

Bold, were mainly concerned with strengthening the administration of each province separately. Thus they reorganised the original Council of the Counts of Holland into a Court of Holland which, however, was by no means a judicature in the modern sense of the word. As for the creation of a central government for all the Burgundian Netherlands, the time was hardly opportune: the Parliament at Mechlin and the occasional assemblies of the States-General were no more than modest steps in that direction.

The whole situation had changed drastically by the time Charles V became ruler over a Netherlands that included Friesland, Groningen, the Bishopric of Utrecht, and Guelders. Now the new political doctrine of centralisation was given full sway in the creation of the three councils of 1531, and in many other ways as well. However, Charles's all-too-Spanish son failed to realise that he could only apply the new doctrine to the government of this important and fertile region, stretching from Luxemburg to Friesland and best known in its entirety as Burgundy, provided he treated it as a new and independent unit in the Western world, and raised the idea of independence to a political principle.

Now, that realisation was quite beyond Philip II and his advisers in Madrid. The Revolt was a direct consequence. The Spanish government rushed into fiscal experiments without making even the least attempt to discover whether or not such experiments suited the economic structure of the country. Next, it introduced such intrinsically reasonable reforms as the consolidation of the criminal law, but without considering how much the whole legal system of the Netherlands was still anchored in the medieval concept of privileges, and hence how opposed it was to any kind of central authority, no matter how desirable.

Here we need not speak at length about the Revolt, nor is it possible to assess the part played in it by religious faith or by the person of William of Orange. One point cannot however, be emphasised enough: it was due to an irreducible chain of special events and not to 'ethnic' predestination that the poorer North, lacking the glory and tradition of Flanders, Brabant and Hainault, should nevertheless have surpassed them in power and renown when North and South went their separate ways in 1579.

To the United Provinces, victory meant not only the supremacy of the Protestant faith, but also—and this ran counter to the entire political current of the time—the preservation of urban autonomy, of provincial government by the Estates, and of the rather antiquated industrial system that went hand in hand with this outlook. The Union of Utrecht was, in principle, no more than an *ad hoc* military alliance aimed at bringing the common struggle to a satisfactory conclusion. The only reference to long-term aims in the treaty occurs in the first article, which declares that the contracting provinces agree to remain eternally united. But how many treaties and pacts have not been signed for eternity only to be dissolved again! The treaty of union was not expressly concerned with political freedom and independence, nor was it intended to be the constitution of a free state. That it became just that, was entirely due to external circumstances which also—and unavoidably—revealed its inability to play so exalted a part. The basis of union had been the medieval concept of municipal liberty —a weak foundation, indeed, on which to build a new state. Thus the demand in the treaty that all major decisions should be unanimous went back to a time when the principle of majority rule was not yet recognised. In the earlier Middle Ages, important decisions were, in fact, made in the belief that all counsellors must be agreed in their opinions, seeing that the Holy Ghost inspired them with the correct choice. In the practice of modern government, however, the demand for unanimity merely impedes the efficiency of the legislators. Even more of a handicap in the long run was the complete lack of means for dealing with the deadweight of opposition, or for forcing the minority to submit to the will of the majority. No wonder then, that precisely those articles of the treaty that involved central action, for instance the general imposition and collection of taxes, were never translated into practice. The Republic, you may say, was never intended to be a new state—after all, the King had not been disavowed in 1579—so that, when unexpected circumstances forced it to behave like one in 1587, it did so without due preparation and hence imperfectly. Moreover, its structure was based on antiquated ideas and not on conscious political principles. How anomalous the situation really was may be seen from the fact that while the sovereign himself was rejected, his delegate, the Stadholder, was retained in a position where, without possessing any of the king's attributes, he was nevertheless endowed with royal powers, including the right to grant free pardons—in a position, what is more, that could neither be called authority over the provinces nor service under them. Nor was the Stadholder's office the only constitutional anomaly in the Dutch Republic—that of Grand Pensionary of Holland was at least as strange. This title, formerly used in Zeeland, replaced that of *Landsadvocaat* (Advocate General) after the tragic death of Oldenbarnevelt in 1618. Circumstances had helped to turn the learned counsellor of the States of Holland into an official who combined the offices of State-President and State-Secretary and who, above all, exerted the greatest possible influence on the States-General. As he was in constant contact with foreign ambassadors, it was natural for foreigners to look upon him as Prime Minister of the entire Union. Finally, he knew more about the finances of Holland, and hence of the entire country, than almost anyone else.

And as if the continued existence of Grand Pensionary and Stadholder, viceroy now without a king, was not strange enough, the latter office, originally a purely provincial one, was to have its very basis changed in time. Before 1589, there used to be separate Stadholders of Guelders,

Overijsel and Utrecht, but then Maurice combined their offices with his own. As a result, the entire stadholdership fell into the hands of the two branches of the House of Orange-Nassau. Later, when the Frisian branch fused with that of Holland, there was room for but one Stadholder in the entire Union, and so it remained for fifty years.

Truly, the constitution of the Republic was a strange edifice, but the fact that it had not grown out of any political theory made it in no way inferior. Possibly it was even an advantage that the treaty should have left open the vexed question of sovereignty which, after 1587, came, in any case, to be vested independently in the States of each province. The theory expounded by Hugo de Groot (Grotius) in his *Treatise on the Antiquities of the Batavian now Hollandish Republic*[1], was based on the assumption that, even in olden times, the Estates were in the habit of delegating their powers to a duke or count. In fact, the Estates as governing bodies or states were late in emerging in the North, and when they did, their powers were by no means full and, in any case, differed from region to region. We have already mentioned the weakness of the clerical Estate: in most provinces the clergy was not even represented as such; in Zeeland, the style of Abbot of Middelburg disappeared with the Revolt; in Utrecht, clerical representation was but a weak echo of the old position of the chapters. Since, outside Friesland and Groningen, the peasantry was not represented, the electoral colleges in most of the country were in the hands of but two classes: the urban patriciate and the landed nobility. The latter predominated in the States of Gelderland and Overijsel, but neither of these had a lasting say in the affairs of the Union. The Dutch nobility did, it is true, enjoy great renown, but it was numerically small and hence unable to counterbalance the influence of the towns.

[1] The Dutch translation 'revised by the author' appeared in the same year as the Latin original (1610). Note that Grotius ignored all provinces other than Holland.

not have become a race of warriors. There would seem to be a marked difference in this respect between the Dutch and the Swiss or even between the Dutch themselves—on land and at sea. However, on closer inspection, the difference begins to dissolve. As regards the Swiss, it was the repeated need to defend their freedom in 1300–1500 that helped to turn this Alpine people into a nation of mercenaries. Time and again, the old, closed communities in the cantons had to rush to the defence of causes that, in the last analysis, were the concern of all. This military interlude came to an end quite suddenly when freedom and peace seemed assured soon after 1515. The continued martial reputation of the Swiss was really due to that class whom poverty had forced into soldiering. With limited trading and industrial prospects and, unlike the Netherlands, unable to enter claims for new territory, the Swiss could find no employment for their excess population other than service in foreign armies. This unsavoury source of prosperity proved a means of power and profit to only a few aristocrats in each canton. The rest of the upper class was not much more warlike than it was elsewhere; farmers, clerics and magistrates together constituted the national type.

Now, if even conditions in Switzerland failed to produce a militaristic society, how could the Eighty Years' War have implanted a martial spirit in the Netherlands? Even in 1568–1597, it was only rarely that the Dutch themselves bore arms against the enemy. They suffered rather than waged the war; fighting was left largely to troops recruited abroad—mainly in Germany and French Flanders. And so it remained during the later phase of the war, when Frederick Henry went into battle. The Dutch peasantry had no need to follow the Swiss example: most of their land was fertile; trade and industry, the building of polders, shipping and fishing were all clamouring for hands—in short, there was ample opportunity to engage in work other than soldiering, an occupation that was nowhere held in high

In short, the Republic wielded a minimum of central power, and that minimum in the interests of the urban oligarchies. The weakness of its political structure was clearly illustrated by the absence of a supreme court of law. Thus, when they had to try Oldenbarnevelt and his supporters, the States-General—incidentally, with very little formal right—were forced to institute the special Bench of the Twenty-Four, who judged only to be judged by history in turn.

If we add to the list of the Union's shortcomings the fact that the Council of State, though intended to be a central organ of government on the model of Burgundy and Austria, paled beside the mighty States Provincial into an insignificant organ of financial control, then we have shown that it was not perfection of political form that ensured the welfare of the Dutch state and, at the same time, that the spirit of the age was not here, as elsewhere, embodied in absolutism. For this imperfect state not only prospered for two centuries but governed a country and a people better and more benignly than any of its European contemporaries. Slow, clumsy and defective though they undoubtedly were, the States-General and Provincial nevertheless provided the Republic with a policy that was able to alter as circumstances demanded and yet remain fundamentally unchanged, and one that, moreover, compared most favourably with the perilous and often ruthless political experiments of the Stuarts, Vasas and Bourbons. Many foreigners believed that the policies of the United Provinces had but the one aim of flattering the greed of avaricious merchants, and while that motive was certainly strong, people of good sense or good will would have seen that these very policies also benefited the country as a whole, and that they were considerably wiser and more humane than the dynastic adventures of most European monarchs.

The conscious and consistent pursuit of prosperity is at one and the same time a policy of peace and reconciliation.

And peace has been the aim and ideal of the Republic from its birth in bloody battle. As the horrors of the Thirty Years' War continued, the longing for peace became more insistent still. 'Europe bare and stricken sore,' wrote the poet Vondel, 'gasps for respite from the war, for peace in union evermore'. Yet peace-loving though the Republic was, no one could have called her pacifist—when peaceful negotiations and reconciliation failed, the Dutch never flinched from armed conflict.

What power for good the Republic exerted sprang from the greatest anomaly of them all: the position of the House of Orange. Royal yet not sovereign, treated with the respect normally reserved for kings, and often leading his armies in the field, the Prince had an invisible sway over the hearts of his people, a love that was founded on gratitude to the 'Father of the Fatherland', and that, in times of need, always prevailed over the will of the ruling merchant-aristocracy.

Even so, it was only in part due to the exertions of its own small community that this young state succeeded in reaching a position of such eminence in Europe. For the rest, it was the perilous condition of their rivals that enabled the Dutch to exploit their new-found freedom and limited resources to the utmost degree. Germany was embroiled in the Thirty Years' War; France, which had but recently emerged from the religious wars, still faced the task of keeping the Hapsburgs at bay; post-Elizabethan England was increasingly dissipating her strength in a constitutional struggle; mighty Spain failed to recover from the Dutch disaster. In short, at the turn of the sixteenth century, most European countries were far too busy with their own troubles to play a serious role abroad. From these circumstances the Republic of the Seven Provinces profited to the full, not only politically but also economically—the weakness of her neighbours left full scope to her own industry and commerce. For almost half a century, the Republic was not

troubled by tariff restrictions. German trade and shipping had ceased to offer serious competition—the Hanseatic League had become an anachronism. Spain and Portugal had changed from merchants into mere customers; France was still awaiting her Colbert, and England was still lagging a fair way behind.

All these political and economic advantages were fast fading by 1660. Still, the loss of an advantage need not be fatal. Politically and economically, the second half of the seventeenth century was the heyday of the Republic and it was not until 1700 that the Wars of the Spanish Succession brought tragedy to the Netherlands. Forced as a great power to join in the European conflict, the Republic played her part with honour at the cost of her former position. In the resurgent Europe of 1713, in which England was to rise to eminence, in which Austrian power waxed strong, and in which Prussia and Russia had begun to play a leading role, the Republic withdrew into the illusory safety of her 'Dutch barrier' and sank into a sweet slumber, to enjoy dreams of durable peace and the clinking of ducats. And yet, it strikes one again and again, people take too unfair a view of eighteenth-century Holland. The real history of our country during that period has not yet been written—a subject to which we shall be returning at the end of this essay.

II

The social structure of the new, free nation which came of age with the creation of the Republic was based on customs rooted in bygone centuries, and hence only explicable—if, indeed, the essence of a people can be explained—in terms of the past.

Take the unwarlike character of the Dutch people. It might seem odd that after so long a war, which the Netherlands waged with fortitude and honour, her people should

esteem. Let no one, then, call cowardly a people that preferred the constant dangers of the sea to the vicissitudes of the battlefield. Thus it came about that, although the landed nobility, and particularly those families who had remained Catholic, would encourage their sons to choose a military career, most of the officers were recruited abroad, chiefly in Germany, France, Switzerland, England and Scotland. More than one foreign family entered the Dutch aristocracy in this way. Things were somewhat different when it came to the navy. True, the foreign—chiefly Norse—elements was not entirely lacking here either, but it was chiefly the Dutch themselves who served at sea and who made the sailor a type far more symbolic of our nation than the soldier ever was. Naval officers rarely came from abroad, and service at sea not only had a great nation-building effect but also acted as a kind of social cement. Our naval commanders—as every Dutch schoolboy knows—were drawn from all sections of the population: Piet Hein, Tromp, De Ruyter and the Evertsens were the sons of sailors, Van Ghent, the three Van Brakels and Warsenaer-Obdam were the sons of nobles. There is little doubt that life at sea had a levelling effect on Dutch society as a whole.

The contrasting popular attitudes to war at sea and war on land were clearly reflected in Dutch art. Few of our important paintings portray feats of arms on land, the conquest of cities, the battle of Nieuwpoort (1600), or other great encounters. This is for a number of reasons. The eye of our great masters looked for better subjects than unpaintable sieges or bogus compositions and confused battle scenes. True, Wouwerman or Meulener have given us canvases of cavalry engagements, but these they did not paint as clearly and truly as we expect of Dutch masters. Indeed, no one in our country has produced anything to match *Las lanzas*, Velazquez's glorious poem in colour. In short, battlefields appealed as little to our painters as they did to our military commanders. That does not mean that our artists did not bother with soldiers, far from it. But on their many familiar canvases, soldiers are shown smoking, drinking, courting, visiting, or bragging, while the company looks on with no small measure of suspicion. It is all part and parcel of Dutch genre painting.

Now look at our artists' view of engagements at sea. Every great naval battle has been the subject of outstanding canvases, by Vroom, De Vliegher, Willem van der Velde and a host of others. True, all these paintings, too, are compositions, but how much that is best in Dutch art is reflected in them, how great is their pictorial impact and how much love has gone into them!

In most periods of history the social life of the army has been closely linked to the glamour of princely courts. In the Netherlands, too, what social life the army enjoyed centred round the Stadholder's Court in The Hague. Yet how much less sparkling it was than so many foreign palaces! Most of us know under what extremely modest, almost meagre circumstances Prince William I did his duties. Even under Maurice, the Court was still lacking in pomp and riches, and only after the death of Frederick Henry, when his widow built the famous royal villa, the *Huis ten Bosch*, and had it embellished by pupils of Rubens, was there a clear desire to display the panoply of regal life, justified not least by the marriage of the young prince and successor to the English princess. A new centre of courtly life in Baroque style might well have arisen here, had the right conditions prevailed. As it was, the cultural life of the Republic did not revolve about the Stadholder's court, especially in the middle of the century when Amsterdam was extending her girth with canal after canal and her fame with a new city hall. Moreover, the fall of Charles I robbed the English royal connection of its political importance and of much of its lustre. As we have said, the House of Orange lacked regal magnificence even under Frederick Henry; his immediate circle continued to live fairly simply and the leading spirit among them, Constantijn Huygens, had nothing of the courtier about him. The Prince's entourage was somewhat divorced from the cultural life of the rest of the country. The estrangement between the Stadholder and the urban aristocracy, quite especially in Amsterdam, increased considerably under Frederick Henry, and was more than a mere difference of political views. During his later years, Frederick Henry took a path that led him further and further away from what was the very crux of our national life, towards dynastic power politics in which the nation's interests and prosperity no longer took first place. He and his son—and this may sound harsh in view of Frederick Henry's invaluable contribution to the safeguarding of our State—failed to understand the Netherlands or to grasp the spirit of her people.

Less still did social and intellectual life revolve about the nobility. Their castles, usually not very luxurious or even reasonably well-equipped, were no palaces, and life in them was neither socially nor intellectually stimulating or fruitful. The torch of culture burned instead in the merchants' town houses or nearby countryside villas which, though many of them were manorial strongholds and still protected by moats and gates, had lost their feudal sombreness and epitomised instead the kind of agreeable country-life in which Vondel heard the song of blackbirds and nightingales. No doubt the cruel pleasures of finch-hunting took pride of place over pure love of nature, but that, too, was not entirely missing.

Amsterdam, more than any other town, had its commuters, though theirs was not a daily or week-end but a seasonal migration. Here were the handsome gentlemen whom the poet Joost van den Vondel was pleased to call his hosts and benefactors. It often seems to us that their names have something of that sparkling optimism that belongs to this poet, and belongs to him in more noble measure than to most of those who stepped so confidently into their spiritual shoes.

In about 1648, Amsterdam must have had some 150,000 inhabitants and was thus one of Europe's greatest cities. Three times in fifty years it extended its size by means of that masterpiece of town-planning, the concentric canal, and three times the canals were edged on either side with rows of stately houses, rich yet simple. The result, judged not only from the social and economic standpoint but also as pure architecture, was greatly preferable to Versailles. If the atmosphere of the century can be captured anywhere, it is surely beside Amsterdam's canals on a Sunday morning in spring or on a late summer evening.

However, the Dutchman is bound to recall not only the greatest of all his cities but also all those other towns whose vital arteries Amsterdam never severed and which she never reduced into mere copies of her own greatness—flourishing towns all of them albeit some were as small as Hoorn and Enkhuizen, and all with their own character and atmosphere. It would be a thankless task to decide which town in the Netherlands has best preserved the charm of its past—until some fifty or sixty years ago all of them succeeded equally well. Then tramway lines, concrete, asphalt and motor traffic destroyed their ancient face, just as the glory of sail waned with the disappearance of full-rigged ships. This lament must not be dismissed as the reactionary sulkings of an old man; the younger generation does not, indeed cannot ever, know the kind of beauty of which their elders only just managed to catch a glimpse.

The happy diffusion of trade and prosperity over a large number of independent centres enabled even those towns that lagged far behind Amsterdam—Haarlem, Rotterdam, Leyden, Dordrecht, Delft, Utrecht and Middelburg—to become cultural centres, each in its own right. Nothing reflects this so well as the appearance of schools of paintings in so many of our towns. No doubt, political rivalry between the towns did much to encourage this autonomy and diversity. In principle, all, with the exception of the very smallest, had as much say in the States, and hence as great a share in the running of the country, as Amsterdam, their mighty sister. None felt too mean to bear their own variant of the letters SPQR on their arms, or to see their civic dignitaries praised as senators in verse. All had reputable Latin schools; a fair measure of classical learning helped to turn the towns into fertile soil for the intellectual seeds that the development of trade and industry could bring to germination and fruition.

The general social structure which underpinned and nurtured Dutch culture in the towns is well-known. Though it preserved rare vestiges of ancient democratic rights, Dutch municipal government was predominantly oligarchic. The Confederates of Groningen, the Council of Eight of Dordrecht and their counterparts elsewhere were respected as antiquities but had no real power. The families from whom rulers and legislators—town councillors, aldermen and burgomasters—were recruited, usually belonged to a circle that was closed purely by convention and hence neither legally nor completely. In about 1600, this circle could hardly have been called aristocratic, let alone a regent class. It was not sharply divided from the more substantial burghers or even from the less well-to-do. Riches or a well-arranged marriage often gained outsiders admission to the municipal hierarchy.

At the beginning of the seventeenth century, most of these magisterial families were still engaged in trade. In Amsterdam, they would live in the Nes or Niezel, in houses that were still of the small step-gable type with deep cellars and large lofts for storing merchandise. But many had already begun to buy up manors and to hanker after knighthoods—from France, England, Denmark or the Kaiser.

Their children began by studying law in Leyden and then went on a 'grand tour' of France and Italy. Meanwhile business life, in the shipyards, on the quays, in the office and the exchange, kept the new patriciate in constant touch with the common citizens and artisans. They were still burgher enough themselves to respect the old virtues of thrift and simplicity. Moreover, there was no room yet, in the literal sense of the word, for the great builder, though, soon afterwards, when the canals were completed, it became *de rigeur* for every patrician to own a stately home, in the new style that was grafted on alien roots. Every one commissioned or collected pictures, all were patrons of poetry, of the church and of learning. As a result, the urban upper class was gradually transformed into a true burgher-aristocracy—a strong, healthy and, above all, widely scattered group of people interested in culture and the arts.

Dutch historians have for a long time gone out of their way to point to the many shortcomings of this 'regent class.' Their authority, we are told, was corrupt, slow in action, and only concerned with the furtherance of narrow class interests. However, the critics seem to forget that the seventeenth century was not offered a choice between an aristocracy on the one hand and ideal democracy on the other, but merely between a monarchy and an aristocracy, and that both these systems were equally fraught with human failings. It is safe to say, although it cannot be proved in every particular, that corruption and inertia were far more pronounced abroad than they were in the Netherlands, where everyone, as it were, had a finger in the public pie. In fact, it would be extremely difficult to find another ruling caste that governed a country for so long with so little coercion and generally with so much benevolence.

We have said that the Dutch magisterial class was interested in culture. What of the men who supplied their cultural needs? In general, we might say that a civilisation is the healthier the more closely the circles of intellectual creation and intellectual curiosity coincide, provided only that the entire process is not confined to a narrow élite. It goes without saying that the circle of creative artists must not be equated with that of the intellectuals. If we identify the two, we ignore not only peasant and popular art, but also our great masters, for few of them were educated men in the full sense of the term. If, on the other hand, we define culture as widely as we ought, then even the illiterate masses can be said to have played a part in its development, and quite especially the peasantry with their carvings, primitive paintings and decorations. On closer examination, it might well emerge that an equally important contribution was made by the small burgher, fisherman and sailor. Indeed, the only ones to take no marked interest in culture, either as producers or consumers, were the landed gentry of the eastern provinces, who lived in their remote castles and stuck to their primitive agrarian concerns. Throughout the nation, however, from the highest to the lowest, the medieval love of song and dance, play and proverb was gradually ousted, as prayer became the chief intellectual diet. It is quite wrong to put all the blame for this cultural decline on Calvinism, as so many have done; in the first place because Baptism, too, played a major part in damping the love of life for the Lord's sake, and secondly because it remains an open question whether the regions that remained Catholic preserved more of the genuine popular culture than the rest.

In any case, the basis of seventeenth-century Dutch culture was urban society. Within it, cultural creation was singularly independent of rank or wealth. In the great task of encouraging new art-forms and expressing new ideas, the patricians and members of the learned professions—lawyers, doctors, clergymen—worked hand in hand, almost fraternally. Even the deep gulf between Protestants and Catholics did not preclude individuals from co-operating in

41

this task, as witness the friendship between the daughters of Roemer Visscher and the circle round Hooft.

Side by side with the learned professions, a broad stratum of traders and members of the lower middle classes also participated actively in cultural events. Here as elsewhere, this process expressed itself not least by way of social recreation. Thus two forms of association, the Civic Guards and the Chambers of Rhetoric, both going back to the late Middle Ages, were chiefly responsible for providing the social framework in which cultural activity could take place. Elsewhere, too, the seventeenth century saw the rise of new intellectual forums. Ever since the Renaissance, Italy could boast of Academies, institutes of learning and literature, with such strange names as *Crusca* (chaff) and *Lincei* (lynxes). France saw the emergence of the literary salon, England that of the coffee house followed by the birth of that backbone of English social life—the Club. In Holland, however, people remained conservative, and despite Coster's Academy of 1617, continued to rely for social intercourse on the two old associations we have mentioned. Now it was precisely this Dutch dislike of throwing the helve after the hatchet that was responsible for maintaining social communication between the rising patriciate and the bourgeoisie although their political and economic interests diverged increasingly. There remained a kind of cultural homogeneity which had repercussions in the material sphere and prevented the emergence of crude class divisions. In the *Doelen* of the Civic Guard and in the Chamber of Rhetoric, small shop-keepers and great merchants would meet and enjoy a literary education. Intellectual life was not greatly affected by the aristocratic manners with which the magisterial circle tried to improve itself, and the cultural outlook even of the patricians remained essentially bourgeois. The preservation of a measure of social cohesion was further encouraged by the sedulous pursuit of classical learning as the basis of all education. Now, classicism made no fine distinction between honourable men of greater and somewhat lesser substance; it was based on Roman and Greek traditions, and these the greatest gentleman was no better placed to emulate than the humblest burgher. When it came to poetry, all alike were Greeks and Romans.

Nor did things change greatly when poetry gradually began to shed the antiquated and stilted style imposed by the Guild of Rhetoric. The Muiden Circle of Hooft provides the outstanding example of a literary group which, in the castle of one who was but a second-generation patrician himself, freely absorbed bourgeois elements.

It is easy to exaggerate social distinctions in seventeenth-century Holland, but those who make a close study of our literature, art, or other expressions of social life (outside purely official relations) at the time, are bound to gain the impression that, despite all pompous displays of caste and social distinction, life was extremely sociable, almost familiar. Very small indeed was the difference socially, personally and intellectually, between such men as Vondel, Bredero, Hooft, Cats and Huygens, two of whom were the sons of tradesmen, middle-class people as we might say, and three of whom belonged to the rich magistrature. Hugyens especially provides us with an excellent illustration of the absence of social distinctions among, and of the predominantly bourgeois tone of, the Dutch élite. This very paragon of versatility, at once witty and serious, playful and strong, was secretary to two Princes of Orange, a diplomat, a polyglot, a man of the world, an outstanding connoisseur of classical and modern art, a fine musician, a devout Christian, and much more besides. In his writings, however, he remained a true Dutch burgher, Dutch despite his multilingual accomplishments, and a true son of the people despite his high rank and position. In his satires and epigrams, in *Hofwyck* as much as in *Trijntje Cornelis*, he regularly takes us among the people, indeed, among the lowest classes. His whole attitude, his concern with simple and ordinary, sometimes too ordinary, situations, his warmth, his jovial morality and down-to-earth humour, are far more expressive of the soul of the people than of the patrician. His deep love of nature and, country life (down-to-earth, moreover, and not romantic) a love that sought its expression neither in the pastoral nor in the idyllic, but welled up freely and easily from the heart, more than compensates us for those of his writings whose excessive intellectualism and exaggerated reasonableness we find so irksome. Truly, those who wish to understand seventeenth-century Holland must read Huygens as well as Vondel, the man who captured the style, enthusiasm and greatness of his age. Huygens', like Vondel's, poetry is full of classical and Biblical allusions, but precisely because he does not invariably take us into the loftiest spheres, he, more than Vondel, shows us the true, everyday Holland we know so well from our great painters and engravers.

It is well known that our seventeenth-century compatriots had little appreciation of Dutch art and, where they did, they liked it for the wrong reasons. Poets rather than painters were held in high esteem. This point has recently been dealt with in an excellent paper by Gerard Brom[1]. Most painters were of petty-bourgeois origin and their social prestige rarely exceeded that of their class. None of them was honoured as Rubens, Van Dyck or Velazquez were abroad; in fact, they were not deemed worthy of much, if any, notice, and even Jan Vermeer or Hercules Seghers were generally ignored or completely forgotten. Our painters were uneducated men, and our noble regents would write to them, if at all, with a measure of kindly but unmistakable condescension. Only Rembrandt succeeded in gaining attention, not so much by his work as by leading the life of a semi-bohemian recluse, but that, too, did not prevent him

[1]Proceedings of the Eighteenth Congress of Dutch Philologers (1939), pp. 11-26.

from ending his days on a note of suffering and proud defiance, as his last self-portraits show us only too clearly.

Now this disdain of art and artists had a remarkable consequence. For had the artist's path taken him from his master's studio and years of study in Italy straight to a high position among the ranks of merchants, churchmen and magistrates, perhaps the greatest masterpieces would never have seen the light of day.

The fact that painting and drawing were by far the most important expressions of Dutch art in the seventeenth century cannot be explained—if it can be explained at all—by a single well-defined cause. No doubt, the very special conditions under which our culture arose played an important part in this process. Almost all the proportions were small—down to the size of the country, the distances between towns, the differences between the various classes. Hand in hand with these small gradations went a high degree of general prosperity and a lively interest in culture and intellectual pursuits. Artists in our country had to rely almost perforce on the decoration of plane areas, i.e. on painting, drawing, or etching—there was little scope for great architecture or sculpture, not so much due to the absence of stone as to the lack of patrons. Palaces and elaborate monuments are the prerogatives of great princes, cardinals and nobles and in Holland such men did not exist.

These very circumstances, however, gave a great impetus to the graphic arts, and especially to painting as it emerged after the Renaissance—divorced from altar pieces and murals (which latter, in any case, could not have flourished in the wet climate of Holland) and destined instead for the town hall, the poor house, or even the private dwelling. And art with this social function demands little more than love of the look of things, artistic skill, and a large number of enthusiasts clamouring for its products. Now the demand for paintings was far greater and more constant in the Netherlands, with its prosperous population, and in Holland in particular, than in any other country. Nor were the patrons to be sought exclusively among the richest and noblest, as a mere glance at commissioned portraits will suffice to show. Rembrandt and Frans Hals did not merely paint mayors and leading dignitaries but also writing-masters, preachers, Jewish physicians, engravers and gold-smiths. From the study by Fruin[1], we know that foreign visitors to our country were taken aback by the widespread desire to own works of art. Good paintings could be bought in Rotterdam fairground booths, and were wont to grace the walls of even the humblest houses. You will not find a cobbler, an English traveller wrote, who does not own a painting. Another suggested that the Dutch bought paint-ings as a form of investment; it was no rarity, he said, for a small farmer to spend a fortune in this way. In view of the general availability of much sounder investments, this sug-gestion strikes me as a little far-fetched. Thus in 1696, during the riots in Amsterdam, when a number of houses were sacked, and the damage was assessed, people deplored the fact that the mediocre family pieces of Mayor Boreel were thought to be more valuable than the exquisite art collection of Captain Spaaroog, a simple soldier.

It is regrettable in a way that our ideas about the past are so largely based on paintings. Even literature takes second place to art with most of our people, and when it comes to political and social history, the great majority is completely at sea. This applies to some extent to all of us, and we cannot possibly help it: the visible beauty of a painting casts an irresistible spell over our spirit. We shall return to art and literature again, but before doing so, we must first look at two other aspects of our culture: religion and science.

---

[1] *De Nederlanders der zeventiende eeuw door Engelsen geschetst* (English opinions of seventeenth-century Dutchmen). Selected Works, vol. IV, p. 245.

III

Because it is other-worldly and also because of its very message, the Church invariably tends to break down sharp divisions between social groups. We have already seen that, in the Netherlands, these divisions were, in any case, less sharp than in most other countries. Nevertheless, even here the Church could play this part, and Calvinism, once it became the dominant religion, worked in that very direction, not so much by deliberate intent as by force of circumstance. The pastor called at the castle as well as on the shopkeeper. His was an important yet exceedingly delicate position. For the most part, the clergy was recruited from among the middle-classes. By the very nature of Calvin's church, the servants of God's word were preachers first and shepherds of their flock second. Hence they saw their task chiefly as one of addressing, admonishing and persuading —their office led them automatically to judge, and often to condemn, state and society alike. The servants of the ruling church thus became the upholders of views that, albeit they could not yet be called public opinion in the full sense of the term, nevertheless had sufficient authority not to be dismissed as mere whims. Quite unavoidably, the pastor's views had a democratic flavour. A son of the people himself, he proclaimed the Word of God in the tongue of the people. That voice was not at all revolutionary. The aristocratic system as such was not even questioned, yet there was a clear wariness of complacent government from the cushioned eminence of the mayoral chair. From the church, the sounds of non-aristocratic, popular notions constantly filtered through to the town hall. Although the clergy had no voice in the town or the States and although a magistrate would from time to time call them to order with a: Come, come, gentlemen, leave us to deal with our business while you mind your own, the temporal authorities

47

knew perfectly well that the opinions and attitudes expressed by the Church could not be ignored for long.

The relationship between Church, bourgeoisie and aristocracy was much like other relationships in the Netherlands: there were no sharp divisions. The anti-aristocratic tenor of church life did not meet with strong opposition from a patriciate that owed its learning and culture far more to the parson than it did to the grammar school, and which, in spirit and manners, remained firmly rooted in the Protestant faith. Simplicity remained the hallmark of even the greatest dignitaries, and a sober attitude was kept alive by continual contacts with the Church, from Sunday to Sunday, and during all family events. Once her authority was accepted, the Church for her part raised no objections to the regents' display of pomp; on the contrary, she would help frame the epitaphs and memorials to the great and inscribe them on escutcheons on the church walls.

The stranger interested in our history, generally has the idea that the Republic was a wholly Calvinist state. We ourselves know better than that. The Dutch Reformed Church, our particular brand of Calvinism, prevailed in the form laid down by the Synod of Dort. This does not mean that country, people and culture were completely moulded in the Calvinist stamp. The reformed faith was never a state or established religion, as Anglicanism, for instance, is in England. It held sway in the State, was supported by the State and was even granted a kind of public monopoly; if you like it was the Church of the State, but it was never a state church in the full sense of the word. Its position was not anchored in the political institutions of the Republic. The fact that all political offices were filled by its members was a matter of political practice tacitly accepted, if not openly avowed, by all; it was never raised into a principle.

We all know that the presence of a large Calvinistic majority in our country was the result of a lengthy historical process. During the early years of the Revolt it was strong and resolute Calvinistic minorities that, in the towns of Holland, Zeeland and Utrecht, came to the fore as leaders of their people. Did they clash with the Spaniards because Calvin's doctrine so guided them or did they rather follow Calvin because they would not put up with oppression? In either case, it was they who braved untold dangers, who kept up their own courage and helped the people to persevere, and it is to them that the Dutch owed their final victory, inasmuch as it was a victory of spirit no less than of arms. But to what extent was it that, and from what period onwards are we entitled to speak of victory? Here a flood of memories takes us to the very heart of our history: the laborious and painstaking diplomacy of Prince William, his unflinching perseverance in the face of impending disaster and lack of resources, even unto death; the shattering blow of the failure of the Pacification and the Anjou experiments, the loss of Antwerp, the progress of the Union and the misgovernment of Leicester. Victory? Surely, that word cannot be applied to the cause of the Revolt before 1594–1600.

And even when the Republic—now free except in name and, barring unforeseen contingencies, safe—moved towards an era of unprecedented prosperity, the various religions continued to co-exist. There was never any question of enforcing Calvinism. It gained in numbers as the provinces gained their freedom. Only Drente was more or less systematically converted, and here the Old Church gave hardly any sign of life and offered no resistance. In all other provinces, the relationship between the churches became stabilised quite early on, except that within the Reformed Church itself the increasing contrast between the moderate and orthodox elements threatened a definite break. The spirit of Erasmus was too deeply rooted, for Calvin's doctrine to have a clear field. Before 1600, many a serious man, particularly among the educated classes, had not yet made a final choice between Catholicism and the new faith.

Everywhere, in town and country alike, large minorities continued to adhere to Rome, even in Zeeland, the Protestant stronghold. It is proof positive of the lack of proselytising fervour among the Reformers that round the very foci of the Revolt—round Alkmaar and Leyden—most of the villages remained predominantly Catholic. Most of the rural nobility in the Eastern provinces, too, held fast to the old faith. Then, when Dutch Flanders and most of what is now North Brabant, Maastricht and Overmaas were added to the Republic, the number of Catholics was doubled, though this increase did not mean a proportionate increase in influence in the state, because the inhabitants of these regions were excluded from all political say, and played no important part in either the public or the intellectual life of the Seven Provinces. The state remained Protestant although not exclusively Calvinistic since, from the very start, the Reformed Church was forced to share the Protestant territory with a small Lutheran and a very large Baptist community and soon afterwards with the Remonstrants. A lasting reminder that Lutheranism was a factor in our past can be found in the round Lutheran Church on the Singel in Amsterdam—that peculiar example of Protestant church architecture, a subject to which we shall be returning.

What the Remonstrant presence meant to Dutch culture is a question so closely interwoven with our political history that we can do no more here than recall that the old Erasmian faith and the spirituality of Coornhert found their firm expression in the Remonstrant doctrine.

All-pervading yet difficult to define was the Baptist factor in Dutch culture. The Mennonites were the oldest Protestant group to emerge as a distinct sect among the people, albeit they had neither a creed nor a clear-cut organisation. During the persecution, the authorities had no difficulty in hunting them out; the entire sixteenth century seemed full of the scent of the dreaded and detested Anabaptists. They were the people condemned to the stake

—simple burghers such as Dirk Willemszoon of Asperen, the martyr who rescued his persecutor from the ice, was arrested by the self-same man, and thrown into a fire which would not catch properly, so that Dirk Willemszoon could be heard 'squealing like a stuck pig'. How is it that a religion whose zealots were responsible for fanatical excesses in Amsterdam and Munster should have subsided so gently into decorous piety, and that the many disciples of Menno in the northern provinces, in Haarlem and in Amsterdam, became the most peaceful citizens of all? They were exempted from oaths, offices, and arms, they were given the cold shoulder by those in the 'big' church, people would joke about their ultra-puritanical dress and manners but would not really begrudge them the fruits of their labours or their 'Mennonite' houses—narrow in front and all with fine gardens. The state came to look upon them as contented people without a history, and left them to bicker among themselves like the rest.

As for the Jews, their role in the Republic and in Dutch culture constitutes a unique chapter in world history. In Holland there was resurrected what formerly arose in Spain and Portugal and was later expelled—a Jewish community tolerated and even esteemed by its neighbours: the 'Portuguese' community of Amsterdam, the circle in which Rembrandt sought his inspiration, subjects and friends, and the circle which produced Spinoza. True many Jews, streaming into the eastern provinces from Germany or else crowding into Amsterdam, shared neither the prosperity nor the great respect enjoyed by their Portuguese brethren. People and state alike thought them deceitful and often felonious; they were made to share the age-old obloquy of Israel, but not too harshly. They were neither persecuted nor cut off from the rest of the population.

The Calvinistic element in the young Republic was, as everyone knows, greatly re-inforced by the influx of refugees from those regions over which Spain succeeded in regaining her hold and where every trace of heresy was brutally stamped out. From 1567, but particularly after the fall of Antwerp in 1585, these refugees poured in from Flanders, Brabant, Hainault and Artois—some speaking French and some speaking Flemish. It was by no means the weakest of them who preferred exile in this still hazardous backwater —for that is what they must have thought of Holland, Zeeland and Utrecht—to a settled life under Spain and Rome. Unrestrained by the many traditional ties that made them conservatives in their homes, they constituted a naturally radical element of political life—as emerged clearly in Leicester's day. They had everything to gain and no more to lose. And they did gain a great deal, not least wealth from trade. Once persecuted themselves, they became unyielding in matters of faith and, after 1600, greatly strengthened the counter-Remonstrant faction.

Here it is not necessary to describe in any great detail the ecclesiastical and political quarrels during the years of the Truce. All that matters in this brief account is to point out the incidental repercussions of these quarrels on the cultural life of the time.

From that point of view, the victory of 1618 barely deserves the name. For however orthodox the Protestant majority had grown since the crisis, it would be untrue to say that Dutch life and culture in the seventeenth century, seen as a whole, was dominated by the spirit of the Synod of Dort. How quickly were the Remonstrants rehabilitated! In the very year in which Grotius failed to make a permanent return from exile, Amsterdam opened its Athenaeum Illustre with the *Mercator sapiens*, a play by Barlaeus, the very man whom the Synod had deprived of his post at Leyden University, the friend of both Hooft and Huygens, and in many respects the most perfect representative of Dutch culture in the seventeenth century.

After 1618, when Calvinism had gained the upper hand

and no longer needed to be so blatantly aggressive, it inevitably ceased to be the driving force it had been. The spirit of Voetius might reign in Utrecht, which raised her old school to the rank of a university, but it never held sway over Holland. Soon, in Descartes' philosophy, there arose a force that, without uprooting the Calvinistic doctrine, nevertheless undermined it by way of Cocceius's opinions.

The tenor of seventeenth-century life, as it is reflected in art and learning, in manners and morals, in private pursuits and amusements, in industry and politics, was by no means wholly puritanical. Here we have a striking contrast to that other country in which Calvinism ruled supreme, namely Scotland. The Scottish Presbyterians were far churchier than their Dutch counterparts. Despite all its touches of Protestant orthodoxy, Dutch life followed the voice of Erasmus rather than that of the great Genevan. The fusion of piety with love of learning and culture had taken root here long before Calvin proclaimed his hard doctrine in the year of Erasmus' death. Humanism[1] in a specifically northern form, and differing characteristically from the Humanism of the Italians, French and Germans, has always been the soil on which Dutch culture flourished.

A few words now about the political aspects of the crisis during the Truce. In 1609, when the safety of the state was assured for the next twelve years and peaceful conditions were restored, the unimpeded development of Oldenbarnevelt's political system would undoubtedly have proved extremely dangerous. Strict provincial autonomy, unchallenged mastery by the town patriciate, the Church open to the freer and wider tendencies of Arminius's doctrine and

[1] I should like to stress in passing that I use the word 'Humanism' to refer to the intellectual phenomenon that appeared towards the end of the Middle Ages, and that reached full maturity in the first half of the sixteenth century. I do not approve of the common habit of applying the terms 'Humanist' and 'Humanism' loosely to all sorts of modern doctrines and views.

Grotius's ideas—to Gomarus and his party, all these trends were so many serious threats to the authority of the Church. Behind Oldenbarnevelt also stood all who had Baptist or spiritualistic leanings. And what if things had been allowed to run their course, if the advice of Jeannin, the French envoy to Holland had been taken, and the country had been granted complete religious freedom? In that case the Catholics would undoubtedly have gained the day.

We know how things went: Maurice's purely political choice between the two parties, the short and almost bloodless conflict, the expulsion of Remonstrant town councils, the commitment of the Church's cause to the national synod, whose views were known in advance, and then victory, but victory marred by the type of bias that had seemed so reprehensible in the enemy—all these events led to the country's tragedy in the *Binnenhof*, to Oldenbarnevelt's condemnation and death.

And so Calvinism, cleansed of the Arminian heresy, continued as the Church of the State, yet without becoming established. Official positions were henceforth reserved for those who subscribed to the doctrine of Dort, though this restriction never became law, nor was any special oath or test expressly laid down—just another typical example of how much the new state disliked all cut and dried formulations. The system governing religious beliefs could be called neither one of religious freedom nor one of religious tolerance, rather was it one in which officialdom, by closing an eye and accepting the occasional bribe, helped to temper the lot of those outside the official Church. Catholic worship was officially proscribed, but everyone knew where clandestine churches could be found. Even the exclusion from public office of those who did not adhere to the tenets of the 'true Christian Reformed Religion' admitted of exceptions, inasmuch as Catholic nobles were allowed to sit as judges in some provinces, and to rise to high rank in the army. Protestant dissenters—Lutherans and Baptists—hardly suffered from this law for, like the Jews, they did not seek public office.

Hence the position may rightly be called a permanent *status quo* with respect to the conditions prevailing in 1618—on the whole, things were left more or less as they had been. At the critical moment, the central authority was able to bring the conflict to some sort of close but it was never strong enough, nor even seriously inclined, to exert further pressure or effect large-scale conversions. In many respects it was this very weakness that preserved the kind of religious climate from which the dissenters benefited so greatly.

As we have said, though the year 1618 may have brought victory to the Reformed Church, politically it meant little more than a slight shifting of power, and culturally little more than a compromise between two ways of life. The replacement of officials did not involve a change in the system of government nor in the outlook of the ruling class. The latter now became more observant, but neither renounced its views of freedom within the state nor the Erasmian basis of its personal ideals. It never became Puritanical in the English or Scottish sense—the Netherlands in the seventeenth century produced neither the Roundhead nor the Cavalier type, and this for a variety of reasons.

In England, two distinct cultures confronted each other as early as 1600. On the one hand there was the puritan ideal of the sober life in strict accordance with the Old Testament, a life in which thought, speech and manners are all suffused with the word of God, and this ideal was shared by Anglicans, Presbyterians, Congregationalists and Brownists alike. Opposed to this ideal was everything that, in England, went by the name of Renaissance and Humanism. There you had a large number of aristocrats, from the gentry to the highest nobility, who tried to revive the ideals of chivalry and courtliness by living a life in which the clash of arms, bold sea voyages, hunting and poetry all had their place and complemented one another. Those who grew up in this atmosphere did not necessarily have to be merely worldly, polished and witty—here, too, there was room for worship and the serious life, as witness the earliest of the Cavaliers, Sir Philip Sidney. Though he was, of course, a member of the Established Church, his outlook was that of the Calvinist. In that respect he was an exception. Most of his party felt at home in the Established Church precisely because of the ties between Anglicanism and Roman Catholicism. The hierarchic structure, the strong national tradition, the learned, conservative theology all went wonderfully well with the spirit that the English gentleman loves so well.

In England the two cultures clashed violently for half a century. Puritanism seems to have gained the upper hand with the end of the Civil War, but, despite a leader of the stature of Cromwell, it proved unable to govern the country or to become the permanent expression of the will of the people. However, the Restoration was no mere reaction, no simple return to unseasonable Cavalier life. It meant a temporary rise of licentiousness; atheism openly reared its head among the upper classes. Moreover, Charles II was not the man to stem the tide of corruption that flooded all spheres of life. Still, the sound sense of the English prevailed in the end, and modern England was born of the fusion of the two older streams.

How different was the short struggle in the Netherlands! Here neither the social nor the cultural differences between the contending parties were very great. The counter-Remonstrants cannot really be compared with the Puritans, nor their opponents with the Cavaliers. True, there were many similarities between Remonstrants and Anglicans, and it was no accident that English Puritans imported the name of 'Arminians' from Holland in order to revile their High Church adversaries with it. Grotius and William Laud felt very close to each other. However, the Dutch patricians, albeit they boasted manors and foreign honours, bore little resemblance to English aristocrats—for one thing they utterly lacked the latter's courtly and military splendour. The contrasts were accordingly much slighter in Holland, the issues less controversial, the conflict brief, and insufficient to undermine the foundations of the polity, or to impair the smooth functioning of the state machine. A fusion of the more liberal and the orthodox parties took place almost unnoticed. We may safely say that Dutch culture in 1625–1675 was at a more developed stage than its counterpart in England. Conflicts of the kind that split national life wide open and threatened cultural stability across the Channel, found a fairly harmonious solution here.

From this digression we must now return to a problem we have left unsolved, namely the extent to which Calvinism stimulated the development of Dutch culture. Was it no more than the leaven in the lump of religious life? Or was it rather the driving force behind the intellectual and social improvement of this young nation; did it help to crystallise Dutch thought, to fertilise Dutch art? Those who try to answer these questions will quickly find that they are working with imponderables. What is certain is that in the building and preservation of the state, Calvinistic zeal, courage, faith and steadfastness all played a very large part. Calvinism helped to steel the people's resolve, albeit far too often into obstinacy, and inspired such men of action as Jan Pieterszoon Coen to perform his great deeds. It was upheld by all who served the state and all who were in authority. Does that mean that the spirit of Calvinism suffused our culture in all its aspects? The answer is found in the history of our universities. Towards the end of 1574, only a few months after the relief of Leyden had averted the worst danger, and when no one yet dared to dream of an independent state, but at most hoped for a satisfactory compromise with the King of Spain, the Prince, in consultation

57

with the States, founded the University of Leyden. All the relevant documents, from the Prince's letter to the States on 28th December 1574 down to the charter and statutes, show that his love of freedom and national unity were as strong as his thirsting after the 'knowledge of the Lord'. The university would be a 'bastion and guardian of all the lands, and hence a lasting bridge not only between the lands themselves but also between them and the neighbouring provinces'. From the very beginning, the teaching was not to be confined to theology but extended to 'all the honest and liberal arts and sciences'. The university was to be 'a sure and safe support of freedom and honest government not only in matters of religion but also in all things concerning the welfare of the common citizen'. Has anyone been better able than Prince William of Orange to grasp and express the deepest significance of a university? The belief that universities must serve as nurseries of orthodoxy was much stronger in Leyden's successors: in Franeker, Groningen, Harderwijck and Utrecht. Yet not even these bastions of Calvinism clung as closely to the apron strings of Mother Church as the latter might have liked, or were the paragons of orthodoxy their statutes proclaimed them to be. Leyden had Remonstrant teachers until after 1610 and, after 1650, all Dutch universities became platforms for or against the Cartesian doctrine. The supremacy of the Reformed Church in the seventeenth century was in many respects one of form rather than substance.

The Dutch universities were also very fortunate in that they were new foundations, and as such unencumbered by the weight of a medieval past. Not that scholasticism did not make its oppressive influence felt here as well: Aristotle reigned supreme in the Netherlands as elsewhere. Nevertheless Dutch universities enjoyed exceptional freedom and far better opportunities than most to develop new branches of learning or to add to the old. In the last analysis, it was not theology, but classical and oriental studies, and the rising sciences of anatomy, astronomy, botany, physics and chemistry that earned our universities lasting fame. Now, all these studies were completely beyond the reach of Calvinism or of the Calvinistic spirit.

As, therefore, even in the university, which the Church considered her very special preserve, Church domination did little to frustrate intellectual progress, it follows that the influence of Calvinism on those who engaged in independent intellectual pursuits must have been very much slighter still. To the thought of Grotius, not to mention Spinoza, Calvin's doctrine was entirely alien. However greatly we may prize Calvinism as a factor in our civilisation, it remains an undeniable fact that Dutch intellectual life in the seventeenth century, seen as a whole, was but partially rooted in the doctrines promulgated at Dordrecht.

In this connection we must also mention a fact that, in my opinion, cannot be stressed enough whenever the discussion comes round to the recent history of European culture, namely that we gave up the atrocities of witch-hunting more than a century earlier than our neighbours.[1] While Professor Carpzovius of Leipzig could still boast about the wholesale extermination of witches in the middle of the seventeenth century, while Richelieu himself had a hand in condemning Urbain Grandier for bewitching the Ursulines of Louvain, while Scotland and Switzerland continued to try witches until far into the eighteenth century, the last great Dutch witch trial took place in 1595 in Utrecht, then the centre of strict Calvinism.[2] In the province of Holland, one such trial ended in an acquittal in 1610; it was on this occasion that Jacob Cats earned his laurels as a young lawyer. Apparently this was the last time witches or sorcerers were brought before a Dutch court. That does not, of course, mean that the people had ceased to believe in

[1] Cf. my *Erasmus, The Dutch Spirit*, and many of my other writings.
[2] Cf. the diary of Arend van Buchell.

witches, or that their pastors had ceased to encourage them in this superstition. All of us know how Balthasar Bekker was called a blasphemer and heretic by the Church and removed from the ministry in 1691, when he published *The World Bewitched*, a work in which he expressed his disbelief in magic and sorcery. No, the humane tenor of Dutch life was fostered by an enlightened and humane magistracy, the very regent class that has so often been derided for its shortcomings.

Here we need not dwell on the delicate question of what part the Church played in the general decline of popular art. Church bells were silenced, except at funerals, and church organs came within an ace of sharing the same fate. (All the merrier was the sound of the bells in the clocktowers of even the smallest towns.) Incidentally, as we saw, the general fading of colour from popular life was probably as much the deliberate work of Baptists as it was that of Calvinists.

To sum up, we can therefore say that, though it cannot be defined in detail, the influence of Calvin's doctrine and spirit was undoubtedly decisive in the rise and preservation of the new, free state of the United Provinces, and in the foundation of the Dutch empire overseas. There is no doubt, moreover, that the life of the people was cast in a Calvinistic mould. This is not the place to discuss the repercussions on religious life, on piety and the intensity of faith of the doctrine and practice of 1618—the idea of eternity cannot be measured with an historical yardstick.

As for the rise of science in the seventeenth century, Calvinism had no specific bearing upon it, and this despite the fact that many great scientists were highly orthodox in their beliefs. Poetry, on the other hand, owed much of its inspiration and of its subject matter to Calvinism. Architects were given most of their greatest commissions by the Church, though by the Church as an institution rather than as a preceptor, and it remains an open question whether or not the results had a strictly Calvinistic character. The same is true of the rare works of sculpture, and especially of tombs and cenotaphs, for on these the accents of the doctrine were muted by boasts of military glory and the quarterings of nobility. The painting of the century did not owe overmuch to the Protestant faith, and even less to Calvinism—the sanctity of Rembrandt's religious scenes transcended all denominational differences. Of the greatest Dutchmen of them all, those who created new forms or new concepts, not a single one was a Calvinist—not Grotius, nor Vondel, nor Rembrandt.

IV

Before we can pass from our brief discussion of the basis and general trends of Dutch culture in the seventeenth century to a review of two of its most tangible aspects, namely art and literature, we must first look briefly at the everyday life of the Dutch people, and this inevitably brings us to one of their qualities that is neither lofty nor very spiritual and yet is of very great importance: their simplicity and, closely related to it, their thrift and cleanliness. Simplicity lay not only in their dress and dwelling, in the tenor of their social life and intellectual habits, but also in the very lie of their land. A flat country with few tall trees, without the many great ruins so typical of Southern countries, offered the eye the peace of simple lines, of hazy distances and gradual changes. Sky and cloud, then and now, helped to calm the troubled spirit. The modest towns with their moss-covered walls were surrounded by greenery or water—the oldest element in all creation, upon whose face the Spirit of God had moved in the very beginning, and the simplest as well. No wonder, therefore, that even the people were simple—in all they thought and did. Dutch and Spanish extremes came together in their love of sombre colours. Huygens spoke of 'Holland's glorious simplicity', a virtue in which modesty and moderation went hand in hand with tradition and great dignity. Moderation did not, of course, stretch to food and drink, for temperance in these is something that has never been counted among our ancestors' qualities.

Not even the coming of great prosperity succeeded in eradicating our simplicity. In 1676 still, Pallavicino, the Papal Nuncio to Cologne, visited our country and was struck everywhere outside The Hague by 'the old simplicity of manners, dress and furniture', and by the way in which 'the people create wealth for others instead of grasping their own share'. It is the general custom, he continued, 'to spend less than one earns, and it is considered a shameful extravagance and indeed loose living to do otherwise'. When he visited Amsterdam, the town had but recently been extended by a new circular canal, to make room for new districts with a host of fine houses. Only a nation—Pallavicino went on to say—that does not squander its wealth on clothes or servants, could have succeeded in doing all this with so little fuss. 'In this way the people of Holland are making a lasting contribution to their country's beauty and glory.'[1]

Now, if a foreign visitor was struck by the simplicity of our great towns, what would he not have thought of life in the countryside! Adriaan Leeghwater, by his works and foresight the very embodiment of our people's common sense tells us in his curious memoirs[2], that there were only three pairs of shoes in his native De Rijn, and that these were requisitioned by the aldermen whenever they were called to The Hague on matters of state.

Just one word about the proverbial cleanliness of Dutch streets and houses. This phenomenon, which was especially striking in towns north of the Ijsel, was partially due to economic causes: the important work of cheese-making took place inside the farmhouse, and since the slightest impurity could ruin the work of many weeks, everyone realised that

[1] Proceedings of the (Dutch) Historical Society, xxxii (viii) p. 83f.
[2] *Klein Chronykje* in the *Haarlemmermeerboeck*.

dirt had to be kept out at all costs—long before microbes were heard of.

Perhaps though, our love of spit and polish has far deeper roots than that. Our people have always loved simple things —it is part of our religious outlook to prize them as God's gifts, to enjoy their beauty as such, and hence to care for them as best we can. In this we are greatly helped by the ample presence of water, and by the fact that a moist atmosphere and frequent sea breezes generally keep our air free of dust.

It may have been a homely virtue, our cleanliness, but it was anything but crude materialism. For cleanliness went hand in hand with a strong feeling for reality, inasmuch as, philosophically or otherwise, objects were deemed to exist in their own right and valued as such. Thus our cleanliness reflected a little of our national ethos and religion—this point is emphasised in the writings of Jan Veth on the links between Dutch cleanliness and the art of Jan Vermeer.[1]

Such truly Dutch qualities as simplicity, thrift and cleanliness and, if you like, sobriety and a rather pedestrian outlook, bring us quite naturally to one who will help us to move on from culture in general to literature in particular, namely Constantine Huygens. We have already met him as a man of honour and rank, who yet remained a thorough burgher in spirit and attitude. We must now look at him more closely, for this highly talented, though not truly great, man was one of the purest representatives of Dutch culture in his day. Constantine's father, Christian, was born in the barony of Breda, became one of Prince William's secretaries as early as 1578 and, on the latter's death, a secretary to the Council of State. He gave his sons a carefully balanced education, in which games and physical exercise complemented intellectual training to produce healthy, courageous, simple, free and natural men, in accordance with the ideals of the Renaissance. And throughout his long life Constantine

[1] *Beelden en Groepen*, Amsterdam (1919), p. 105.

proved worthy of his education and faithful to its ideals. He was one who lived his life to the full and a man of outstanding ability. He spoke several languages, drew reasonably well, and was an accomplished musician with hundreds of compositions to his credit. He wrote poetry in Dutch, Latin and French, and dabbled in theology, natural science, astronomy, philosophy and literature besides. He was a model secretary to the Prince, one who conducted important business for the House of Orange in Southern France and London while already in his seventies. He was 91 years old when he died in 1687, and he himself edited his voluminous and multilingual correspondence with a host of writers, nobles, scholars, diplomats and great ladies. Not surprisingly the writings of this indefatigably active man included a tirade against sleep:

> Fell sleep thou art no friend of mine
> Had I my way, I would not lie supine,
> On pillows soft a nightly death to die,
> But would with hearty labour thee defy . . .[1]

Fittingly, this honest poet, who was not quite poetical enough, this man of unblemished character, went into deep mourning for his wife Susanna, one whom he never forgot.

Though his poems were full of classical allusions and references, he remained Dutch to the core of his being, and he even succeeded in giving authentic Dutch renderings of Italian, French, Spanish and English literary works of the sixteenth and seventeenth centuries.

Few people nowadays read Huygens for other than academic reasons, partly because of a regrettable decline of interest in, and hence neglect of, our national heritage. To the man of average education, the *dramatis personae* are no longer as close, their circumstances no longer as familiar, as they used to be in the days of Van Lennep and Potgieter. Few will be able to tell you how the States of Holland worked, or how the Act of Seclusion came about, or who

[1]*Hofwyck, De Koren-bloemen,* 1658, p. 599.

Nicolaus Witsen was; most prefer to leave all that to the experts. This loss of contact with our country's history (despite the existence of many illustrated works on the subject) is also responsible for the general neglect of Huygens. His poetry is too dry and too time-worn for us. Such satires as his *Kostelyck Mal*, together with his symbols, maxims and epigrams, moral reflections and didactic poems, have become literary curiosities, and the blame is not entirely the reader's. Huygens' work had many serious flaws. The elaborate style demands too much concentration; the learned undercurrents can be prodigiously tiresome. He makes excessive use of the oxymoron, a rhetorical figure by which contradictory terms are conjoined to give ironical point to a statement. His mind was fresh and penetrating enough, but his humour, at which he tried his hand again and again, has grown stale, and stale humour, like stale bread, is unpalatable. When all is said and done, Huygens was far too serious at heart to succeed as a humorist.

And yet, whosoever wishes to savour the spirit of seventeenth-century Holland as he would old wine, let him sample *Hofwyck*; he will find more good sense than poetry in it, but he will also find our country and people as they were when every board that could bear paint, was a merry blaze of green or white or red or yellow or blue.

Although it is only a step from Constantine Huygens to Jacob Cats, it is not, as is so often claimed, a step from the sublime to the ridiculous, for Huygens was not sublime nor was Cats ridiculous. We have become accustomed to speaking of the poet whose works could be found alongside the Bible in every Dutch house for two whole centuries, with a certain embarrassment and with many excuses. We have come to think of him as the *enfant terrible* of our great epoch, as one whose level was too low, although his unexcelled popularity proves clearly that he, as no other, saw the people of the Netherlands as they wanted to be seen. Was it possibly because he came from Zeeland and not from Holland, that Cats failed to rise above his circumstances? I would have no one think that I am lacking in appreciation of this, the most charming of our provinces, where the lights are softer, the skyline more sweeping, the meadows greener, the villages cosier—and where the towns used to be more beautiful than anywhere else. Yet is it not a fact that its plain-speaking inhabitants—brave sailors, good fishermen and kindly farmers—produced very little during our heyday in the way of great writing or painting? And was the song of the 'Zeeland Nightingale' really much more than a frog croaking merrily in the reeds?

Perhaps it would be safer and fairer to blame Cats' poetical shortcomings on his preoccupation with worldly success. He studied in Leyden, took his law degree in Orleans, became an advocate and climbed, more through skilful negotiation of the prevailing political rapids than through talent or merit, to the highest office in the Republic. He, the Zeelander, became Grand Pensionary of Holland, simply because Frederick Henry did not like to see a strong personality in that office. Cats never became a great statesman, but he did become an English knight and, through his early work in land reclamation, a very rich man. He was a good Calvinist, always surrounded by parsons, but expressed pietistic and moralistic rather than strictly doctrinal ideas, so that the Catholic South, too, could read and continue to enjoy him without taking the slightest offence. His work even achieved great renown in South Africa.

No matter how we explain it, Cats' great and durable popularity remains somewhat of a blot on our national character. True, in purely formal respects, he was a far better poet than most modern critics will grant, but why had it to be his pedestrian mind, his calculated morality, his circumspect sensuality, his complacency and his untuned lyre which, of all things, captured the imagination of our people? Because he gave the masses what they understood and liked, because the whole nation recognised itself in his often entertaining and always instructive musings and in the utter banality and prosaic sobriety that mirrored their own. In order to understand Cats we must grasp him not with our poetic but with our historical sense, and see him as the (often turbid) pool in which an entire age is reflected.

The more the heavy volumes of Cats' works have been relegated to the bottom of the bookcase, the keener has literary interest grown in the writings of Gerbrand Adriaenszoon Bredero. The contrast between these two could hardly have been greater. One was the master of Zorgvliet who, though he lost his heart to poetry while still a child, yet did not begin to write verses till fairly late in life and, laden with honours, offices and worldly goods, steered a safe course and lived to the ripe age of eighty-three. The other was an Amsterdam shoemaker's son who, sparkling with wit and poetic fire died at the age of thirty-three. One had studied the classics (he composed Greek and Latin verses). The other, like the swan of Avon, had small Latin and less Greek. Bredero himself said of his education that 'a little school-French still rattled in his head'. Although Bredero, too, would go to the classics for inspiration, and even based his *Moortje* on a French translation of Terence's *Eunuch*, he was perhaps less given than any of our other poets to embellishing his verses with smatterings of great learning. Not that he ignored the Renaissance, for he could surely not have written his passionate love poems without Petrarch, and his earlier dramatic material was taken from the chivalric *Palmerin of England* novels, themselves a continuation of *Amadis of Gaul*. He also made a remarkable return to the style of medieval folksong. But what of his masterpiece and final work, the *Spanish Brabanter*? He took the theme from *Lazarillo de Tormes*, a picaresque novel, and what he made of it was more typical of Holland, indeed of Amsterdam, than anything else he wrote. If ever a slice of popular life and culture spoke straight from the pages of a book, then it was in the *Spanish Brabanter* and in the best pages of *Moortje*, the little Moor. Here you can see the generation of Vondel, Frans Hals and Jan Pieterszoon Coen large as life—with all their vitality and all their coarseness as well.

Bredero's two greatest comedies were neither plays nor were they really comic, albeit his contemporaries must have laughed most heartily at their homespun humour. But brisk dialogue and droll situations are no substitutes for dramatic effect, nor bawdiness for humour. To find a true writer of comedies we must go to Ben Jonson. Despite all that, we would not exchange Bredero for anyone, for he, as no one else, takes us back to our own past and the Amsterdam of yore. The most fitting epithet for Bredero's art is 'graphic'. And for that very reason he is not really humorous: his writing is too pictorial, and humour described makes us laugh as little as tragedy described makes us cry. Bredero, who was trained as a painter and who first earned his living as a draughtsman, really belongs far more to painting than he does to literature.

It is not our aim in this brief sketch to give an exhaustive survey of Dutch literature. Hence we shall pass in silence over a host of other poets, and go straight on to Hooft and Vondel.

What can Pieter Corneliszoon Hooft who, unlike Bredero, came from the burgomaster's and not a shoemaker's house, tell us about life in Amsterdam in his time? Like most other leading families in the town, the Hoofts were not patricians of long standing—most of the old patriciate had disappeared when Amsterdam espoused Protestantism. Hooft's father had risen by trade and shipping, and the son, too, was intended to become a merchant. But while studying in France and Italy he became fired with the spirit of the Italian

Renaissance. In 1605, he persuaded his father to let him relinquish the study of commerce abroad for that of jurisprudence in Leyden, and before he was thirty years old, Prince Maurice appointed him Warden of Muiden, Bailiff of Gooiland and Chief Officer of Weesp. It would seem that he did not neglect his official duties, but his life—in Muiden Castle during the summer, in winter at Amsterdam—was nevertheless that of the man of letters without any worldly cares. What strikes one as so remarkable in Hooft is that, despite his *Nederlandse Historien*, he should have been so unlike most of his Dutch contemporaries in manner and spirit. In his historical work, say what you will, the Dutch sounds are often muffled by the pervasive strains of Tacitus. For my part, the dry historiographer, Bor, often gets far closer to the crux of things than Hooft with all his fine style. In his mannered poetry he remained Romance at heart; the simplicity of his language and prosody, the soft stress, the warm sentiment—all this seems little related to the harsh element in our character and past. Yet is it precisely the softer, sweet qualities of his poetry that make Hooft so much more accessible to the modern reader than any other of our seventeenth-century writers. His warmth and gentle pathos, his light though often profound touch—all these appeal far more to our modern sensibilities than do the stern and rough manners of his contemporaries. Nevertheless, we recognise far too well how much credit Hooft, as host of the Muiden Circle, deserves for providing his country with a centre of cultural life, to go any further into what set him apart from his fellow citizens.

We now come to Vondel, the greatest of them all by far. We Dutchmen know that Vondel must be counted among the finest writers of all time. We also realise, and are resigned to the fact, that the world neither knows him nor is ever likely to do so. Is it simply because he wrote in Dutch? Surely not, for if that were the case, he would have earned world renown in translation, just as Cervantes and other Spanish writers did or, more recently, the Russians and Ibsen. No, he must rather have been lacking in certain qualities that make a writer universally admired.

Any attempt to survey Vondel's work briefly, without entering into too many details or stating too many well-known facts, had best begin with an appreciation of the formal excellence of his writing. If we do that, we find that the words 'resounding, 'majestic,' and 'perfect' spring to our lips. True, now and then he would sweetly blow the pipes of Pan or else rouse us with a blast on his trumpet, but his work as a whole remains orchestral in the fullest sense of the word. Or to use another set of metaphors: Vondel's poetry is an unusually lavish mixture of colours. 'Colourful,' 'lavish,' 'resounding'—metaphors from the realms of two different senses—do they fully express the force, ease, and liveliness of Vondel's rhythm? I cannot tell what proportion of his work was written in alexandrines; what I do know is that when we sometimes weary of him (and how often he tires me!) it is not due to the quality of his metre. Yet, when he occasionally expresses himself in a different rhythm, it often seems as if he had escaped from a cage. Again, we may call Vondel's poetry brilliant, noble, or Elysian. Until, in the face of so much praise for the formal excellence of his metre, it begins to dawn upon us that nothing at all has been said about the excellence of his thought. Is it because there is very little to say about it? And if so, how greatly does that detract from his poetic merit?

It is as well to go directly from Vondel's great qualities to his many shortcomings, as they affect the general reader rather than the philologer or the poet. Do we read him often and with pleasure, do we know a great deal about him, is he part and parcel of our stock of phrase and fable? It is hard to answer all these questions with an unqualified yes. I, for my part, freely confess that a play by Vondel—unlike one by Shakespeare—makes great demands upon my patience, and that even on reading one of his choruses, my interest begins to flag or even to evaporate after only a few lines. How is it that not only Shakespeare but even Racine seem so much closer to us? Is it the dead weight of ancient and Biblical imagery that oppresses us, or the superabundance of players and scenes? We can no longer absorb Vondel through our poetic pores. With the exception of a few lyrical poems or lyrical passages, his voice has ceased to filter through to us. We read him much as a non-classicist with a smattering of Latin may occasionally pick up a copy of Virgil.

But even the severest critics will not be able to discover anything ignoble or mean in Vondel's spirit. They will tell you of his failings as a poet, but few of these made him a lesser, and none a colder, man. His poetry was often spoiled by his boundless naiveté and his amiable ignorance of the world, to which the lack of dramatic interest in his plays is due and to which his extremely primitive psychology must be attributed. His characters are for the most part puppets, moved by the simplest strings, radiant in their unsullied virtue or detestable in their dire intent. Vondel knew the force of temptation and of inward struggle, but in his treatment of them he rarely if ever deviated from the scriptural or hagiographic pattern. Deep reverence, in the fullest sense of the word, was one of Vondel's most trenchant characteristics. How childish and modest this reverence really was is perhaps best appreciated from the diligence with which the great poet began studying Latin at a time when he was already at the height of his power, the more faithfully to follow his classical models. In writing a tragedy, in laying and unravelling a plot, what charming ingenuity or rather what lack of design—in complete contrast to Shakespeare or Racine! To put it bluntly, Vondel worked with a strictly limited number of poetic stereotypes.

Vondel's outlook was typical of Holland. Few of his Antwerp antecedents affected his work, but he joined Cologne, his birthplace, to Amsterdam in a song of praise, a vision in which the everyday was transformed into the Christian millennium, with Cologne triumphant as the seat of St. Ursula and humbler Amsterdam a Christian Troy. The hero, Gysbreght, was an obscure Aeneas whom Vondel raised from shadowy existence in old chronicles to a seat on Olympus. The reader may remember that before he was allowed to stage his *Gysbreght Van Amstel*, Vondel was forced to remove a number of passages smacking of those 'Popish superstitions' he was soon afterwards to embrace.

But even when he did so, he did not abandon his earlier Arminian strains or many of his Baptist ideas, with the result that his poetic world became suffused with a primitive Christian atmosphere of saints and martyrs. That did not prevent his dipping into the here and now, into the vortex of Amsterdam or the lush greenery of Het Gooi or Kennemerland. You may call Vondel a heroic visionary, but you must also grant that he was a thorough realist, in the literal sense of that word, a man who firmly believed in the reality and importance of ordinary things, much as St. Thomas Aquinas had done long before him and, in fact, most Dutchmen did in his own day. It was this ready acceptance of things as they appeared to the senses by which Vondel is related to such lesser men as Huygens and, indeed, to most writers of the time. Vondel saw the world of his imagination in the rounded forms and luxuriant draperies of the Baroque: all simple and straight lines were blurred by the rich imagination of renascent Catholicism.

All his life long, Vondel remained an occasional poet. But then so did great poets in all ages, the Greek dramatists no less than the minnesingers, Virgil no less than Dante. Opportunity makes a poet as well as a thief; the idea that a spontaneous flow of verses is the only mark of the true poet is a Romantic fiction. Vondel, in his simple faith, his warm spontaneity, his lack of prudence in dealing with envious detractors and with authority, remained the eternal child, and in this he was at one with nearly all truly great minds. He had a strong and fervent appreciation of the joys and hardships of family life—of which latter he had an ample share—and of everything that was healthy, honest and simple. It was just like him that, despite the many wedding songs he composed for others, the only poems he composed for his own family were lamentations.

This modest man may truly be said to have lived his whole life in an atmosphere of exalted virtue—to have truly been one of that band which are merciful and which do hunger and thirst after righteousness.

The differences between Vondel and Hugo Grotius seem far greater today than they did in the seventeenth century. To us they are the differences between poet and scholar, art and learning. Even though Grotius, too, wrote some 10,000 Latin and a similar number of Dutch lines of verse, we hold that he was much too closely associated with the law and the university to be placed in the same category as Vondel. Yet it was not until much later that literature in the sense of *belles lettres* became lumped together with music and art, and we must not forget that poetry along with history, philology, philosophy, grammar and sometimes even jurisprudence used to constitute letters or *literae* in the seventeenth century, while the term 'art' referred to painting, sculpture, music and craftsmanship—the last being very close to what we would now call science. To seventeenth-century man, therefore, the step from Vondel to Grotius was not so very great—both were men of letters. Two points deserve brief mention in this connection: Grotius's role as representative of Dutch culture, and the importance of letters and learning in his day and age.

It is easy to show that Grotius was a typical Dutchman in

every fibre[1]. This is perhaps most clearly borne out by his *Truth of the Christian Religion*, a work at least as dear to him as the *De Jure Belli et Pacis* and one, moreover, on which his fame was largely founded. He wrote it at Loevestein in Dutch rhyme, and for whom? For Dutch sailors, men who mixed with all the nations and were thus the obvious bearers of God's message, if only that message be explained to them in simple enough terms. Here we have Grotius in a nutshell: the simple-hearted teacher, the gentle optimist, the universal peacebringer, one who put his trust in the strength of honest argument, in the spirit of harmony and religious tolerance, the opponent of unyielding orthodoxy —in short, the Remonstrant.

Vondel and Grotius were united in their love of freedom, as they understood it: freedom for the individual to develop his potential powers under a moderate, orderly, benevolent aristocracy. They were also agreed in their views on justice. Vondel, just four years younger than Grotius, outlived him by thirty-four years. Thus Grotius was mainly a figure of the early part of the seventeenth century, one who gave his best in his forties, at a time when, in his Parisian exile, he had become somewhat estranged from the progress of Dutch culture. He lived to witness Vondel's conversion to Catholicism, but he never saw its ripest fruit, Vondel's *Lucifer*. In any case, Grotius's own Catholic tendencies were quite unlike Vondel's wholehearted passion for the mysteries of the Church. To Grotius, the Old Church seemed bathed in the soft glow of that universal peace, harmony, tradition, style and form that also filled him with admiration for the Church of England. Yet this was a far cry from Vondel's worship of the saints, from his passionate surrender to the power of the Sacrament. When all is said and done, Grotius remained far too much the rationalist and classicist to walk

[1]Grotius himself preferred to think of himself as a Hollander (cf. p. 30), and to treat the other provinces as mere allies or *socii* of Holland in accordance with the Roman model.

along Vondel's path. With his *De veritate religionis christianae* (which quickly followed the publication of the Dutch text) in which he based his defence of religion more on historical and philological than on theological and philosophical grounds, Grotius prepared the way for the coming of rationalism, the more so because what he wrote was exceedingly simple to understand.

Grotius was one who drew on firm knowledge and proved with irrefutable logical argument, not one who delved into the unknown until he found what he sought. That is precisely why he accepted the firm authority of the Bible and of classical ideas. He measured the vast multiplicity of daily events against the simple backcloth of ancient history, and interpreted the here and now in terms of what had gone before.

In the absence of a continuous stream of daily news, seventeenth-century man could devote much time and care to the pursuit of literature in its older, wider sense. It formed the chief ornament of intellectual existence, a noble pleasure, and it was closely bound up with everything festive or solemn. How much literature did not arise as an act of homage, celebration, consecration or remembrance, as eulogy, dedication, epithalamium, epitaph!

Quite different was the position of systematised learning, or rather of that portion which, at the time, began to break away from *literae* as *scientia*. Natural science had not yet taken its rightful place in society—those in search of nature's mysteries remained outsiders and still went in fear of being mistaken for sorcerers, alchemists, or quacks. Their work was considered to involve such vices as idle curiosity, daydreaming and base lust for gold, though the contributions of some were valued for their direct results: the improvement of tools and the solution of practical problems. However, in no sense was the pursuit of science considered a proper occupation, let alone a true vocation. And yet, despite all this,

Stevin, Snellius, Leeuwenhoek and Swammerdam followed their chosen path, and even found a modicum of fame along it. In only one case did scientific genius go hand in hand with social prestige, respect, recognition and a carefree life —in the case of Christian Huygens.

Although his father, Constantine Huygens, died only eight years before him, Christian seems like a figure from quite another age or world. Moreover, father and son led quite disparate personal lives; Christian, the bachelor, who lost his mother early on and was educated by his father; Constantine, absorbed in his children. They shared many things, among them a great love of music, a firm practical hold on life (Christian himself polished the lenses for his astronomic observations and discoveries) and an astonishing versatility. For Christian, too, was a man of many talents: Latin scholar, mathematician, lawyer and fine draughtsman—it was he who drew the portrait for Cornelis Visscher's engraving in Constantine's *Korenbloemen*, a work that appeared in the same year and under the same imprint as Christian's own *Horologium*. If I could look more deeply into Christian's heart than my historical training permits, I should no doubt discover many more points of agreement between the son, whose essential Dutch character not even years of absence in France could wipe out, the father and even the grandfather, and thus adduce glowing proof of the inheritance of talent in three generations of what was, from the outset, a highly gifted family. But in this brief sketch I can hope to do no more than recall that Christian Huygens was a brilliant scientist who lived at a time when the concept of science, as we understand it today, was barely born.

Indeed, in this essay we are forced to ignore a great many matters that played an essential part in the cultural life of the time. I am thinking in particular of our mills, dikes and fortifications; of our shipwrights, of the work of Nicolaus Witsen and Cornelius van Yk; of our travellers and explorers; of our laws and our administration. I should also have liked to discuss at some greater length our precocious attempts to provide a measure of social welfare based on Christian charity—our reformatories, workhouses and orphanages, primitive though they were by modern standards, were far in advance of anything found in most other countries.

Finally the greatest gaps of all: in this essay devoted to the age and country of Spinoza, we must keep silent about philosophy, nor have we the space to discuss music in the age of Sweelinck. In accordance with the intentions declared in the Preface, we shall therefore proceed directly to the subject of Dutch art.

v

Art is probably the one aspect of seventeenth-century Dutch culture with which the modern reader is fairly familiar. Most of us have daily contact with it in all its forms—painting and engraving, architecture and sculpture—and it would seem that, barring details of peculiar interest to historians of art, the subject could hold few secrets for us. Is there anything we can usefully add in these few pages? In fact, what we shall have to say will be more in the form of questions than of positive statements.

We have mentioned the connection between the mainly urban and bourgeois structure of seventeenth-century Dutch society and the predominance of painting over sculpture. Painting had its *raison d'être* in the wealth and vitality of the well-to-do burghers; among them it found its inspiration, protectors and patrons. There were no great Maecenases among them, mark you; instead there was a vast number of art lovers. Paintings could be found everywhere: in the town hall and other public places, in orphanages and offices, in the houses of patricians and burghers alike—in brief, everywhere except in the churches.

What was it that the well-to-do and cultured burgher—merchant, advocate, public servant—expected from art and saw in it? What, in other words, was the social and aesthetic function of art? Let no one answer: the quenching of a thirst for beauty. It is an anachronism to project our own aesthetic views into the minds of seventeenth-century men, for our views stem very largely from cultural developments in the eighteenth and nineteenth centuries. The artistic approach of most of Rembrandt's contemporaries was primitive in the extreme. True there was a direct response to colour and line—the result of centuries of decorative endeavour: medieval man had painted anything that would take colour, and in the seventeenth century this enthusiasm was not yet forgotten. Only forty or fifty years ago people felt it incumbent upon them to remove the colour from the stone figures that adorn so many of our gateways and gables and to reveal them in bare sandstone or freestone. Since then we have learned better. Colour has been used throughout the ages and, indeed, respect for brick and stone can go too far and become historically perverse.

Of course, an innate love of colour does not in itself suffice to explain the extraordinary development of Dutch painting. Much more essential was the intense enjoyment of shapes and objects, the unshakable faith in the reality and importance of all earthly things, a faith that had nothing to do with philosophical realism, but was the direct consequence of a deep love of life and interest in one's environment.

All those aesthetes who, at one time or another, have decried or depreciated Dutch art and all those who have called our painters unoriginal hacks and mere copyists, have mistaken the real meaning of representational painting and its true value. A drawing or painting is always more than a mere copy; it is always an attempt to grasp what is hidden beneath the visible form, of what cannot be expressed in mere words.

And seventeenth-century artists must, indeed, have had an irrepressible need to grasp things. Nothing in their environment was too slight to be noticed. In addition, they also depicted figures from the world of their imagination, allegorically transformed into symbols. Here the vision of the subject was strictly circumscribed by style and tradition, and variety of expression very small indeed.

And what did the buyer of paintings or engravings expect from the artist? This question is as important to our purpose as that of the artist's own intent. First and foremost, they demanded a suitable subject, one, moreover, they could admire and that was presented in the way in which they were wont to see it. Next they sought and valued artistic skill and sheer technical accomplishment. They expected to derive pleasure from their paintings and also liked to show them off. The choice of subject was often determined by the particular wall on which the painting would be hung. This does not mean that seventeenth-century houses had special studies, guest-rooms, etc.—these were a later innovation, though meals were, of course, always served in the same place, and it was here that a still-life depicting fruit, game and other delicacies would usually be hung.

As a result of the great demand for paintings, many a mere owner was transformed into a collector with a gallery of his own—and not only among the very rich. In this way, the emphasis gradually shifted from enjoyment of good likenesses towards the sheer love of art and beauty. However, even the collector was not a collector in the modern sense of the word. He was far more concerned to own works of every genre than of every great master. The average buyer greatly preferred possessing a country scene, a landscape, a seascape, an allegory and above all his own portrait to owning a Van Goyen, Steen, Hals or Porcellis. There were, of course, exceptions to this rule, and a really first-class gallery was expected to include a Dürer and a Holbein—hence the many suspected forgeries.

Any attempt to assess the artistic appreciation of earlier generations runs the danger of involving too many modern criteria. It would be ridiculous to contend that people of the time did not appreciate the full beauty of a work, simply because they failed to praise it in flowing prose. What they did write about was, in fact, the skill of the artist, the extent to which the picture accorded with the prevailing canons and its apparent faithfulness to nature. In all these matters they expressed their opinions in measured terms—and that is surely no drawback.

The question of the faithfulness to nature raises a delicate problem: many of the older generation will remember how the advent of photography changed our ideas on trotting horses, which ceased to be suitable subjects for painting. Moreover, seventeenth-century painters were quite unable to depict lions, monkeys, or elephants in a way we should call true to nature—in sharp contrast to the matchless accuracy with which Adriaan van de Velde, for instance, painted domestic animals.

One more word on the choice of subject matter by seventeenth-century Dutch artists. The modern art-lover must be careful to avoid the temptation of looking at the painter's ideas or subjects in the light of his own views and hence seeing more in them than was there. Luckily, critics have ceased to see Dostoevskian tragedies behind every Breughel, Jan Steen and Adriaan Brouwer, but this gain is offset by the fact that our artists' crude satire and coarse humour has lost much of its appeal. Thus, if we are to view their work in the way we have set out to do, namely as the cultural expression of the age in which they lived, we must try to feel our way back into the cheerful vulgarity of their minds and tastes.

Part of their art will forever elude us. It is full of arcane allusions and many of these we cannot hope to fathom even after the most careful research. Thus every bloom in every flower piece is a symbol, and the subject of every still life has emblematic as well as a natural significance. The same is true of many undecipherable details in the bearing of a market stall-keeper, servant or musician—types whom our painters and engravers so often chose as their subjects.

Because of their social function, i.e. because they were mainly intended as a form of home decoration in a bourgeois setting, paintings were automatically restricted to small dimensions. Even when they were destined for public display—paintings of regents, Civic Guards, naval battles—it was only the exceptional canvases that swelled to vast proportions. The atmosphere in which art flourished demanded neither large perspectives nor great imagination. Is it to be regretted that our artists were not expected to give vent to the passion of a Rubens? Did their imagination become stunted because there was no demand for it? Here in the North there was no resurgence of Catholic church art to encourage the painter to expand on a Rubensian scale. Lack of opportunity to develop in the grandiose Baroque manner led him to neglect large areas of poetic fantasy, and kept him out of the century's artistic fashion. Not for our artists the dazzling brilliance, pomp, ritual and majesty so dear to their colleagues abroad or the intense love of sacred mysteries. Instead, they concentrated on the intimate details of everyday life and the dreamy contemplation of far-away distances. All the essential aspects of the late Baroque: its majestic elegance, its grandiloquence, its histrionics, its loud accents, were as alien to Dutch art as the bustle of city life is to a remote province.

But we must not carry such contrasts too far for, dissimilar though Dutch art was to the work of Claude of Lorraine, Murillo, Ribera or the Italians, yet it was not entirely unrelated to the work of such famous painters from abroad as Le Nain and De la Tour, not to mention the obvious affinities between Frans Hals and Velazquez. If, in this brief space, we are to consider painting purely as an element of Dutch civilisation, we must refrain from entering into too many technical details and confine ourselves to a number of general observations. As we saw, our painters were mainly expected to portray simple everyday objects. Even if it was not deliberately Protestant, their art was nevertheless produced in a predominantly Protestant environment, and thus had no use for the figures of saints or for liturgical motifs. Again, no matter how greatly mythology may have influenced our literature, it seemed out of place in paintings for the merchant's house. Mythology and ancient history still played some part in the decoration of town hall or tribunal, but they were never sources of inspiration to our painters. All the same, one might have thought that Biblical and particularly Old Testament scenes would have been used far more often than, in fact, they were, yet religious canvases of the kind painted by Rembrandt and Barend Fabritius remained the rare exceptions. Was it Calvinistic severity or too literal an interpretation of the second commandment that stood in the way of the use of religious subjects? Was it a lack of creative imagination? Or, finally, a pious renunciation, a view rooted in religion itself, that these subjects were beyond the reach of human powers? Perhaps it was by way of compensation that our painters turned their incomparable talent to the portrayal of church interiors and exteriors—Peter Saenredam and Emanuel de Witte are two of our greatest artists.

There seems little doubt that Protestantism, by limiting the painter's choice of subject, stunted abilities that would have flourished in earlier times. In the absence of any call for painting in the ornamental style, something of the approach of Jan van Scorel or Maarten van Heemskerk died away— our art lost its ideological momentum. Whether or not that was a disadvantage is a question we shall not attempt to answer here.

Any discussion of seventeenth-century Dutch art seems inevitably to involve the word 'realism.' When we speak of realism in art, do we mean the belief that the external form of things must be reproduced as faithfully as possible? Surely not, for that is merely a question of honest skill, of the probity of art, as Ingres called it, and that skill was shared by artists of all periods, in Egypt and China no less than among the modern impressionists. The differences between them arise because truth and accurate draughtsmanship are not necessarily synonymous. Now, our painters did not really bother their heads about the distinction. They were too uneducated, too naïve, too unacademic to do so; they were simple men who knew their job exceedingly well but scarcely knew the meaning of style, who painted as best they could, in accordance with the motto chosen by Jan van Eyck. Did they perchance also try to capture the 'meaning' of 'life'? Yes, if you like, though that was not really what inspired their work. They invested life with little fantasy but with a great deal of mystery, which in fact it has. 'Realists' in the philosophical sense they may have been, though unwittingly, but there is little doubt that they were realists in the sense in which the word is commonly used, i.e. they were firmly convinced of the substantiality of things.

If, in our discussion of seventeenth-century Dutch art, we are to proceed from the simple to the more complex, we must speak of Frans Hals before we turn to Rembrandt which, of course, is also the chronological order. Frans Hals was above all a spontaneous man—nothing in him was calculated or deliberate, nothing studied or affected. Whoever came under his brush might wear his best suit and smartest collar but had to leave his vanity behind. Even the noble Van Heythuysen did not get more than he deserved. Hals made no attempt to depict plain burghers with the graces of princes or heroes. We like to think of Hals's subjects as men of solid and healthy appearance. If we look more closely, however, we shall find a number of sickly and seedy-looking faces among them. It remains one of the wonders of art how Frans Hals, almost eighty years old at the time, contrived to immortalise the 'Lady Governors of the Home for the Aged', these old ladies with their withered everyday faces, in such a way that, albeit we know nothing of their names and doings, we remember them as clearly as we might great princes or poets. Do not call it psychology, do not tell us Hals succeeded in probing deep into their souls—far from it. But his vision and skill were mightier than he himself knew or could have known, with the result that he created a poem redolent of a whole era and an entire people. And here, for once, he did something that Velazquez could not have equalled.

We are deliberately ignoring the Flemish school because the task of including the South would take us too far afield. Yet we must make a brief comparison between Frans Hals and Van Dyck, because that comparison sets off the typically Dutch character of Hals better than anything else. For whereas Van Dyck had grandeur, elegance, refinement and distinction—qualities that were lacking in seventeenth-century Holland and have, in any case, lost some of their lustre over the centuries, Hals had candour and honest simplicity, and these strike even the foreigner, who cannot fully understand our country and people, as the more enduring of the two.

What can we say about Jan Vermeer of Delft, one of the great masters whose work transcends all technical categories, one who humbles all the precepts of aesthetics? Let us be brief and simple. Superficially speaking, Vermeer, like so many of his friends, was a painter of every-day life. Why did he, as far as we know, so rarely seek it in portraiture? Surely not because he failed to fathom the depth of his subjects. He will show you a man, or preferably a woman, doing the simplest task, in simple surroundings, with loving care, reading a letter, pouring milk from a jug or waiting for a boat to arrive. All the figures seem to have been transplanted from ordinary existence into a clear and harmonious setting where words have no sound and thoughts no form. Their actions are steeped in mystery, as those of figures we see in a dream. The word realism seems completely out of place here. Everything is of unrivalled poetic intensity. If we look carefully, we see that Vermeer's figures are not so much Dutchwomen from the sixteenth century as figures from an elegiacal world, peaceful and calm. Nor do they wear the costume of a particular period; they are dressed like visions, symphonies in blue, green and yellow. Glowing, living reds were not very close to Vermeer's heart —even that glorious masterpiece *The Painter in his Studio* is neither loud nor glaring. It may be rather bold of me to say that Vermeer fails precisely when he depicts holy scenes, for instance Christ at Emmaus. For it is not with the Gospel story itself that he is primarily concerned; rather does he treat the subject as a brilliant exercise in colour. Despite his unique qualities, Vermeer is a truly Dutch painter, at least inasmuch as he, too, propounded no theses and, in the strict sense of the word, lacked a fixed style.

In discussing landscape painting, we must clearly distinguish between those artists who are ruled by the laws of composition and those to whom every theory, every clear-cut rule, seems anathema. To my mind, Dutch landscapes are at their best when, unlike Ruisdael's *Jewish Cemetery*, which Goethe admired so greatly, they are non-picturesque —Van Goyen's bare banks of Haarlem Lake with its broad turbulent waves, or so many landscapes by Lambert Doomer, Janson van Ceulen and, above all, Hercules Seghers. The lack of theories and stylistic principles, and the simple devotion to their trade caused them to discover vast and unexpected possibilities—merely by following the irresistible flow of their hand. Our painters were at their best whenever, instead of subscribing to any particular style they let themselves go and thus discovered unexpected, and often unappreciated, shades of beauty in everyday life.

85

Their work at its best may be called a kind of pictorial
laissez-faire policy.

A factor contributing to this freedom was undoubtedly
the kind of training Dutch painters enjoyed. Only a few of
them went to Italy, to become lost in the hurly-burly of the
typical painter's life with all its conventions. In the Netherlands themselves, they found neither Bohemia nor Academe,
but learned their trade in one of the many painter's work-
shops that could be found throughout the country, but were
particularly widespread in Holland.

As an indication of culture, the engraver's art is probably
a far more reliable guide than the painter's—from the rise of
woodcuts and copperplate printing in the fifteenth century
to the advent of modern photographic methods of book
illustration, engravings were almost unrivalled media of
cultural diffusion, reaching as they did all strata of the population. We can hardly imagine today what the enjoyment
and possession of engravings—from the simplest to the most
highly perfect products of the taille douce, mezzotint and
stipple methods—meant to their seventeenth-century
owners. For whereas great paintings were kept out of the
public view in private houses or displayed in public
buildings that were not always accessible, everyone
could afford to collect cheap prints and recognise himself
and his surroundings in them.

Moreover, engraving was governed by special principles,
and remained far more a branch of trade and industry than
did painting. Thus no matter how high, in Dürer's and
Holbein's hands, was the standard of wood-carving in the
sixteenth century, engraving only became an important
cultural factor in the life of the people with the advent of the
copperplate—in the Netherlands, with Goltzius and Jacob
de Gheyn, soon followed by Jan van de Velde and so many
others. The man wielding the burin generally worked to a
publisher's orders, be it to produce calendar pages or series

of town or village views, castles, ships, costumes or what have you. He also illustrated books, reproduced portraits and supplied emblems or vignettes. Generally speaking, his subjects were familiar—he was expected to depict what he knew and what he could see. Did he always do just that? Perhaps not, for though he kept to the model when he produced a portrait or to the architectural features of a given town view, as soon as he was left any freedom, for instance in the cycle of the months by Jan van de Velde, he would temper his faithfulness to nature with a few drops of the fantastic and romantic, and would often spoil some of his best work by placing a typical Dutch scene against a background of mountains.

In his art, he obeyed a number of conventions, for instance he would balance a group of trees in the left foreground with light and space on the right, yet he did so with a great deal of latitude which often inspired his happiest effects.

Closely though etching and engraving are related, yet their cultural function and significance are quite distinct. The etcher is free of all the restrictions and bonds that make the engraver a true craftsman. However, we must step carefully here. When we think of etchers we think primarily of Rembrandt, but we cannot really ignore Roeland Roghman, Simon de Vliegher and, above all, Hercules Seghers. Still, it is true that though the etcher, too, might work to order, he worked primarily for his own satisfaction or for that of the connoisseur. Often he himself was a painter first and foremost. The more he was left to his own devices, the more freedom he could give to his versatile needle, or to exploring the endless possibilities of applying ink in different measure. Nowhere do stylistic norms matter less than they do in etching. Here the pure artist's instinct reigns supreme, almost more directly even than in drawings, and we are often touched more deeply by the drawings than by the finished work of the great masters. Drawing strikes us as springing more directly from the heart and soul. This quality is fully shared by etching. Is that the reason why more than one of our great painters, an Ostade or a Potter for instance, gave his best in that medium? In any case, there is little doubt that the spirit of etching, the spirit of reverie and dreaming, suits our national temperament exceedingly well.

In art as in literature, the greatest are not bound by the prevailing rules—they make their own. In the case of Rembrandt it would be ludicrous to suggest that his etching is preferable to his painting, to call him a better draughtsman and etcher than painter. There is really no sense in comparing a full orchestra to a single fiddle. When we look at his *Syndics* or at *Saul and David* or the *Blessing of Jacob* the idea of etching or drawing does not even arise—not because they are inferior techniques but simply because they belong to a different world. All that was most profound and serious in Rembrandt, he could only express with the brush.

No one can object if, in this brief essay, no attempt is made to praise Rembrandt's true greatness once again in glowing phrases, and if, instead, we direct our attention to the limitations of his genius. However, even the severest critic has to admit that what failings Rembrandt may have had must be sought in his paintings alone—his etchings and drawings, however simple—are as perfect as can be. The reader may think that applying the word 'limitation' to Rembrandt is in any case pedantic, or worse still, an attack on what is greatest in our heritage. If we use it nevertheless, it is because Rembrandt's stature as an exemplar of Dutch culture is conditioned by some of his least qualities as much as by some of his greatest.

Rembrandt forever tried to depict a life different from that lived in the bourgeois Dutch Republic. Thus in the *Portrait of Saskia*, the *Painter and his Wife*, *Hendrickje Stoffels*, he decked out those nearest to him in great finery, not in order to show them as they were but simply to create good pictures. The necklaces and golden chains, the feathered hats, the loose hair, the colour—all these were not signs of the time but sheer fantasy tempered with historical and foreign elements, a flight from the present into the magnificently beautiful and splendidly noble world of his imagination. Was he fully successful in his attempts to express that world, to show us his visions in all their glory? Or did his fantasy fall a little flat, so that his figures hover in the no man's land between the exalted and the trivial, to which simple Dutch reality is greatly preferable? The near-vulgar flourishes of the Kassel *Saskia* or the Dresden *Rembrandt and Saskia* make an almost painful contrast not only to what Rembrandt himself expressed in his greater portraits but also to the work of Frans Hals. Quite certainly, these semi-fantasies lack all the inexpressible depths that Rembrandt brought to his Gospel scenes.

On the other hand, some of his Old Testament canvases seem to share in what I make bold to call Rembrandt's weakest side, for his visions of Oriental splendour, too, are lacking both in formal beauty and greatness of style. An example is his *David and Absalom*, formerly in the Hermitage Museum: David with his Sunday turban, no less than Absalom with a fancy-dress sword, looks ridiculous.

At the risk of being accused of sacrilege, I must confess that I even find some of this lack of serenity in the *Night Watch*—despite all the shades of light and colour and the wonderful inventiveness, I cannot help feeling that Rembrandt aimed at something far greater than he actually achieved.

Only once was he called upon to paint a truly heroic scene. For the subject of the banquet and pledge of Claudius Civilis was far more sublime than that of the march of Frans Banning Cocq's Civic Guard: the uprising of the Batavi against Rome, which culminated in that pledge, ushered in what seemed like the birth of our nation, and to portray it for the new Amsterdam Town Hall was truly the greatest commission that any artist could have been asked to execute. Rembrandt rose fully to the occasion, and in so doing greatly surpassed his Civic Guard painting in depth of heroic imagination and in unrivalled greatness of style. But alas the good burghers of Amsterdam disapproved of the work, the masterpiece was not completed, the main fragment ended up in Stockholm, and Rembrandt was made to taste of the bitter tragedy of greatness once again.

If it is true that Rembrandt's limitations must be sought in the grandeur of his style, his strivings for monumental and classical effects, then it follows quite naturally that his etchings must be free of these faults. For here monumental or stylistic effects are out of place, here the artist can give free rein to his mood and inventive genius. And, in fact, though he did not deliberately discard everything that tradition and stylistic norms seemed to demand from him, in most of his etchings he surrendered freely to the magic of the needle and with a few quick strokes of his hand drew from the depths of his unfathomable spirit the most direct and telling reflection of the mystery surrounding all things. And what was true of his etchings applied, *a fortiori*, to his drawings, in which he could let himself go even more completely.

In his deepest heart, Rembrandt was the true son of his country and his people: you grasp the Netherlands through Rembrandt, and Rembrandt through the Netherlands. His portrayal of scenes from the Gospel, be it an etching of the Nativity, or of the Circumcision or a painting of one of the men of Emmaus, not only transcends all denominational and doctrinal differences, from Rome to Dordrecht, but even the thorny question of whether or not a particular painting is in the Baroque style. In the original draft of this essay, written in German some ten years ago, I ended this section with the following words: 'The dream-world Rembrandt sought is not entirely the world of the Baroque.

But did he not wish it to be just that? Did he not fail to assimilate the Baroque spirit simply because his innate Dutch disdain of formal style kept pulling him back into the narrow confines of his native bourgeois world? Or was it simply that in Dutch art and above all in Rembrandt an eternal and all-pervading sense of beauty triumphed over stylistic precepts? If it was, the triumph must have been one of honest craftsmanship, and of a simple heart.' So much for my earlier version. Today I would be inclined to scrap the whole passage, and say: Leave the word Baroque alone whenever you can. Far from adding to our understanding, it usually beclouds it.[1]

Let us now look briefly at some other aspects of Dutch art in the seventeenth century. On sculpture we can be very brief. As we saw, its scant contribution was largely due to the prevailing social and spatial conditions. In this land of polders, the ground had to be parcelled out in small pieces and the towns, the obvious places for statues, were generally small and their streets narrow—which does not, of course, mean that a town with large squares necessarily brings forth great sculpture. Space would surely have been found had it been wanted, but there was also the far more serious lack of patrons. Sculpture is dependent on patronage: it needs the support either of great art-lovers or else of a state ready and able to dispense largesse. Neither was present in the Dutch Republic, and this lack made itself felt over a far wider field than the one under discussion. In the Netherlands, money raised by taxation went mainly into the municipal coffers, and only to a small extent to those of the state, and the men controlling finances were for the most part burghers and merchants who preferred building almshouses and orphanages to commissioning public works of art. The churches, too, were completely closed to

---

[1] I realise that my definition of 'Baroque' differs somewhat from that found in Schmidt-Degener's excellent and absorbing *Rembrandt und der holländische Barock* (Studien der Bibliothek Warburg, IX, 1928).

sculpture, with the result that sculptors had to rely for their commissions on the family pride of the leading patricians. The church did, however, help to the extent that it allowed the erection of imposing tombs and gravestones so that, in the end, most sculptures owed their existence to the Protestant Church, after all.

Quite apart from whether or not the country, state and popular character were favourable to the rise of sculpture, we can also ask how far what little sculpture was, in fact, produced in the Netherlands during the seventeenth century expressed the special character of the Dutch people. In general, sculpture offers less possibilities for expressing national characteristics than any other form of art. The greater its works, the closer they are to the prevailing general norms and to a near-perpetual ideal: the perfect representation of the human figure. Although it is easy enough to find appropriate adjectives to describe a number of Dutch characteristics in the work of Hendrick de Keyser or Rombout Verhulst, to do so serves little purpose, and we shall, accordingly, leave it at that.

The relationship between art and national culture has always been much clearer in architecture than it is in sculpture, particularly during the early seventeenth century when many countries reached new cultural heights, each in its own way: Spain with Cervantes, Velazquez, Lope de Vega and Calderón, England with Shakespeare and his contemporaries at home and her great expansion overseas, Sweden with her unexpected political ascendancy. The Dutch Republic was unique in reaching eminence in all spheres simultaneously—in politics, trade, navigation and industry, and as a centre of art and letters. But nowhere is the typically Dutch character of our culture more striking than it is in our architecture, an instrument that seems to have been created with our state and nation in the very struggle for freedom. Of course, things are not quite as simple as that, firstly because architecture, just like any other of the arts, has its roots in the past, and secondly because in our country, with its strong regional differences, it everywhere bears traces of local character. What is remarkable is that, despite the strong Flemish influence in the South and the rich German influence in the North East, a special style should have developed that may truly be called Dutch. How much more beautiful our country would have been had the nineteenth century not scrapped so ruthlessly what the eighteenth century had allowed to fall into decay! How pitifully little has remained of the older, north-eastern style to which Groningen, for instance, owed its Great Market, one of the most beautiful squares in these parts! The small, relatively young towns of the Province of Holland, with their slender façades, supplied the overall pattern: narrow buildings with step-gables. The typical house was a development of what was originally a wooden structure, of which, however, only a few vestiges remained. Neither the half-timbered fronts nor the overhanging upper storeys were taken over, nor was the house built round an inner court. The simple form of the most usual type of house was once again the product of bourgeois simplicity, of the needs of family life with few servants. This type of building left little to the architect's imagination. In 1600, there was hardly any call for town houses with imposing interiors or staircases, and the country houses of the nobility generally preserved the massive form of the late-medieval castle, with small windows and thick walls, as they can still be found in Limburg and elsewhere.

Other buildings in demand were town halls, orphanages, assembly halls for the Civic Guards, warehouses, exchanges, depots for the great overseas trading companies, and finally country houses for the rich merchants, set in large parks and woods. Last but not least came the churches. Many of the old ones were taken over for Protestant worship, and this despite the fact that they were unsuited to the much more austere service; others were left to decay or fell victim to wilful destruction. Meanwhile, the new faith and the new prosperity seemed to call for the building of special places of worship. Here our architects' creative talents found their worthiest and most fertile field. It was not so much originality and imagination that were demanded of them as a new interpretation of the most sacred traditions and themes, and for these they turned towards Italy and the late Renaissance. From Italy came the type of building in which seventeenth-century Dutch Protestant church architecture excelled, and which was so largely inspired by Santa Maria della Salute in Venice: the Marekerk in Leyden, the Oostkerk in Middelburg and the Nieuwe Kerk in Groningen, to name but a few. In all of them, the foreign elements were translated with simple dignity into the spirit of Dutch Calvinism. And where the central scheme was not applied, there appeared such truly national masterpieces as the Westerkerk in Amsterdam, the Nieuwe Kerk in Haarlem, and the countless village churches which followed the great examples from afar—almost all with clean proportions and beautiful in their simplicity.

If we look at secular public buildings, we find that our architects did little more at first than apply the principles of domestic architecture to them. However, a Lieven de Key who built the Fleshers' Hall in Haarlem in the simple style of a dwelling, nevertheless applied the decorative element so brilliantly and on so large a scale that his great masterpiece combines the grace of the small with the proportions of the large in unexcelled harmony. Was it also he who designed that resplendent façade hiding the medieval Leyden town hall behind a front with four gables, gay yet stately, and tranquil despite all the decorative inscriptions and flourishes?

With the exception of a few large buildings, the strength of Dutch architecture did not lie in the monumental. Yet it is one of the strongest proofs of the expansive energy of our people that our builders were called upon to produce monumental works abroad. Thus, in Denmark, they supplied their princely patrons with a host of buildings in royal dimensions but of a style that was more typical of the burgher's house. No wonder that these Danish castles strike one as being somewhat hybrid in character, as being too obviously transplanted growths.

The imaginative element in our architects was given free rein in designing towers for whatever buildings could support them. The great church towers, with their rather clumsy combination of wood, lead and copper, their bulbous forms and pinched waists, were among their less happy creations—with the exception of such masterpieces as the spire of the Westerkerk. Much more successful were the towers of the town halls: graceful to the point of whimsy, in complete harmony with the carillon inside, the embodiment, as it were, of everything that is gay and light, delicate and graceful in the Dutch character, all that reminds us of the lyricism of Hooft and Vondel. Here everything speaks of solid happiness, good humour, and faith in the future. If we compare seventeenth-century Italian architecture with our own, it is almost as if the traditional roles of the two nations had been reversed: in the Italian *seicento* heaviness and sombreness, in the Dutch counterpart an almost Japanese delicacy. Despite the speed with which the old landscape is now being buried under new buildings and the demands of fast traffic, this lighthearted aspect of our seventeenth-century culture is still best and most vividly preserved in its architectural remains. Only while, but fifty years ago, the old canals, houses and streets could still be found almost everywhere, and every corner of old Amsterdam was still as beautiful as Middelburg, we must now search ever more laboriously to recover the past amidst the banal signs of subsequent neglect and of still later bungling. It was through architectural beauty that seventeenth-century man himself best appreciated the environment in which he lived. Not, mark you, in the words of the modern art critic or art lover—seventeenth-century man felt beauty rather than expressed it in words. How else could our painters and illustrators have drawn street scenes with so much love, with so much touching devotion to detail, combining the accuracy of a Van der Heyden, a Berckheyde, a Beerstraten, with the poetical vision of Vermeer's *View of Delft*? Perhaps nothing fills us with greater longing for that sunny age, for its healthy life, simple outlook and firm faith than a seventeenth-century street scene.

And our artists truly preserved the characteristic aspect of Dutch town life, with its pleasant streets or canals and simple houses. But the spirit of the times, here as elsewhere, longed for a less familiar kind of beauty—for the exotic and exalted or the fantastic and romantic. Ruisdael was not so much renowned for depicting the peaceful dunes of Kennemerland as for his romantic rocks and currents. This eternal dissatisfaction with the known explains why our patricians so quickly tired of Dutch architecture, new and original though it was, and why it came to be looked down upon as part of a past that was altogether too restricted. The ideals of a noble and disciplined classical tradition wafted across from France and Italy and spoiled the taste for sandstone and plain brick. The step gable would no longer do but must be hidden behind rounded gable ends. When the city fathers of Amsterdam deserted the narrow streets of the 'Oude Zij' for 'de Gracht', that splendid triple ring of canals was soon adorned with houses of the kind designed by Philip Vingboons, single or double fronted, built in freestone or in black brick, all with cornices instead of pointed gables and all, however humble, based on the French *hôtel* or the Italian *palazzo*.

It sounds almost symbolic that Amsterdam, at the peak of her wealth and glory, in the very year peace was declared, should have given orders for the building of a new Town

Hall and that, before it was completed, the medieval Town Hall nearby should have obliged by burning down. Van Campen's masterpiece rose up as 'the eighth wonder of the world' praised by Vondel in a festive song that had the sonorous aspect and almost the length of an epic. And Constantine Huygens praised Van Campen who

> From our stricken and disfigured face,
> The Gothic squint and squalor did erase.

What strange views, what remarkable bias! Did the good Constantine really and truly think that all that went before Van Campen—for instance the work of Hendrick de Keyser and Lieven de Key and everything we call the Dutch Renaissance—was nothing but 'squint and squalor'? I cannot believe it. For Huygens of all people was not smitten with French classicism, the sickness that sapped our culture of its national strength.

VI

With this last remark we impinge upon a question with which I should like to conclude this essay, namely why Dutch civilisation went into so rapid a decline, and in no sphere more suddenly and more markedly than in architecture. Now, it is a fact that, as soon as our architects began to hanker after rigid forms, they lost something of that crisp and rich quality we associate with our heyday and love so well. Our architecture could remain truly Dutch, truly national, only while the note of happy fantasy and native love of decoration remained dominant, while it aimed at ease rather than grandeur. Once in search of magnificence, it was irresistibly driven to imitate the model of the Romanic countries, and so lost its national identity.

In this connection, we must return to a question that I raised at the beginning, namely the relationship of Dutch art to the Baroque style, understood in its modern and, alas, far too general sense. Dutch civilisation, we said, had few affinities with it, some of the work of Grotius and Vondel notwithstanding. In particular, Dutch painting and architecture at their most typical were anything but Baroque, and we showed that wherever Rembrandt, the greatest master of all, strove after Baroque effects, he failed most profoundly. If this view is correct, then the conclusion that the Baroque style could not have been the driving force of our culture becomes inescapable.

Now the fact that Dutch art was so independent of the general trend further emphasises its individuality and special merit. Is the same true of Dutch literature as well? At first sight, literature would seem far less bound to stylistic fashion than art, which after all bears the whole weight of the present: art involves the use of raw materials and technical aids; it is produced in a studio, and it cannot escape from traditional craft and labour practices. The writer, on the other hand, can apparently give his imagination free rein as often as he likes or whenever his spirit drives him. And yet what do we see happening, not only in seventeenth-century Netherlands but elsewhere, too, and at all times? We find that literature remains far more tightly imprisoned than art in old formulas, patterns, concepts and laws. Seldom did our writers, even the greatest among them, dare to fly in the face of the new classicism. It oppressed their work with the weight of ancient figures. But however closely they tried to follow the classical pattern, their spirit kept breaking its bonds and returned to the atmosphere of Dutch meadows and dunes, precisely where Ruisdael and Cuyp found their noblest inspiration. Vondel himself wrote his best poetry when he transcended the classical norm.

Dutch writers are mainly visual in their approach—they see things just as the painter sees them. Bredero's comedies are picturesque, and so to all intents and purposes are Vondel's tragedies—this is precisely why they are bad theatre and why most of them owe their immortality to the bookshelf rather than the stage. Although Catholicism in-spired Vondel with the glorious choruses of his *Lucifer*, it could not turn him into the kind of dramatist who, like Shakespeare, makes us tremble with emotion, or like Racine, makes us thrill to the noble sound of his stylised passion.

We still have not determined precisely how and when our all too short-lived seventeenth-century civilisation came to an end. The answer 'with the end of the century itself' is unhelpful. A cultural period does not change with the calendar, however tempting and useful it may be to identify some historical periods with centuries. In fact, what we are after here cannot be put in a few words, but involves answers to a whole series of questions. When did the strength ebb away, the flowering stop, the drive slacken that turned our civilization into a worthy, albeit less illustrious, successor to Florence and Venice? What precisely was the nature of the cultural decline which unmistakably divides the Nether-lands after 1700 from that of the preceding hundred years?

Let us take the most familiar case—that of our painting. As Rembrandt entered the twilight of his later years, the great age of Dutch painting was about to pass away. For when a Lairesse could succeed in captivating public taste, and one as lacking in grace as Romein de Hooghe could become the foremost book illustrator, we can no longer speak of a great age, even though a number of our greatest painters survived the 1670's. What causes such periods of greatness to decline as if they were human lives? In this particular case, was it the rise of French fashion, was it because the old style had lost its appeal, was it pictorial repletion, or was it rather the decline of talent and skill? The change can hardly be ascribed to a social and economic decline: the country was richer than ever, and the demand for painting as great as before. Nothing stood in the way of new masters and yet they failed to appear. It would almost seem as if civilisations were born and died like so many cells or organs, though all such comparisons are, of course, deceptive and dangerous.

The decline of literature seems to have been steeper still. For who was there to wear the poet's crown once Vondel's golden voice had fallen silent? Surely not Antonides van der Goes, whose rolling verses, at best, preserved Vondel's decorum.

Here we come face to face with an agonising fact: the general collapse of Dutch culture in the eighteenth century. The extent of the collapse is often exaggerated, but the collapse itself is an undeniable historical fact. The disturbing thing is that, at the same time that the Netherlands fell into a deep slumber, the countries round us—France and England followed by Germany—were enjoying a great cultural revival. In the years 1685–1715, which Paul Hazard has so aptly called the years of Europe's *crise de conscience*, what was it that stopped us from writing the kind of prose that could be read and read again? What was the cause of the withering and calcification of Dutch letters? Was it because the prose of Hooft, our early master, was too artificial and contrived to serve as an example to others? In any case, very few great writers came after him. Letter writing became bogged down in committee jargon and French phrases; scholars wrote in Latin or in Latin style, and the rest of our prose was given over to sermons. Still, even sermons can be great. Why then were there no Dutch Bossuets or Bourdaloues? Had Calvinism lost its impetus? Why no authors like Swift, Defoe or Lesage? Why did Van Effen come out grudgingly in Dutch four years before his death, after having written in French for most of his life?

We gain an even worse impression of Dutch intellectual life upon comparing such great French periodicals as the *Journal des Sçavens* with such products as the *Boekzaal* which a Pieter Rabus was able to peddle in this country.

Leaving aside art and literature for a moment, we may

also ask whether, before the end of the seventeenth century, the Dutch people also lost some of the national qualities from which sprang our great cultural upsurge.

There is no doubt that circumstances changed. People themselves changed, too. In the course of the seventeenth century, the intellectual outlook of the Netherlands was gradually being transformed by such new factors as the rise of natural science, greater tolerance, the waning of superstition (the year 1682 brought an explanation of the real nature of comets) and, above all, the gradual accept-ance of reason as a standard of life and action. Except for a few disciples of Spinoza or strange sectarians, the Dutch remained good Calvinists or Catholics, but the old rigidity, the old violence and the old religious passions gradually lost out to the spirit of the times, the dry and sober spirit of the dawning eighteenth century. As the mark of Calvin became less prominent, so the great counter-current that has in-spired so many Dutchmen since the sixteenth century, gained momentum. You may call this counter-current Eras-mian, if you will. You may even wonder whether, in the formation of our national character, it was not, in fact, the main current rather than the counter-current. In any case, it went with a set of ideals that became increasingly typical of us: forbearance, mildness, a very strong sense of justice, a dislike of hairsplitting and sonorous phrases, a love of tranquillity. Now, depending on our interpretation of it, tranquillity may be a very low or a very high ideal, border-ing as it does on both sloth and the contemplation of eternity. Tranquillity need not be tantamount to passivity. Even in the seventeenth century, when the Netherlands pro-duced extremely active traders, sailors and soldiers, and diligent workers and builders in all branches of industry and learning, our people longed for the serene tranquillity of a peaceful country life, surrounded by books and good friends—the kind of life so dear to Erasmus and praised by Huygens, Cats and Vondel. Yet the state was ready and able to defend their rights and possessions by force of arms, and the individual to perform great acts of courage, perseverance and ingenuity. However, not the long struggle with Spain, the repeated clashes with England, nor the bitter strife with France was able to turn our people into militarists;—unlike the Swedes who, after 1700, succumbed to their warlike pretensions. The Republic looked upon her part in the War of the Spanish Succession as an onerous task and a hard trial. When it was over, tranquillity seemed to be within the grasp of most of our people, and general prosperity assured for a long time to come. Whole regions of the Netherlands were covered with summer houses, from the castles and manors of the richest and most distinguished down to the smaller, domed villas of the well-to-do tradesmen. It was a way of life of a standard unrivalled in any other country, and one that went hand in hand with a high degree of public safety. The foreign visitor must truly have looked upon our country as a paradise.

However, our widespread prosperity also had its social dangers. One result was that, even in the seventeenth century, our merchants gradually turned magistrates and our entrepreneurs investors. Were we becoming a nation of rentiers? There is no doubt that the governing and moneyed classes still produced men of great energy—economic life continued to offer enough challenges even to those who did not pay daily visits to the office, exchange or wharf. But for the average regent the main business of the day had become running after his gardener or talking to his steward or notary—apart, of course, from the routine ceremonial of town government and the more serious but not too time-consuming duties of the bench. At the same time, the pursuit of classical and theological studies and flirtations with poetry gave way to the acquisition of natural history cabinets, for these had become a *sine qua non* of fashionable life. The overall result may have represented a gain for science, but there is no doubt that much of our national energy was dissipated in the process.

Had the Netherlands become too peaceable? Had we lost something of our heroic mettle? These are dangerous questions that may cause us to become bogged down in mere words and phrases. All the same, our general and undeniable cultural decline in the eighteenth century is closely connected with them.

For the hustle and bustle of the seventeenth century, the eighteenth century substituted a way of life that may be compared to dozing in the sunset of a long summer's day. Even the fact that it was the age of Boerhaave and 'sGravesande does not rid us of the impression that it was also an age of cultural decline, and this impression is further heightened by the realisation that our only great eighteenth-century statesman, Simon van Slingelandt, failed to speak out until it was far too late.

Historical assessment of an entire period is bound to involve some distortion, not least because we tend to measure the past with alien standards, and hence fail to give credit where credit is due. Thus we are inclined to deprecate the dry rationalism and all-too-sober outlook of eighteenth-century Dutch life, because they fall far short of our own ideals. But if we judge them instead by the needs of those who, born in the seventeenth century, had not yet succeeded in shaking off the confusion of its thought, we shall, no doubt, think less harshly of the events that drew a veil over Rembrandt's century.

Some sixty years ago, educators and writers alike were wont to speak of our golden age. Thus in 1897, when P. L. Muller brought out his most worthy *The Republic of the United Netherlands in its Heyday*, the publishers insisted on changing the title to *Our Golden Age*. Now as Colenbrander has rightly observed in his biography of Muller, that title really belies the work. For there was no glitter at all in the author's matter-of-fact treatment of the state, the army and navy, the church, trade and industry, shipping, the founding of the colonies, provincial government and history, social life, literature and art. And indeed, the name of 'Golden Age' smacks of the *aurea aetas*, the classical Fools' Paradise, which annoyed us in Ovid even while we were still at school. If our great age must perforce be given a name, let it be that of wood and steel, pitch and tar, colour and ink, pluck and piety, fire and imagination. The term 'golden' applies far better to the eighteenth century, when our coffers were stuffed with gold-pieces.

We in the Netherlands know that what made our country and people great in the seventeenth century—vigour, determination, justice and fair play, charity, piety and faith in God—is lost neither to us who live today nor to those who will come after us.

The Spirit of the Netherlands[1]

I. THE ORIGINS OF OUR NATIONALITY

When I lived in Haarlem, I never passed through Zijl-straat without glancing at a modest house whose stone tablet bore the inscription INT SOET NEDERLAND flanked by two sandstone pennons with ICK BLYF GETROU and ICK WYCT NYET AF.[2] I cannot tell why an unknown burgher should have chosen this particular slogan for his house soon after 1600, though it certainly betokens a deep love of country. As an expression of patriotism in the seventeenth century, the inscription is as eloquent as a poem by Vondel or a painting by Frans Hals or Jan van Goyen. In all of them sounds the symphonic theme of our nation and its people.

Patriotism that is not mirrored in the past is evanescent, for a nation, just like an individual, *is* its history. Its form and significance, sense and direction, stem from the living past. One who would cut himself off from this organic memory loses all vital orientation. Every valid idea of state and nationhood calls for knowledge and awareness of its history.

For us, in the Netherlands, this is especially clear. The origins of our country as an independent member of the European community lie in the relatively recent past—some four or at most five centuries ago. Most of our sister countries are older than we are. Portuguese, Danes and Poles could already count themselves nations (insofar as the term nation applied under medieval conditions) when even the name of 'Netherlands' was not yet in use. But, you might

[1]First published by A. W. Sijthoff's Uitg. Mij. N.V., Leyden, 1935.
[2]To the dear Netherlands. I shall be true. I shall not waver.

argue, was there not a Dutch-speaking community uniting Flanders and Brabant with Holland, Zeeland and Utrecht, and distinguishing them from the Low German and the High German regions, as long ago as the thirteenth century? Certainly there was a process of linguistic, political and cultural differentiation from the German Empire, under the persistent influence of the French, who had long introduced the distinction between *Thiois*, the inhabitants of the 'Dutch' areas, and *Allemands*. But this no more determined the eventual separation of the Netherlands from the German Empire than it made inevitable the political amalgamation of all those territories—Walloon, Flemish, Lower-Franconian, Saxon and Frisian—into what would one day be known as the Netherlands.

As always in history, this process of separation and fusion involved general factors of a formative kind as well as others of a purely incidental character. If we attribute a decisive importance in the whole development to geographic and ethnic factors, we must yet admit that these factors were quite different in the South and North; and, again, in the regions facing the sea and those more inland. We like to speak of the water that has borne us (our inland waters, mark you, no less than the sea!), teaching us self-reliance and turning us into dike-builders and dike-reeves—in short into defenders of our land. But is it not, in fact, our old Hollandocentric spirit that makes us speak like that? A Netherlands based on the sea is one that comprises at most Holland, Zeeland, the Frisian North together with the Betuwe region. The hydrographic factor will not explain the original amalgamation of *all* the Netherlands, South and North together, into a single unit. The similarity and connection of Flanders, Brabant, Hainault to one another and to the Northern regions does not spring from their maritime or riparian character.

In the search for such over-all explanations, we run the danger of losing ourselves in idle speculation. In fact, the

separation of the Low Countries from the German Empire
(in the case of Flanders and Artois from feudal ties with
France), their combination into a single state, the speedy
break-up into two—the free North and the Spanish South—
none of these can be explained by general factors of whatever kind. The actual and assignable cause of all this was
the policy and fate of the House of Burgundy, from the first
Philip, towards the end of the fourteenth century, to Charles
V and Philip II in the sixteenth.

True, we can suggest many good reasons why, as early as
1500, the Flemings differed from the Hollanders, and
Quantyn Matsys from Lucas of Leyden. But the decisive
thing is that, between 1578 and 1632, a piece of Flanders
and half of Brabant, together with an odd fragment of
Overmaas, were broken off from the rest, and that this was
the result of the military exploits of Parma, Maurice, and
Frederick Henry. Theirs alone? Yes, theirs, inasmuch as
their personalities were borne onwards by the irreversible
tide of events.

Now for what most concerns us here. Only after the unexpected emergence of the United Provinces did the people
of the Netherlands combine their forces and come to realise
their right to independent existence. This process of nation-
forming was not, however, accomplished overnight. As long
as part of the Republic was treated as a conquered province,
there could hardly be any question of national unity. Indeed, it took the Catholic population in the South almost
the entire seventeenth century to find its way towards a
sincere and mature adoption of the Dutch national idea.
Even apart from the old differences between Generality
lands and Seven Provinces which so long persisted, the
Dutch people never (luckily, some will say) achieved the
sort of homogeneity in which the periphery was completely
assimilated to the hub. How could it be otherwise in a state
like ours, which takes pride in balancing local autonomy

against a strong centre? Here we meet again what I have called our Hollandocentrism. On that subject I must now add a few further remarks.

The predominance of Holland has been unavoidable, and indeed most salutary. Without Holland, no Netherlands. We can readily adapt to our country the old allegory of the belly and the rebellious members with which a patrician pacified the discontented Roman crowd. In our Republic, the other provinces have often had to make do with the supporting role or even the part of audience in the drama of national life. That is no longer so. The conduct of a small modern country allows a measure of political and national partnership that supersedes old animosities and subordinations. The provincialism of the Groninger, Limburger or Zeelander is no longer exaggerated, nor an obstacle to full participation in the life of the nation. If national unity depended solely on social and geographical conditions, we should have achieved it long ago.

The Republic of the United Provinces, which helped us to become a nation, was something of a contradiction—old and small yet glorious and beloved. After the death of William of Orange, a whole series of vicissitudes led to the consolidation of our independence. The circumstances under which the rebellious provinces unexpectedly combined into a republic in 1584–7, were really a series of setbacks. The vain offers of sovereignty to France and England, the fall of Antwerp, and hence the loss of the south, the miserable failure of Leicester's administration, all this seemed much more likely to lead a people to subjugation than to political independence. The latter was never anticipated; it was born of need.

Wonderful as was the emergence of this state, its nature was singular and its growth perplexing. In a century in which absolutism was almost everywhere the rule, in which governments did away with the old medieval liberties wherever possible and replaced them with a strict autocratic system, the Dutch state proved that it was still possible to build a nation on the basis of the ancient principle of local autonomy. From the viewpoint of modern constitutional law, the Union of Utrecht must seem like a formula for failure. The demand for a consensus of opinion in all major decisions, the lack of a binding authority, the equivocal position of the Stadholder, the absence of a practical financial system and of a Supreme Court—all these strike us as so many evils in the body politic. And as Slingelandt was to testify in the eighteenth century, they did, in fact, undermine our political system. We are entitled to ask, paradoxical though it may sound, whether it was not precisely the failings of the Union which repeatedly saved the state.

Be that as it may; the history of the Republic in the seventeenth century has shown that provincial independence not only could be built on these makeshift foundations, but that the structure that rose up on them was in many respects better and safer than the proud edifices of princely supremacy. In the free Netherlands there was thrown up, as it were, everything that in seventeenth-century Europe went under the name of culture. The material soil for this was provided by our vast economic expansion and by our relatively high standard of living. High also was the standard of science and art—and, if our science was necessarily international, our art was so intensely national that it became the most profound expression of our character. Freedom was greater here than elsewhere and so, more through circumstance than from conviction, was the spirit of tolerance. Traffic was safer and faster, crime rarer, care for the poor and destitute more effective, the public spirit more enlightened.[1] And in the purely political sphere, our domestic and foreign interests depended on the preser-

[1] It cannot be stressed too often that, notwithstanding popular superstition, our magistrates have allowed no witch trials to take place since the seventeenth century.

vation of prosperity and peace everywhere, in contrast to the dynastic lust for power which caused remorseless wars on every side of us.

All these advantages and qualities of the Netherlands were due neither to individual merit, to the excellence of the political system or ideas, nor yet exclusively to a chain of circumstances. Those who wish to express the causes in a phrase, can do no better than speak of divine benediction. History may teach other people to be proud and boastful of their glorious origins, for us its lesson, if it is well understood, is one of humility alone.

II. THE DUTCH CHARACTER

My sketch of Dutch life in our great age, with the characteristics it had even then, has shown that we are essentially unheroic. Our character lacks the wildness and fierceness that we usually associate with Spain from Cervantes to Calderón, with the France of the *Three Musketeers* and the England of Cavaliers and Roundheads. How could it be otherwise? A state formed by prosperous burghers living in fairly large cities and by fairly satisfied farmers and peasants is not the soil in which flourishes what goes by the name of heroism. Even the deeds of our sailors and settlers overseas hardly answer to the common notion of the heroic. But then our age is particularly prone to squander big words on self and party and to belittle others. For that matter, has there ever been a time when group sentiments were not vented in inflated slogans and empty words? These, rather than sound convictions as such are what popular movements and ideas live on.

In every society, certain words are charged with feelings of aversion or affection. These words may originally have been based on religious, cultural or political convictions, but in the minds of the many who embrace them as slogans, the original content is swamped by partisan emotion. Thus,

once upon a time, in the days of the Convention, the innocent word 'federalism' became a term of abuse applied
only to traitors and splinter groups. So too, in the nineteenth century, 'bourgeois' became the most pejorative
term of all, particularly in the mouths of socialists and
artists, and later even of fascists. As Jules Renard put it so
incisively: 'Le bourgeois, c'est lui qui n'a pas mes idées'.
And what a devilish sound the word 'capitalistic' has assumed! So repulsive, in fact, that even those who are firmly
convinced that personal and inherited property is the basis
of all culture and that it is not within human power to replace the existing system of production with a better one,
no longer dare to call themselves 'capitalists'. And what a
sinister sound had the word 'orthodox' in the liberal Netherlands of seventy-five years ago! The free-thinking Dutchman with average prejudices saw nothing but bigots and
hypocrites under that label. Or how does the term 'liberal'
itself now sound to our socialists, fascists, and Rightists?
The revulsion of an entire generation seems to have been
focussed on it.

The most recent trend in Europe, that of extreme nationalism, bears 'heroism' as the brightest pearl in its crown.
But, sad to say, only artificial pearls can be mass-produced
—heroism can no more be a point in a program than can
sanctity. It can be attained in the lonely sick-bed or stuffy
office no less than on the battle-field or in the air. I know
perfectly well what noble aspiration drives this modern
generation; what spirit of self-sacrifice and what thirst to
bathe life once again in poetry and beauty. But it is impossible to *strive* for the heroic life. The title of hero is
bestowed by the survivors upon the fallen, who themselves
know nothing of heroism. Devotion and a sense of duty are
all we can undertake to bring to our deeds. In modern
'heroism', however, such as is being peddled and praised
by the political demagogues, one hears the roar of arro-
gance and barbarism. It is the intoxicant of the regimented

masses. This false heroism is one of the moral plagues with which our age is visited, perhaps the worst, and of all thoughtlessly misused terms the most dangerous.

How useful it would be from time to time to set up all the most common political and cultural terms in a row for re-appraisal and disinfection. Some would undoubtedly end up in the rubbish-bin as useless or threadbare, others would have to be scrubbed clean of all the dirt that has stuck to them. For instance, *liberal* would be restored to its original significance and freed of all the emotional overtones that a century of party conflict has attached to it, to stand once again for 'worthy of a free man'. And if *bourgeois* could be rid of all the negative associations with which envy and pride (for that is what they were) have endowed it, could it not once more refer to all the attributes of urban life? In that case, we might remember that Babylonian, Greek, Roman and Western-Christian cultures, and a few more as well, grew up in cities and were fostered by them. It is in this purified sense of the term that the following section has been written.

III. THE BOURGEOIS CHARACTER OF THE DUTCH PEOPLE

The solidarity of the Dutch people springs from their bourgeois character. Whether we fly high or low, we Dutch-men are all bourgeois—lawyer and poet, baron and labourer alike. Our national culture is bourgeois in every sense you can legitimately attach to that word. The bour-geois conception of life is shared by all classes or groups of our people—urban and rural, property-owning or not. It was from a bourgeois dislike of interference with their affairs that our forefathers rose up against Spain. In bour-geois morals are rooted those political qualities of the Re-public that I have outlined above. It was a bourgeois atmosphere that was responsible for our unmartial spirit

and our commercial propensities. Bourgeois life explains
the lack of revolutionary passion in our people and why the
even tenor of our national life remained almost unruffled
by the high winds of great ideas. The reader will notice
that I am not concerned with white-washing our faults.
For in our bourgeois character there are also rooted our
worst national failings: blustering behaviour that can so
often be a nuisance, and that special mixture of courtesy
and niggardliness for which we have so often been reproved.
Our bourgeois ways were, moreover, responsible for the
gradual decline of our national life in the eighteenth century
and the slowness of its re-awakening in the nineteenth.

It is a strange fact that we in the Netherlands so often
have no other response to Dutch life in the eighteenth century than a deprecating smirk. It strikes us as prosaic. Its
language does not move us. Its feelings appear to have been
over-refined and pretentious, or else homespun, trite and
sentimental. The quarrels between the Patriots and their
opponents seem so many comedies of errors. What, above
all, we cannot forgive our ancestors, is their self-satisfaction
and self-admiration. We prefer to consider them not so
much as forefathers as, say, distant relations. Of their century, we retain only the stale smell of their tobacco and the
sickly scent of their powdered wigs.

In this depreciation of a chapter in our history lies a great
deal of shortsightedness on our part. For while it is true
that, in the eighteenth century our great neighbours produced far greater things than we did, our own people displayed a simplicity of spirit and a purity of ideas that we
might well envy today. But those to whom 'bourgeois' is an
unqualified term of abuse may well revile the eighteenth
century, for it was bourgeois to the bone. And bourgeois
also were Rembrandt, Vondel, Jan de Witt and even
Spinoza.

IV. THE FORCES OF NATIONAL UNITY

In the Netherlands, the contrasts between the different strata of the population, and also between town and country were smaller than in most other European countries—as a result of dense population, small distances, easy communications and general education, the rural part of the Dutch people long since adopted bourgeois habits. But this solidarity could only have become a force for good in national life once it was made manifest in active national qualities. Are there any such? I believe so, and I shall now try to describe them.

At the risk of incensing my heroically-inclined compatriots even more than I have done already, I wish to start with a national quality of which we are rather tired, because it sounds so prosaic, namely our much-vaunted Dutch cleanliness. It is an odd fact that in our language, a single word—*schoon*—expresses cleanliness and purity as well as beauty. What other language uses the same word to describe a clean plate and a moonlit scene? May we therefore also take it that, with us, outer cleanliness goes hand in hand with a special love of inner purity, of logical, ethical and aesthetic orderliness? If only it did! The geography I used at school added to its praise of Dutch cleanliness the words: 'more in house and clothes than in body'. If that were also true of the spiritual sphere, then it were better we rolled in the mud but scrubbed our souls!

Yet there is one quality no one can deny our people: a high measure of respect for the rights and opinions of others. It was our history and our position as a small country surrounded by large ones that taught us this quality. But tolerance is a virtue that can become a vice. Respect for the rights and opinions of others far too often leads to respect for their wrongs. Though in our country, a high standard of public honesty prevented widespread corruption, we must nevertheless grant that the Dutchman, bourgeois in this too, is apt to close an eye to mild indulgence in jobbery or favouritism to friends. Still, there is no doubt that our easy-going attitude is an important and valuable ingredient of our character.

How about another quality that we may grant ourselves without immodesty, since it is again somewhat in the nature of a shortcoming, namely our relative insensibility to myth and rhetoric? It may be a handicap to our imagination and enthusiasm, but as a political quality, this deficiency must undoubtedly be counted a positive and salutary factor. Alas, the advantage is partly cancelled by obstinate adherence to opinions once adopted, love of parish-pump politics and the like. Moreover, our indifference to high-sounding phrases is akin to a lack of spiritual inspiration and leads far too easily to political apathy or aloofness. We must try to let the facts speak for themselves.

The Dutch people have always been averse to strong expressions of political extremism. The troubles that cost the De Witts their lives do not fall under that heading—they resulted from an outbreak of panic, left by neglectful authorities to run its course. Our active anarchism was limited to young Bohemians in the nineties who would now and then threaten to blow up this or that. Post-war communism never really took root here. The future of Rightist extremism is unpredictable as yet. It is likely that it will gain in strength, for extreme nationalism is as fashionable today as Social Democracy used to be with young people in about 1900. Many have embraced fascism under the delusion that its victory will consolidate conservatism. Modern psychological techniques of suggestion, propaganda and technological regimentation make every kind of extremism more dangerous and unpredictable than ever before. No matter what the future holds, an extremist government in the Netherlands would, in all probability, be a moderately extreme one. Even a short period in power, however, might

compel either a Communist or a Fascist regime to German-
ise our country to such an extent that the basis of our independence would be threatened.

Political extremism and rhetoric flourish where there is a
national sense of inferiority, the germs of which may go back
for a hundred years or more. Oppression, declining reputation, waning self-confidence, are the most common causes.
Not our own desert but a favourable destiny has saved us
from them. However reprehensible it may seem to all those
who esteem themselves courageous and passionate, as a
nation and state we are sufficiently pleased with our condition, and it is our patriotic duty to remain so. Just to do
that is likely to make great enough demands on each and
all of us.

If we do not feel politically inferior, we do not feel superior either. One of the virtues with which we can credit
ourselves is that we do not easily lapse into self-glorification.
Compared with other peoples, we sing our own praises in a
minor key. The naïve strains of Helmers[1] and those like him
have long died away and any loud insistence on national
excellence strikes us as rather ludicrous. A self-critical
people is so conscious of its failings—of which indeed we
Dutch people have not a few—that it may go to the opposite
extreme, self-ridicule. Nevertheless, our popular virtues of
sobriety and quiet patriotism are good ones. They are closely
connected with a very important quality, which likewise
owes more to our situation than our merits, namely our
ready appreciation of foreign elements. We keep all our
windows open to every wind that blows. The centuries have
made us familiar with the French, English and German
spirit. If there is one thing in which our country may be
said to excel, it is that it has known better than any other
how to absorb the streams of three distinct cultures smoothly
and to grasp the spirit of them all in full measure. It is a

[1]*Jan F. Helmers (1767-1813) wrote a bombastically patriotic poem, 'De
Hollandsche Natie', in 1812. A.J.P.*

precious luxury that we enjoy—our understanding and response to foreign influences. We are forced into it, because we live in their midst, and we can enjoy it because all we ask of anyone is free intercourse—commercial, cultural and spiritual.

What makes it possible for us to absorb foreign cultures without being assimilated by them, is that we have a language of our own. It may well prevent our word reaching the rest of the world, but it preserves our national identity while enabling us to recognise others. As long as we possess our own way of thought, of which our language is the form and expression, and absorb foreign influences in it, there is no need for us to defend ourselves against external influences. Exaggerated cultural purity is a sin. For modern civilisation is becoming ever more international and it is a blessing for a language when it is in a position to absorb, without damage to its own structure, the countless terms of Latin and Greek origin in which society is forever expressing itself anew. Let us preserve our language in such a way that it remains good Dutch and becomes as international as possible!

What applies to the language applies also to social and intellectual life. We cannot avert alien influences, nor do we wish to do so. Foreign motor cars and films are welcome to us, and so are ideas keyed to our sense of values. International contacts are growing apace, and this despite the agues that shake humanity from time to time. Wisely indulged, the dialogue with others can help us to preserve our equanimity.

These, in few words, are the qualities we may call virtues in our people. You may possibly feel that I have pitched them low, even made them seem humdrum. Perhaps I should have given less offence if I had called them our common faults. But nonetheless, if I have not been too wide of the mark, we may ask how far such modest virtues can contribute to the national unity we all desire? Can they help us both to resist whatever evils may threaten the integrity of our state and the welfare of our people, and to surge forward to deeds that may redound to the credit of us all?

V. THE CULTURAL CRISIS

Indeed, in view of the gravity and magnitude of the cultural crisis which, all may agree, threatens both East and West, we must first look to our defences. How far can such qualities as those we have adduced strengthen our people to resist tendencies that threaten all cultures with destruction and decay?

The oppressive feeling of living in a world that hovers on the brink of annihilation has not been known with such intensity as we in Europe know it today, since the end of the Middle Ages. Then, the sense of impending disaster was tempered with belief in divine salvation for the deserving, the belief that the end of the world would usher in the Day of Judgment. But nowadays, all those who see dark days ahead, including those whose Christian faith remains unshaken, generally hold that it is men who can and should reverse the downward trend. Our collective sense of responsibility is far greater than it used to be in the past, and this very fact gives us real grounds for hope. For the world is not only much worse, but also a little better than it used to be. The belief in continuous progress, which survived into the present century, was not altogether a delusion. The healing forces have not gone down to final defeat. Hatred and humbug fill the world, but we know what they are and can fight them as we do insidious diseases.

Let us look at one aspect of the patent decline of culture since the eighteenth century. In 1778, when France participated in America's war against England, the French government instructed its naval commanders that, should they come across Captain Cook, they were to show him every courtesy and do all in their power to help his voyages of discovery. In 1813, Sir Humphry Davy (and his assistant Faraday) was allowed to travel through France in the midst of the war to fulfil engagements with a number of learned societies, and everywhere he received respect and acclaim. In 1917, on the other hand, Albert Schweitzer, the man who cured the sick by the hundred and strengthened tens of thousands by his own example of Christian living, was thrown into a French internment camp. The other warring nations behaved little better.

That humanity nevertheless progressed at the same time and in many ways is shown by the amelioration of the penal code, the greatly improved treatment of mental illness, and the acceptance of social responsibility for the poor. How then can we explain that, while social and personal behaviour improved, political conduct deteriorated? By reference to what are also the main causes of most other aspects of mankind's astonishing cultural decline: the adverse effects of the mechanical and technical revolution on social life in general, and the rise of narrow nationalism in particular. Forces unleashed by our own reason now threaten to subject us all to a wave of lunacy that we all abhor but can no longer prevent. Prometheus is once more chained to the rock, and the eagle which daily attacks his flesh is sent by the grim idols of technocracy and over-organisation.

Man has become enslaved to his machines. Like a mill run mad, the world grinds out foodstuffs and throws them into the sea because the hungry cannot pay, while murderous armaments find greedy purchasers. The Word has become a slave of wealth and power and proclaims for all the world to hear what avarice and ambition command.

All social life is based on organisation. To exist at all, human society must create forms of social life, allocate functions, determine the rights and duties of the individual *vis-à-vis* society, in short it must organise. In the early phase of culture, all this happens naturally, or at least seems to us to have done so. But as culture advances, social organisation becomes more and more a conscious art both in great matters and small. In modern society, the technique of social organisation has been so sophisticated by printing, better communications, and general education that it no longer changes in accordance with changed needs but has become a law unto itself. Organisation itself is the final arbiter. Every fully developed organisation is kept going by its own momentum and makes of its own perpetuation an end in itself.

Given a measure of energy, some shrewdness in diagnosing human weaknesses and a smooth tongue, any superstition, any bagatelle, any kind of quackery and vice can be organised, so that it appears in works of reference in imposing type. Under such pressures, the human being is levelled down, or rather—to coin a word—massified. Or else he is exalted to a fame to which no true hero would aspire. Joseph de Maistre noticed all this long ago, when he described the men of the Terror. 'Ces hommes excessivement médiocres,' he wrote, 'exercèrent le plus affreux despotisme . . . Plus on examine les personnages en apparence les plus actifs de la révolution, plus on trouve en eux quelque chose de passif et mécanique.'[1]

Organisation means power, and power as an end in itself is evil. It can only be salutary if it is subordinated to personal moral responsibility.

Social organisation remains indispensable, but nevertheless poses a very grave threat. It turns man into a machine and deprives him of some of his personal responsibility. Every organisation means a restriction of freedom, the imposition of mediocrity. It entails a certain rigidity of thought that can have a thwarting effect on social life.

The dire consequences of these two closely connected phenomena—the supremacy of technical power and the channelling of the social instinct into soulless over-organisation—are so frightening because changes in social life, ever

[1] *Considerations sur la France*, 1796.

increasing in tempo and intensity, coincide with a considerable weakening of judgment, and also of morality. The belief that what is evil becomes good if only enough people want it is one of the most terrifying aberrations of the age.

Paradoxically, this decline of morality has gone hand in hand with a formidable gain in knowledge and understanding since 1800, a gain that has been extensive—in that it has involved the spread of general education and the full intellectual emancipation of women—as well as intensive— scientific knowledge has become far deeper and far more detailed. Nevertheless, it would be over-optimistic to declare that mankind as a whole has grown wiser. And this, too, is partly the fault of mechanised organisation. The average man of small leisure parrots opinions continuously drilled into him by every possible power of persuasion. What in the life of the individual during a less intensive culture period than our own was left to private reflection, individual choice and personal expression, seems largely to have been taken from him in our conformist age. It is not, as the enemies of the intellect declare, that knowledge itself is to blame but rather our intellectual digestion, and this is not so much the fault of the cooks as of the circumstances that compel us to gulp down their concoctions too quickly and too hot.

The real interest of the public is no longer in the works of the spirit, less so, at least, than it was in the eighteenth century, when society was much smaller but also more serious. The attention of the masses is increasingly being directed to things that an unprejudiced student would have to qualify as fairly stupid games (there are, of course, good ones as well). The modern world is sodden with puerility. I shall refrain from listing all the social activities that could be subsumed under this head. The old cultural impulses which found expression in the dances of primitive peoples and the pageants of medieval guilds and fraternities have deteriorated into the modern craze for get-togethers and socials. Those in power make full use of it to regiment their supporters. For the holy festivals of yesteryear we now get large-scale political demonstrations in which a drilled mass disports itself and the people become infatuated. It sometimes looks as though modern man knew no higher communal goal than marching together, all faces frozen in the same amiable or fierce grimace. And just because man takes this sinister nonsense so seriously does it become really evil, does human togetherness spawn its antitype. Not much psychological knowledge is needed to realise that emotive words can very easily be used to cause the unformed intellect to suspend independent judgment, if not forever, at least until there is some rude awakening. When judgment drops the reins, the harnessed instincts run away with the cart. The stampede of unreason is the triumph of mechanised organisation.

Much more serious than the weakening of judgment is the decline of morals in modern society. At first sight we find here the same paradox. Is private and public morality in advanced countries really lower than it was before? Statistics about crime, prostitution, and drunkenness do not tell the whole story. What matters here is not so much breaches of law as the betrayal of the spirit. But how is that to be measured? Must we take every age at its own valuation? And if so, which one—the jeremiads of puritans, satirists, moralists, and literary realists, or the self-congratulations of optimistic dreamers and philanthropists? The unflattering image may be nearer the mark, but it seems likely that neither shows us the whole truth.

What is certain is that the standards of morality and justice which public opinion applies to the events of the day have become dangerously lax. Throughout the world there seems to be a kind of infatuation with misdeeds. This phenomenon is undoubtedly connected with the false heroism we mentioned. The origins lie to a large extent in the Romantic reaction against the conventional respectability of an earlier age. It is fostered by the spokesmen of philosophical immoralism. The cinema, too, gives it daily titillation. And our newspapers revel in the acts of derring-do of 'gentlemen-burglars' and their like. They mean well enough, but the effect is hardly edifying, for they address themselves to a far from high-minded mass of readers. Much more serious, however, is a phenomenon we can observe almost daily—the toleration by hosts of otherwise well-meaning people of flagrant injustice and cruelty, something that can at best be put down to mere thoughtlessness. Thus when Lenin died in 1924, and the corpse was put on show, many Europeans who did not in the least love Communism were willing to pay homage to a man who, no matter what the worth of his ideals or the power of his will, was nevertheless responsible for one of the most blood-curdling massacres in history.

Call this mere transient hero-worship if you will. But what of the official and enforced elevation of the state above morality and justice, which forms the credo of popular despotism? Macchiavelli and Hobbes taught that the state *was* amoral but, if I understand them aright, they never added that this was also *right and proper*. But now even the mask of virtue has been dropped. When the government of a great and cultural country declares publicly and through the mouths of its ministers that nothing but political expediency does and should control the actions of a state and dismisses justice as an illusion and fantasy—when it prescribes deliberate falsifications of history for its school-children—when its teachers proclaim that in the relationship between countries, power is more important than truth, then indeed we must sound the cry of *state to state is a wolf*, much more loudly than the sigh *homo homini lupus* was ever sounded. And whereas the latter was a plaint—alas, that is how things are or seem to be—the former has become an affirmation—that is how things will be if we have our way. And if this view becomes general, the extermination of mankind is bound to follow as night follows day.[1]

VI. THE TASK OF OUR PEOPLE

This long digression on the dangers that threaten culture in general was justified in our examination of the Dutch spirit inasmuch as it showed us the kind of world we live in and what high demands are made by the task of remaining true to ourselves and yet serving the course of culture as a whole.

Are the defences of national unity strong enough to enable us to protect, in the mortal struggle that faces state and nation today, all that justifies our independent national existence? Only if there is brought to them much more energy, much more readiness to give up petty interests than we commonly display in public life. In this realisation of the necessity of a higher and freer activity, there lies, I believe, the true motive of those movements that inspire so many of our young people with patriotic ideas. Things must be *different*.

We are burdened by an antiquated party system, fossilised by the misbegotten idea of proportional representation. In practice, the party system has long since ceased to work— as is repeatedly shown by the impossibility of forming durable governments. Inasmuch as our large political conglomerations ever deserved the name of parties, they have lost the right to it long ago. This is particularly true of the various religious parties. In nineteenth-century Dutch society, the formation of Catholic and Protestant parties was essential, lest denominational interests be ignored in the life

[1]The idea that the state is beyond good and evil is deep-rooted in Germany. Thus one of the best modern German historians, Gerhard Ritter, has dismissed the opposite view as a relic from the Middle Ages (*Die Ausprägung deutscher und west-europäischer Geistesart im konfessionellen Zeitalter* in *Historische Zeitschrift*, 149, 1934, pp. 240-52.

of state and nation. The moment these interests were safe-guarded, religious party objectives became harmful not only to the parties themselves, but to Dutch politics as well. The existence of a Christian Party is only justified where Christianity is under attack—Christianity and power simply do not go together. This does not mean, of course, that Christians must not serve in the government. I, for one, fully subscribe to the views with which Emil Brunner concluded a lecture at Utrecht in 1934: 'Only those of us hold rational political views,' he claimed, 'who believe that the fate of Europe depends on such traditional values as Church and Faith.' In order to make that conviction fruitful in our political life something other is, however, needed than the shaky structure of our party system.

Once in power, every political party, irrespective of whether or not it retains its pure and high ideals in theory must needs run a kind of 'spoils system'. It may be argued that the preferential treatment of supporters does no great harm, provided a fairly regular swing between two great parties from opposition to government gives everyone a turn in power. But it becomes a mockery of true politics if, by tacit agreement between the parties, each is given a fixed allocation of offices, for in this way the wishes of the people are completely ignored. Once this system is adopted the state becomes bogged down in the morass of party manipulation—and the longer the deeper.

The impetus that came to us with proportional representation has spent itself on a threadbare pattern of purely political formations, without any historical, psychological or sociological basis. It started from the naïve assumption that membership in a so-called party really and truly expressed the full political wishes of the citizen. It knew nothing of the inherent evil of organisation and its sterilising effects on human striving. It clung to the inert mechanisation of political life, and displaced the aggressive instincts into fields where they were to prove far more dangerous than in the healthy political struggle for concrete and tangible ends.

But, you may say, proportional representation holds the promise of new and spontaneous party groupings. Alas, we all know what the upshot of that has been. Whenever the masses have been asked to join together on the basis of ideas and convictions, they have responded by combining according to petty interests or catchwords.

Strangely enough, the corporate state with which modern despots want to replace the party state is already implicit in the consequences of proportional representation. Both mean the extreme mechanisation of political life, the departmentalisation of every interest. The result—unprecedented over-organisation—is more likely to spell the death of true communal life.

A state that divides everything up into small blocks is in danger of destroying the very life impulses of its body politic. Now these impulses are largely intellectual and not the primitive passions unleashed by modern demagogues. Men with political views do not join together in parties exclusively for their own material interests nor yet entirely by virtue of faith or reason. Political views have at all times been a matter of temperament and tradition, an overall personal attitude moulded by experience and expectations. What is decisive here is the degree of activity or passivity. Men with political convictions may be said to fall into one of three categories. There are those who acclaim what is, 'those who acclaim what should be, and those who are determined to make the change'. These three categories correspond fairly well to the three main types of political temperament: the conservative, the progressive and the radical.

Nor are these postures restricted to politics. They are general attitudes to life, and were present in society long before there was any question of conscious political doctrines. It is often forgotten that the claim to political competence of the common man has only been admitted in recent times. To that end it was necessary that a large part of the population should feel more or less actively involved in the conduct of the state. Now this condition was first fulfilled in the eighteenth century, and it was soon after the end of that century that the three political attitudes first obtained their modern names. These names all originated in England. *Liberal* was formerly used, in the Latin sense, as an antonym to *mechanical*, also in the Latin sense, i.e. it was applied to the intellectual qualities of the leisured man in contrast to those of the artisan. Burke and Gibbon, as it were, transformed 'liberal opinion' from a cultural into a political concept. As such it reached France about 1800 not, as Balzac thought, following Madame de Staël's characterisation of Alexander I, but in the days of the *Consulate*. The Spaniards first used it as a party name, opposing the *liberales* to the *serviles*. But it was in England, where *Liberal* gradually replaced *Whig*, that the term assumed its European significance. *Radical*, too, first appeared in England, to refer to the political reformers of the last decade of the eighteenth century and the earlier period of the nineteenth century. *Conservateur* was in use before and after the French Revolution as an honourable title. You were the '*juge conservateur*' or '*grand conservateur*' of an order, and the highest legislative body was the *Sénat conservateur*. Chateaubriand spoke of an '*esprit conservateur*', though the political parties that stood for the preservation of the existing political institutions were called by other names in France, even down to the Third Republic. The English term *Conservative* was proposed in *The Times* of 1 January 1830 by J. Wilson Croker as a substitute for the misleading and outworn *Tory* and, although it was really an inaccurate designation, it found wide acceptance almost immediately.

In the course of the nineteenth century, all these terms were charged with the emotional overtones to which we have referred. Except for England, which never broke the enviable continuity of her political life or repudiated her tradition, traditionalists everywhere became more or less ashamed of the conservative label, and adopted instead such names as, for instance, our 'Christian-Historical Party'. This fear of appearing to be old-fashioned (a sign of the worst kind of bourgeois attitude) did much to damage political life in our country. It would have been well if a group of politically informed men had had the courage to continue calling themselves Conservative, in the worthy sense of wishing to preserve what is good and refusing to kow-tow to the fashion of the day. A policy of building on the tested foundations of state and society would in no way have been tantamount to stagnation. In recent times it would have served to counter a host of politically evil attitudes and to convert them into healthy ones.

From the outset, liberalism, although still potent in many countries, laboured under a fatal handicap. This was its kinship to eighteenth-century rationalism and to the ideology of the French Revolution. Moreover, it suffered a lack in evocative power. Changeable as the liberal outlook was, differing in accordance with the prevailing circumstances and everywhere concerned with the next practical step, it had no real identity. It could not appeal to the royal or the holy, to throne or altar. Liberalism lacked a metaphysic and symbols, unless it borrowed them from the Revolution, with which its opponents were only too happy to identify it. And unlike the Revolution, it had no myths. To its cry of *Liberty* the Right replied with shouts of *Order* and the Left with shouts of *Equality*. Liberalism only seemed to be forward-looking as long as it could drift on the tide of an age that believed it had solved the riddle of the ages by proclaiming Progress and Evolution.

Until about 1919, the only radicals or revolutionaries were of the Left. In political temperament and intellectual attitude, the radicalism of the Left differs from that of the Right in certain particulars only. The revolutionary, whether or not he feels personally ill-used by society, is the man who cannot bear the imperfections of this world, who nurses uncontrollable longings for a new state of affairs, and who feels irresistibly that a complete change is possible here and now. His striving may be called a secular longing for salvation, and he wants to be saved before and not after death. The most fitting description of the revolutionary is still the old Latin *rerum novarum cupidus*. Economic injustice, let alone social inequality, are by no means the only spurs to the revolutionary temperament. In the longing for the new, the formulation of needs and demands is only secondary. Heretic and revolutionary are interchangeable terms. Those with shallow roots in social life have forever been susceptible to revolutionary temptations. No wonder, therefore, that every revolutionary movement has tried to weaken family ties.

Once organised into a political party, a revolutionary group does not, of course, find its supporters exclusively among men with a revolutionary temperament. The masses who join it, or other groups for that matter, do so from various, not to say mixed, motives: conviction, class-consciousness, the need to externalise inner conflicts, genuine idealism, etc. Here as elsewhere, rigid organisation is bound to subordinate the individual and to distort ideals.

A state, I believe, will be the healthier, the more directly political life reflects the distinction between the three fundamental attitudes of preserving, reforming and overthrowing the existing institutions. In this it is obvious that the first two attitudes will, whenever necessary, combine against the third. For both conservatism and reformism share principles that are entirely lacking in revolutionary extremism. The Conservative and the Reformer share a belief in gradual development, in which conservatism, as it were, stresses the hereditary element and reformism that of adaptation. Both desire a certain balance between order and freedom, albeit with two distinct emphases. Revolution, on the other hand, and violent reaction, too, for that matter, spell catastrophe to, and the severance of the living process of the state. A state that makes legislative provision for its violent over-throw acts like a man who deliberately swallows the germs of his own destruction. The toleration of revolutionary parties in a free society is irrational in the highest degree.

It is true that the state cannot hope to escape irrational-ism altogether. For the majority system which mistakes the voice of the people for the voice of reason is no less irrational than despotism. That is why so many extremist movements feel free to reject democracy. But even if they did away with all parliaments, they would nevertheless have to re-admit the majority principle by the back-door of the councils or colleges with which even despots have to surround them-selves.

In the spring of 1934, when I first put forward these views to a conference on national unity, I believed that I could affirm the possibility of a rapprochement between our national parties. Starting from a few straws in the wind, I offered this prospect to my compatriots more as a hope and possible ideal than as a definite expectation. The interest which my reflections have aroused, however, now forces me to look more closely at them.

During the year that has passed, Dutch political life has completely rid me of my optimism. I think less than ever of the merits and chances of the Dutch party system. I can no longer see any hope of a rapprochement between groups that fundamentally have so much in common. Moreover, in the reviews of my lecture by various journals of different political colours, the whole emphasis was on my praise of our party system and as little as possible was said about my criticisms.

I have no option, therefore, but to voice my prac-tical misgivings more explicitly. I am now more than ever convinced that I did not overstate the case ten years ago when I wrote *inter alia* that 'the Dutch hen in her innocence has hatched the chick of parliamentary oligarchy out of the egg of general representation'.[1] There has been no true parliamentary government for a long time. The people have as little opportunity to decide what they want as they have of getting it done. The reorientation of opinion and trends in accordance with new circumstances and needs is sorely hampered by our established system of completely antiquated parties. Proportional representation with its senseless consequence, compulsory voting, has petrified our political life. It ought to be abolished immediately and utterly, in the recognition that it was the silliest mistake that has ever sprung from a doctrinaire political theory.

Of course, parties must remain and new ones must be formed. In every community that does not wish to be ruled by mere force, differences in outlook and the formation of political groups in accordance with these differences will forever remain the chief safeguard of political health. Dutch national unity in particular cannot be imagined otherwise than as unity in diversity. And co-operation in the face of differences of opinion demands exceptionally capable men.

The political truth that lies forgotten in the doctrine of proportional representation is that the state, although always swayed by party differences, must behave as if it were above party. It is in the recognition that the crown transcends all divisions, that the formula for a healthy working of the parliamentary system was given long ago. The presence of an opposition to the government majority in no way vitiates that principle. The confidence the crown could place in the executors of its will, its ministers and servants, was set a natural limit in the criticism of the people through the mouth of the opposition. Law, parliamentarianism and democracy could fuse into triple harmony. The fact that, under this system, some sections of the population were prevented from exerting a direct influence or had to join a group whose views they could not share in full was not, as

[1] *De Gids*, 1926, I, p. 249.

an ultrarational political school has taught, a semi-disenfranchisement, but on the contrary an essential benefit. The resulting plasticity of the body politic, the ability to adapt to the needs of the moment, the conditions for continuous contact with the predominant mood of the people, have been best preserved precisely in the United Kingdom where the system has been affectionately described as muddling through.

The decline of democracy and parliamentarianism in the few countries in which the English forms were successfully adapted to local needs, began the moment it was thought possible to perfect these forms by legislation. Democratic theory insisted that every foolish and every reasonable demand have an equal right of being heard and supported. It was assumed that good must somehow come out of the sum total of all political endeavours. Yet politics cannot but continually neglect diverging opinions and harm special interests. The clumsy handling of small parties in our country proved only recently that proportional representation must devour its own children.

The Netherlands with its sectarian tendencies in every field was almost predestined to take parliamentarianism to ill-considered extremes. The result is clear to all who look at the matter objectively. We are now so used to all those organisations in our country that call themselves political parties that we have come to look upon them as essential communal institutions or even as tribunals—it rarely strikes us how completely inept and absurd the party apparatus really is. The Christian-Historical Union, which enjoys the support of all who have conservative or moderate views; the Anti-Revolutionary Party which, in practice, is forced to abandon the theocratic point of view that constitutes its real strength; the Catholic Party which is forever in danger of splitting up under internal stresses; the shrinking Liberal groups which are no longer capable of uniting the liberal-minded section of our population; the Social

Democratic Workers' Party which, though it has long ceased to be revolutionary, yet continues to recruit members with the propaganda techniques of the revolution— none of them deserves the name of political party, in the full sense of that term. The complicated and critical relationships of modern political and social life force them, and will increasingly continue to do so, to share political power. A more or less regular alternation of compact, like-minded majorities is no longer possible. Nor is it possible for so many so-called parties to work together. What they do in fact is not much more than to provide personnel from their executives for the strenuous work of government. Once charged with that task, these persons find themselves forced to govern as best they can, without much regard to party viewpoint or consultation with party members, to whom at best, they can make certain trifling concessions. In brief, the party system, as it exists in the Netherlands, daily displays its glaring inadequacies. At best, it helps to find jobs for pals. If we really wished to organise political opinions so as to translate them into fruitful political action, we had far better abandon the many splinter groups in favour of the three main political platforms of earlier times.

The aim of every political system is good government. If our government still, albeit with greater difficulty than before, stands the test of time, it is not because of, but despite our electoral and party system. Even the ship of state must sail or sink. A government doing its job cannot, as we have said, adhere too closely to a party viewpoint, and must in fact try to steer clear of it.

If our inapt party regime continues, we shall probably witness here what has already happened abroad: the quality of our politicians will keep deteriorating, with the result that men of worth will increasingly break free of party bonds.

In the first draft of this essay I speculated on the various ways in which our present divisions would come to an end.

As I have said, I have had to abandon the hopeful conclusion of a rapprochement between the parties. The corporate state? If that lies in store for us, it will have to be imposed from above, outside all the old party groupings, as an almost wholly *economic* and *social* structure, and one that, *politically* speaking, would in all probability, quickly prove to be no more than a robot or homunculus. Or will the system die out as a result of lack of interest on the voters' part? Not while they are driven to the polling booths like sheep to the slaughter by their well-organised party machines. Perhaps voluntary dissolution in face of realisation that parties have become redundant? Alas, a modern organisation does not usually abdicate but blunders on until it falls to pieces.

Perhaps catastrophe will take a hand? (Rejoicing in the wings.) The nationalist parties with their growing influence are only too ready to push our party system over the brink and liquidate it once and for all. Will things come to that pass? We cannot tell. Nor are we at all certain whether, on the rubble-heap of the parliamentary system, the Right would be able to erect a better Netherlands. Similar upheavals elsewhere are not exactly encouraging.

And yet, in one way or another, the parties of today will have to make way for a political organisation of greater force and fruitfulness. Their lingering on into a distant future is now hardly conceivable, nor is it desirable.

If we wish to give the system of democratic representation another chance, then it will have to be through the abolition of what was adopted in an evil hour—the system of proportional representation. The whole Dutch nation will have to be called upon to put a stop to the fragmentation of our political life into countless 'parties'. It goes without saying that the old party organisations will not surrender without a fight. They will behave as if they were indispensable, try to put up candidates, fight election campaigns. The simplest and most effective way of thwarting them is to follow the British example: the election of individual candidates by a simple majority, without a second ballot. The introduction of the second ballot is the clearest proof that the British system, on which ours was supposed to be modelled, was never properly understood. This is the very reason why parliamentarianism works so much better and is so much more pliable in Britain than it is here. Only by the choice of candidates based on a simple majority can the expression of the popular will transcend narrow party differences. But, you may ask, is such a system not unfair to the smaller groups? Unfortunately, politics, as the implementation of decisions and the performance of actions is bound to be unfair. *Perfect* justice, like *perfect* charity, has no place in the life of a state compelled to act. Only the acceptance of this unfairness towards minorities and defeated parties can help to cure our political life of its worst evils and to restore it to what it could be at its best: a struggle, but a noble one, to the limit of our powers and conviction.

To abolish proportional representation here and now would undoubtedly call for much daring. But the times call for courageous deeds and great decisions. And only by daring shall we be able to prevent the overthrow of the state by insurgent nationalists. We shall have to say to them: Look, this is your chance as well. If you come to us with a program copied from abroad and with regimented mobs, we do not want you; our Dutch sentiments are too outraged. But if your ideals are great and pure enough, then show yourself capable of placing your leaders at the helm of our floundering ship in the name of our own people. It will weather the storm all the better.

As soon as the electoral system no longer forces us to substitute petrified and antiquated parties for living men with courage and real opinions, the old, simple and adaptable political relationships will be restored almost automatically, and enable a parliamentary system of government to survive even now—in a new form but also with increased authority. Spontaneous associations, reflecting real convictions, coupled with confidence in people from whom strength and leadership can be legitimately expected, will be able to avert the danger which the inherently healthy striving for a more effective political life, for radical change and improvement unquestionably runs—the danger of Fascist intervention.

The danger of the Fascist or so-called National-Socialist movements arises from the fact that their justified resentment of exaggerated rationalism in politics has led them to the other extreme of boundless irrationalism. The ancients spoke of Scylla and Charybdis, and Luther compared man to a drunken peasant: if you lift him on to his horse on one side he falls down on the other. Our times seem to be bent on proving the truth of such ancient warnings.

Despite all the differences in belief, tradition and temperament, is there enough that all Netherlanders of good will have in common in their expectation of the state? No one would deny the need for keeping order—order is the very principle of the cosmos. For some, however, the maintenance of order must not override all other considerations. The cry for freedom that once resounded so passionately throughout the world is in danger of being silenced everywhere. The trend of the times is towards submission to leaders and even to blind forces. Freedom has become a dirty word. Many are only too ready to surrender our ancient spiritual heritage of tolerance to differences of opinion.

Do not dismiss freedom too lightly! Most European states have to thank an autocratic principle for their existence, yet there are some that owe their independence and their very souls to the struggle for freedom. One of these is the Netherlands. Freedom, however narrowly conceived, has been the spirit of our nation. Let us therefore guard well our precious heritage!

A wondrous destiny has helped to create our nation, to set us apart from the original stem, and to make us a noble part of Western Europe. Through Delfzijl and Vaals runs the border between Western and Central Europe. In our Western character lies our strength and the reason for our existence. We belong to the Atlantic; our centre of gravity is in and across the sea. Our company is that of Western nations and above all of that great British people who created the modern democratic state and continue as a bastion of liberty.

Authority, yes, provided it is understood in the sense in which Paul Scholten outlined it last year in his lectures on the principles of society—authority based not on brute force but on the subordination of authority itself to the highest law and bound by legal principles that draw their inspiration from it.

Leadership, gladly, provided our leaders are guides and not dictators. We do not wish to be led like Breughel's blind or like a bear on a chain. Our leaders must be men who submit to a higher wisdom, to wisdom that sets its sights beyond the limits of national and state interest, just as the helmsman steers by the stars.

To keep, to point the way, to care, to direct—those are the ancient virtues by whose presence St. Augustine dististinguished the true political task from the evil appetites for power and domination. Political thinking aware of the commands of justice and the limits of human power must always come back to the old images of the steersman who, knowing his own human frailty, holds the oar steady in the storm, of the fallible shepherd who humbly tends his flock. A poet put it into the mouth of him, but for whose labours there would have been no Dutch nation and no Dutch state:

> Your shepherd never sleepeth
> albeit you have strayed.[1]

[1] *From the national anthem.*

The Netherlands as Mediator between Western and Central Europe[1]

Of the subjects proposed by the German Academy of Politics for this lecture, none has appealed to me more than *The Netherlands as Mediator between Western and Central Europe*. I intend to examine it from the historical and cultural, rather than from the political and practical, standpoint, for it is a subject that is more than merely topical—it is based on history and hence impinges on a sphere with which I am familiar through my own studies and to which I have given my heart.

As soon as I started to consider the best approach to the subject I also began to have grave reservations. At first sight, the title, The Netherlands as Mediator between Western and Central Europe, seems to hold few problems for all the terms look perfectly clear; on closer examination, however, it appears that none of them is anything of the sort. Not only are 'Western Europe' and 'Central Europe' protean entities but so also are—at least historically speaking—the 'Netherlands' and 'mediator'; so that I am left with 'between' as the only unequivocal word in the title.

Let us therefore begin by deciding in what sense and with what limitations we shall be using the terms Western and

[1]Lecture given on 27 January 1933 to the Deutsche Hochschule für Politik, and published in Dr. H. Holborn (ed.): *Grundfragen der internationalen Politik*, Vorträge des Carnegie Lehrstuhls für Aussenpolitik und Geschichte an der deutschen Hochschule für Politik, vol. 5, Teubner, Leipzig and Berlin, 1933.

Central Europe. From a purely geographical point of view, the answer is fairly simple, as any school atlas will show you. That point of view is just about good enough for railway time-tables, but for our own purpose we need a classification based on political and economic, or else on cultural and historical factors and not merely on geographical boundaries. Now, political geography is an exceedingly dangerous subject, for it is inclined to be highly selective in its arguments, its concepts are vague and rather wide, the danger of reading all sorts of things into it is grave, and far too often irrational desires, emotions and interests dictate the deployment of its categories.

Oddly enough, when it comes to the distinction between Northern and Southern Europe, Nature herself comes to our aid. Southern Europe clearly consists of the three large Mediterranean peninsulas and, just as clearly, Northern Europe is made up of the three Scandinavian countries, together with Finland and Northern Russia. Between the North and the South there clearly lies a Centre, but here we are concerned, not so much with it as with another Centre —that between East and West.

Now, what we commonly understand by Western Europe is a coherent, albeit very loose-knit, cultural, social and economic whole. Needless to say, it includes England and France. But what of Spain, Denmark and Norway? We are at liberty to include them as well, though the Southern factor is so predominant in Spain, and the Northern in Denmark and Norway, that it is only by stretching our definition to its limit that we can do so. There remain the Netherlands and Belgium. Let it be said straight away that the Dutch—let alone the Belgians—like to think of themselves as Western Europeans. I am convinced that if you were to ask (I myself do not propose to do so) a random number of educated Dutchmen whether they considered themselves Western or Central Europeans, the overwhelming majority would plump for the West.

And rightly so. For the considerations on which such a decision must be based, all point to the West. Our social and political history is, by and large, part and parcel of the history of Western Europe. Our Western connection has helped us to forge our national independence. The friendship and the hostility of both France and England have played their part in our development. Our nation fronts the sea; our centre of gravity lies somewhere in mid-ocean. Only considered as a Western nation do the Netherlands have any real meaning or independent standing.

Let us ignore the situation of the Netherlands for a moment, and ask instead what meaning, if any, must be attached to the conception of Western Europe as a cultural unit. Clearly, the answer can be no more than summary, for what is involved is not a common identity but such general factors as parliamentary government or, at least, political freedom for more than a century, overseas dependencies for more than 300 years, a pronounced, long-term conditioning of culture by capitalistic institutions, and the early emergence of a free and educated middle-class. If we try to go beyond that, the differences between French and English culture become so marked as to render the idea of cultural unity absurd. Look at it as we will, Western Europe remains a vague and variable concept and, in the final analysis, one whose real significance seems to coincide more or less with the geographical.

Does 'Central Europe' constitute a more obvious unit? I think the opposite is true. This claim may seem strange at first, because 'Central Europe' is by far the older of the two terms, and in Germany, for instance, it has been in common use for more than a century, whereas 'Western Europe' does not even rate an entry in most popular encyclopaedias. Yet its title to existence seems to be based on little more than the geographical fact that 'Central Europe' lies in the centre of the continent, i.e. that it forms an enclave between maritime Western and continental Eastern Europe. The boundaries of this area have, however, fluctuated since earliest times.

Actually the importance of this term lies outside geography. Friedrich List, famed for his sweeping economic views, was one of the first to turn it into a political slogan. As such, it was also used by the men of 1848, and again during the Great War, above all by Friedrich Naumann. Today, however, the use and meaning of the term are determined by new factors. In France and Czechoslovakia, for instance, there have recently been vigorous attempts to identify 'Central Europe' with a Danubian Federation. In this identification, Central Europe would comprise Austria, Czechoslovakia, Hungary, Jugoslavia and Rumania, and possibly Italy and Poland as well. German writers, on the other hand, argue that, no matter what its other components, Central Europe is bound to include Austria and Germany. Here I do not wish to discuss the political union of Germany and Austria, nor do I wish to aggravate existing political and economic problems; instead, I shall keep as closely as possible to the historical and cultural aspects of the question. In his *Europäische Gespräche*[1], Harald E. Roos recently re-examined the problem of Central Europe and we cannot but agree with him that, no matter what our particular views, there is no sense at all in stretching the concept to include South-Eastern countries beyond the rivers Leitha and Sava; South-Eastern Europe forms so clear a cultural contrast to North-Western Europe that, in this respect at least, the term 'Central Europe' has an obvious significance.

The Western boundaries, however, owe their justification to economic and political considerations that are not necessarily identical with the assumed cultural realities. 'The term "Central Europe," ' Harald Roos went on to say, 'must not be defined in too narrow a sense; it must include not only Germany, Austria, Switzerland, and Czechoslo-

[1] *Europäische Gespräche*, I, 1932, vol. 9-10, p. 245.

vakia, but Holland and Belgium and indeed the North-European Baltic states as well.' I think it quite possible—though I cannot decide the question—that this kind of association may have a great economic future. But why retain the term Central Europe when, of the nine countries involved, two have a decidedly Western and three a decidedly Northern and North-Western character? I have no desire to enter into economic arguments, but merely wish to stress how loosely the concept of Central Europe is anchored even in the political and cultural life of today.

One is tempted to say that for the time being, at least, the most tangible expressions of its reality are the MITROPA signs on *wagon-lits* and dining cars, and those railway time-tables which we have mentioned earlier and which tell us where and when to put our clocks forward or back. This is no mere fantasy—nowadays communications set the pace everywhere.

The very title of my address bars me from treating the Netherlands as part of either Western or of Central Europe. Even the railway time-table supports me in this view: do we not set our clocks by Amsterdam time? True, Dutch astronomers asked, only a month or two ago, that we forgo this piece of eccentricity and return to Western European time. And who could be a more objective judge of the situation than our astronomers?

This brings me to the first term in the title of this lecture. What do I mean by 'Netherlands'? To begin with I mean that kingdom which you in Germany—and we ourselves as well—generally call Holland. But inasmuch as I am trying to consider the term 'mediator' historically, I must define 'Netherlands' in its broader, historical sense, and include Belgium as well. And even when, speaking of more recent times, I restrict my remarks to Holland alone, the definition of this term is not as simple as it seems. Holland may be called a small country off the North Sea with some eight million inhabitants, or else a circum-Pacific state with a population of more than 60 millions. This last fact is bound to have important repercussions on our mediatory rôle: no discussion of Holland's situation in the modern world can ignore the fact that Japan, the United States, Australia, British and French South-East Asia and even Venezuela are all our neighbours, no less so than Germany and Belgium.

And this leads us straight to our fourth question: what significance must we attach to the rôle of 'mediator' in the modern world, and is it true to say that the Netherlands plays this part?

In view of the parlous state of the world, one is tempted just to sigh and exclaim—if only it did, to whatever small degree! Complicated questions of international finance, squabbles about imports and exports, the increasing tendency of the great powers to settle important problems unilaterally—these are the trends in international affairs that face us every day. Is there then any room for mediation? The question would seem to admit of only one answer.

But what of the past? Was there ever a people that successfully played the part of mediator in the cultural, economic or political life of Europe? Such mediators must not, of course, be sought among the great states, radiating cultural or political power themselves. Thus France in the twelfth or seventeenth century, and Italy during the Renaissance, cannot be called cultural 'mediators'. But Switzerland played that part briefly around 1500, and Denmark, too, acted as temporary mediator between Germany and Sweden. So far as I can see, the only other country that need be considered in this context is the Netherlands in its broadest historical sense, i.e. Holland and Belgium.

The Netherlands' undoubted rôle of material and intellectual mediation is intimately bound up with its emergence as a separate people and state. Let us look briefly at this matter. I shall say little about our very early history, though I cannot ignore it altogether since all discussions of the international rôle of the Netherlands must begin by asking to what extent it was their peculiar political situation and national characteristics that enabled the Low Countries to play it. Such questions can never be answered fully; at best we can hope to discover pointers that help us to explain what actually happened.

Its geographical position in the delta of the rivers Rhine, Maas and Scheldt, undoubtedly explains why from very ancient times, the Netherlands was fitted to the part of economic mediator. Thus the Romans' Caput Germaniae was, in fact, Lugdunum Batavorum; it not only provided the Romans with a springboard for Britain, but was also the starting point on the Peutinger Map of every road running from the North Sea to the Alps. And, after the Barbarian Invasion, when towns once again flourished, Dorestad became a commercial emporium, followed by Bruges, and then, towards the end of the Middle Ages, by Antwerp, and more recently by Amsterdam.

Another factor facilitating the mediatory rôle of the Netherlands was language. The Walloon-Dutch sector of the Romano-Germanic language border has run through the centre of Belgium since olden times. Here the Romanic and Germanic world impinged upon each other in an area that made contacts easier and relations wider than they could have been across the Vosges and Ardennes. It is this state of affairs that Pirenne has used to such good effect when he explained the Belgian national character. For him, the very situation that made Flanders, Hainault, Brabant, Liége, Limburg and Luxemburg meeting places of German and French culture also explained the emergence of an independent, bilingual Belgian nation. Here we cannot pause to vindicate Pirenne's thesis, though the actual occurrence of this cultural exchange can be easily demonstrated by a host of medieval examples—we have only to recall Hendrick van Veldeke and Jan of Brabant, the Imperial House of Luxemburg, with its German and French connections, or that passage in *Meier Helmbrecht*, a thirteenth-century satire against the corruption of the people's state, in which the young peasant speaks Flemish so as to be taken for a knight.

This cultural phenomenon did not, however, involve the northern part of the Netherlands, for in these regions the Romanic and Germanic languages never met. Instead, there was an ethnic factor of a different kind and of equal importance. Throughout the Middle Ages, the coastal regions of the Netherlands, that is the modern provinces of North and South Holland, Zeeland, Utrecht, Friesland and Groningen, were known to all foreigners, including the other tribes of the German Empire to which these coastal regions belonged, as Friesland or Frisia. Now, the Frisians form a separate branch of the West-Germanic people. They are, incidentally, the only Germanic people outside Scandinavia who have maintained themselves and their earliest name at their oldest known—perhaps original—seat. Within the German world, the Frisians occupy a middle position inasmuch as their home borders on that of the Danes in the North, that of the Lower Saxons in the East and South, and that of the related Anglo-Saxons across the sea in the West. Moreover, they not only held a median but also a mediative position. They were sailors and merchants, even at the dawn of history, and archaeological finds help us to trace their rôle of economic and cultural mediation back into prehistory.

It must be remembered that the term 'Frisian' cannot really be applied to the entire coastal region of the Netherlands. For though ancient Frisian law applied in the 'seven Frisian sealands', stretching from the Weser to the Zwin, i.e. to Flanders, not all these regions need necessarily have been Frisian-speaking. Apart from scant traces of Frisian words in ancient place-names, surnames and monuments, we know nothing about the nature of Frisian rule over all of Flanders in Merovingian and Carlovingian times. Frisian, Lower Saxon and Lower Frankish elements are indissoluble components of the Dutch nation.

The eventual independence of the Netherlands and its break with the Holy Roman Empire and France was not determined by the general geographical situation, or by the mixed linguistic character of the Southern Netherlands, or yet by Frisian domination of the North. This emergence, first as a nation hardly aware of its separate nationhood (the Burgundian Netherlands under Charles V), then as two separate areas (one free and one under Spanish domination), and finally as two distinct European states—this double independence was the culmination of a very long series of historical developments.

The break with the Empire began in relatively early times. Whereas three German Emperors—Conrad II, Henry IV and Henry V—died in the Netherlands during the eleventh and twelfth centuries, and so important an event in German history as the deposition of Gregory VII, on Easter 1076, took place in the cathedral of Utrecht, by the thirteenth century the Dutch territories had developed much closer links with France and England than they had with the Empire, which had apparently turned its face towards the South. In about 1340, Edward III used his alliance with insubordinate Flanders and with nobles owning allegiance to the Lower Rhenish dukes to lay the political foundations for a war against France. Even so, this alliance was by no means tantamount to a final separation from the Empire.

It was then that the House of Burgundy appeared on the scene—those dukes of French blood whose statesmanship helped to combine so many territories into a whole, that was to prove far more durable than its ties with France or Germany. And Burgundy with its splendour and dramatic history under Charles the Bold, and with its fortunes joined to those of the House of Hapsburg, determined the shape of

Western Europe and decided the course of European history for centuries to come.

It was not, of course, the personal achievement of the dukes that the Low Countries were able to maintain their new-found, albeit precarious, unity. The new state barely had a name—the term 'Netherlands' had only just been coined, and the new political structure usually went by the name of Burgundy, even though the male line of that House was extinct. All that matters here is that it was not mere political expediency but patriotism that bound together the Netherlands of Charles V, filling its people with loyalty and later with the spirit of resistance to oppression. It was for the sake of their *patria*, fatherland, that they rose against Philip II. In William of Nassau the strains of patriotism, liberty and fidelity combined into a stirring melody.

This is the year in which we celebrate the centenary of the birth of the great Prince of Orange. If we take a very close look at his importance, greatness of spirit and high purpose, we shall find to our astonishment that it was in the name of Burgundy that he raised the standard of revolt. He was, in fact, defending the tradition of the ducal house against Spanish rulers who had failed to respect their Burgundian heritage—he championed the Burgundian state against the House of Burgundy. But he had to pay a great price for his daring. During the vicissitudes of his apparently hopeless struggle with the mightiest ruler in Christendom, there emerged, not a state of seventeen provinces, in which, as the oldest and richest, Flanders, Brabant, Hainault and Artois would have predominated, but a small republic of only seven provinces, a land of seafarers, merchants and fishermen. For the second time, the Burgundian state became a mere torso. Under Charles the Bold, it had looked as if a central state, stretching from the North Sea to the Alps, was an imminent possibility. This pan-Burgundian ideal was buried with the Duke. Precisely 100 years later, when William of Orange, by the pacification of Ghent, united all the provinces against Spain, he hoped that at least that part of the Burgundian Netherlands which stretched from Friesland to Picardy and Lorraine would be successful in maintaining its independence. Until his death, through thick and thin, the Prince of Orange clung to this hope. Things simply had to change for the better. But what, in fact, emerged was far more miraculous than even a great union of all the Netherlands—a tiny Republic with a great empire across the sea, unprecedented prosperity, and a distinctive culture.

To discover to what extent the Netherlands, before its emergence as a new factor in the national life of Europe, i.e. before the separation from Belgium, played a mediatory rôle among its neighbours, we must remember our earlier definition of 'mediation'. There is no doubt at all that the Netherlands acted as a mediator between France and Germany during the Middle Ages, because the Low Countries helped to transmit feudal forms and courtly manners from France to Germany. But when it comes to the transmission of cultural elements or ideas that originated in the Netherlands itself, the term mediation is no longer appropriate. This applies as much to the part played by Netherlanders in the colonisation of North and East Germany during the twelfth century as to the so-called *devotio moderna*, that lay expression of ardent piety whose most fruitful expression was Thomas à Kempis' *The Imitation of Christ*. The influence of the Van Eycks and their school on painters in Cologne and Upper Germany is part of the same process. The Netherlands gave birth to them and hence did not act as mediator. I know of no aspect of German culture that reached France or England through the Netherlands during the Middle Ages and, apart from the courtly manners and ideas we have mentioned, of no traffic in the opposite direction either. If Maximilian really modelled his Austrian government on Burgundian rule in the Netherlands, then we should, indeed, be entitled to speak of mediation. But this question is far from settled.

Until about 1500, the mediative rôle of the Netherlands was mainly restricted to the economic sphere, to the transit of goods and passengers. The details of this type of mediation are part of economic history and we merely mention it in passing.

Yet economic mediation automatically led to a more general type of mediation, for its direct consequence was the meeting of merchants from different countries on Dutch soil, and the exchange of thoughts as well as of goods. This happened in Bruges before 1500 and in Antwerp in about 1500 and later. The central position of Antwerp in the sixteenth century, not only in the world market but also in cultural life, is comparable to that of Venice. Antwerp, the town in which Albrecht Dürer worked and Thomas More conceived his *Utopia*, played much the same rôle in the cultural life of Europe as Erasmus played in its spiritual life. And when it comes to Erasmus, with his gigantic correspondence, with friends and admirers not only in Spain and England but also as far afield as Poland and Hungary—to the man who advised Frederick the Wise on how to deal with Luther, who admonished kings (albeit unsuccessfully) to pursue peaceful policies, and to whom all Europe listened as to an oracle—we may well ask whether he was not mediator first and spiritual guide second. Although he wrote only in Latin and thought but little of his native Holland, Erasmus was at heart far closer to the spirit of the Netherlands than he himself suspected.

When we reach the seventeenth century, the scope of our enquiry narrows to include only the northern part of the Netherlands—to what is now popularly known as Holland. For two centuries, the southern part ceased to be a cultural centre—despite Rubens and Van Dyck—and became a battlefield and political pawn. But for the glorious Dutch Republic there now dawned its greatest day, the peak of its culture and hence also of its rôle as mediator. It is only to refresh your memory that I refer once again to transport, navigation and colonisation, banking and trade, technology and industry, for though all these have a marked mediatory function, they do not really impinge upon our theme. Similarly we again pass over those factors which, springing from Holland itself, had a great influence on developments abroad—for instance on horticulture, agriculture, land reclamation and preservation and also on painting in England, on architecture in Denmark, on mining in Sweden and on navigational methods in Russia. These were simple exports, and not mediation in the stricter sense of the word.

Seventeenth-century Holland was, however, a true mediator in political and intellectual life. The welfare of the Republic was closely bound up with the preservation of the peace of Europe. Every war hampered the Republic's smooth progress, even if it offered individuals the chance to get rich quick. The equilibrium of Europe and of its several parts was a *sine qua non* of Holland's survival—hence her support of Sweden in 1644, and of Denmark in 1658. It is not well known that, in the Baltic, Dutch was used as a diplomatic language throughout the seventeenth century, even in dealings with England. The basic principle of Jan de Witt's policy and that of his successors may not have been purely mediative, but it was always the keeping of the peace. When confronted with the domineering posturings of France under Louis XIV, this policy quite automatically became one of alliances and coalitions, including the Triple Alliance of 1668 and the Grand Alliance of 1689. I am not suggesting that these great events were simply the result of Dutch policy, but the degree to which the Netherlands was recognised as a mediator may be gauged from the fact that the three great peace treaties of 1678, 1697 and 1713 were all signed on Dutch soil—at Nijmwegen, Rijswijk and Utrecht.

If ever it was true to call our country a political mediator it was in about 1700.

Its position of intellectual mediator, too, remained strong. What was this position based on, and how far did it extend? Here we must repeat what we have said when discussing an earlier period: the fact that Dutch culture was itself highly esteemed and some of its expressions imitated abroad does not constitute mediation in the sense we have defined. The fame of Grotius did not make him a cultural mediator, even though he was forced to spend the later part of his life in France. Christian Huygens, the physicist, communicated his discoveries to Englishmen, Germans, Frenchmen and Italians and lived in Paris, but that does not make him a mediator. In fact, Holland owed its rôle as mediator between east and west, north and south, chiefly to its universities. Here people from other countries could meet and exchange books and ideas, as at that time they could do nowhere else to the same extent. The language barrier which today keeps foreign students out of our academies did not then exist—all lectures were delivered in the familiar Latin. Throughout the seventeenth, and for a good part of the eighteenth, century, Leyden, Franeker, Groningen and Utrecht attracted a host of English, French, Scottish, Danish, Swedish, Polish, Hungarian and, above all, German students. At first, a great many of our professors came from France—Scaliger the Younger and Salmasius among them. But then German professors arrived in ever greater number. Thus of Groningen's total of 52 professors in the seventeenth century, 27 were Germans; in Leyden and Utrecht the ratio was roughly one in six. Although most of these foreigners eventually settled in Holland, we are entitled to say that they helped our country to play a continuous and profound mediatory rôle in the field of university education.

Moreover, even outside the university, Holland welcomed a host of foreign visitors and offered asylum to an even larger number of refugees. Descartes was one; others included the Mennonites, driven from Berne at the beginning of the eighteenth century, and the Lutherans who had to flee from Salzburg. The resulting exchange of ideas was intensified by the influx of large waves of French Protestants upon the revocation of the Edict of Nantes. Apart from traders and artisans, the Huguenots who fled to Holland were, in the main, men of intellect and learning. They did not leave us again, becoming Dutch citizens but preserving their French culture. The most famous of them was Pierre Bayle—sceptical philosopher, lexicographer and apostle of the Enlightenment. His name, together with that of Jean Leclerq and the two Basnages, is associated with that important and extraordinary cultural phenomenon: the growth of French literature and the publication of French books in the Netherlands. Our country played a most important part in the history of the Enlightenment, inasmuch as, though the chief proponents were foreigners, it offered them a platform from which to proclaim their views. The effect of their writings was world-wide. Bayle's *Nouvelles de la république des lettres*, Leclerq's *Bibliothèque universelle*, no less than the two journals published at The Hague—the *Journal littéraire* and the *Mémoires littéraires de la Grande Bretagne*—were all media for the international exchange of ideas. Thanks to them, many English ideas in French guise, reached Germany and Switzerland via Holland. True, Holland's own rôle in this exchange was completely passive. The books and journals in question were not written by Dutchmen. But our country provided an indispensable prerequisite: toleration.

From 1700, we pass straight to the present day. The rest of the eighteenth century concerns our problem only inasmuch as our country lost its dominant position almost as suddenly as it had gained it, its cultural activity ceasing to be productive and becoming almost entirely receptive. Holland, which had always welcomed foreign cultural influences, opened the doors even wider to them, now that

Humanism had ceased to produce a kind of cosmopolitan culture. In this process, the marked French influence first became diluted and then counterpoised by English and German contributions. This great turning point in the intellectual life of all Europe, i.e. the ousting of Romanic influences by predominantly Germanic ones, was nowhere more marked than in Holland.

Coming now to the twentieth century and to the present situation, I must repeat that I shall not venture into the realm of economics. Nor need the reader expect me to offer a recipe for solving international import and export problems. (If I were forced to offer one, I should simply say: freedom.) I wish to address you merely as an historian, and as such I would only point out that modern economics are based, to a far larger degree and far more often than economists realise, on irrational considerations. Most economists seem to think that economic motives are susceptible to objective explanation, when they are, in fact, far too often the rationa isation of mere wishful thinking.

But to return to our problem. When discussing the mediative rôle of the Netherlands in modern times, we exclude Belgium from our considerations—its international position and internal problems are such that they can no longer be treated in the same context as Holland's. As for the latter, we shall now consider whether it does and can play a mediatory rôle in modern Europe, and if so whether this rôle is cultural or chiefly political.

Of Holland's geo-political situation we have good reason to say that it has changed in the course of time from a purely peripheral to a predominantly central one. In the Europe of yore, which had its face turned towards the Mediterranean, the Netherlands was a remote region; in the Atlantic Europe which has emerged since 1500, it came to lie far closer to the geographical centre; in the Atlantic-Pacific world of today, it is central in the highest degree. That, in itself, does not, of course, make Holland a mediator. Nevertheless, this position has determined the course of Dutch foreign policy. Politically speaking, we have nothing to gain from any of the great powers. As long as the world does not explode we can do without a special protector—all the great powers alike are interested in leaving us alone. But should the world go mad and a new world war be unleashed, then it makes no difference whether we choose one or the other, since Western culture as a whole seems likely to perish in the flames.

This reluctance to take sides goes hand in hand with great impartiality on the part of our people—though it would be wrong to mistake our lack of bias for indifference. There is probably no other country in which the press reports and comments on foreign affairs more thoroughly, accurately and regularly than in Holland. The educated newspaper reader in our country is fairly familiar with German, English, French and American politics. It is precisely because of this that we have had no favourites among the other nations since the World War. Our foreign policy accords perfectly with our cultural ties.

There is also no other country in the world that is more open to every aspect of foreign culture than we are. And precisely this great openness makes us mediators *par excellence*—even if we did little else—for the very absorption, assimilation, and transmission of cultural elements entitles us to that name.

This openness to foreign influences is rooted in our entire history, for we have had close cultural relations with our neighbours ever since St. Amand came across from Aquitaine and St. Willebrord from England to teach Christianity among us. Even repeated wars have failed to turn us into sworn enemies of France and England. As for the German Empire, we never clashed with it as such—only once did we take arms against a German region, when we fought Munster and Cologne in 1672.

From the nineteenth century onwards, the absorption of

English, French and German cultural elements has been accelerated by fairly widespread and reasonably good knowledge of the languages of our three great neighbours. We take the training of language teachers very seriously. Most Dutchmen have a somewhat exaggerated idea of their ability to speak German, English and French, but it should not be forgotten that our own phonetic system makes it far easier for us than for our neighbours to imitate the sound of all three languages.

The openness to foreign culture also entails serious dangers. The lack of a film and automobile industry of our own is no great loss, for we are happy in the knowledge that we can still build good ships, bridges, and canals. We can even resign ourselves to the fact that our illustrated weeklies have too small a circulation ever to rise above the level of mediocrity. Yet it would fill us with alarm were we threatened with a one-sided cultural traffic and the consequent stifling of our own creative thought. Luckily, we are not faced with that threat in any major field of intellectual endeavour—neither in art nor even in science. For though it cannot be denied that the educated Dutchman, however patriotic, often has the urge to neglect his own for foreign writers, the foreign influences roughly cancel out—perhaps not in one and the same man but certainly in our nation as a whole. And it is precisely the resulting equilibrium which enables us to play the mediator. Thanks to its kinship with German thought, its historical links with England and its cultural bonds with France, the Dutch mind is equally receptive to the influence of all three. And this vast process of cultural assimilation is greatly facilitated by the fact that we have a language of our own.

At first sight, this claim may appear paradoxical. You might think that a bilingual country, such as Switzerland, in which two distinct cultures coexist, is much more suited to the rôle of cultural mediation. But this is not the case. Depending on whether their mother tongue is German or

French, the Swiss are inclined to gravitate to one or other of the two, whereas the Dutch, precisely because they have their own language, that ancient symbol of their national identity and independence, can assimilate foreign influences evenly and quite freely. Without a language of their own, the Dutch could never have become the great mediators they are.

I should like to mention one case in which Dutch mediation has been particularly direct and fruitful. When, immediately after the Great War, intellectual contacts between the former enemies were practically non-existent, it was my old friend de Sitter, the well-known Dutch astronomer, who put his scientific friends in Britain in touch with those in Germany, thus helping the resumption of scientific relations between the two great nations.

True, our mediation is rarely as clear-cut as that, but the Netherlands has undoubtedly acted as mediator in thousands of other cases as well, and in many diverse fields, particularly since the end of the war, when international contacts have been greatly intensified. True, we have only The Hague with its Permanent Court of International Justice to set against Geneva, Basle, Locarno and Lausanne, but does that make Switzerland a more important mediator between Western and Central Europe than Holland? I dare say no.

Mediation, in the sense in which I have been using the word, is not equivalent to a share in the deliberations of the great powers (which we lack) nor to a vote in the League of Nations (which we have). No, the ability to mediate is implied in the very situation and character of a state and people. I hope to have shown that, in this general and somewhat abstract sense, the Netherlands may, indeed, be called mediator between Western and Central Europe. The characteristics attributed to us by other people, and not infrequently by ourselves as well, namely sobriety, phlegm and lack of imagination, go hand in hand with a kind of mental balance, an equable outlook and peace of mind. The resulting intellectual atmosphere makes the Dutchman an eminent critic of all sweeping theories and great plans and, on the other hand, eminently receptive to positive thought from any quarter. This does not mean we have become rootless cosmopolitans—far from it. Precisely because our manifold links with different cultures have enabled us to appreciate the irreplaceable value of each one, do we realise that better international understanding and greater harmony cannot result either from the premature fusion of disparate elements or from the baseless denial of very real differences. Acknowledgment of the alien as such, entering into its spirit and yet maintaining one's own—these are things that all nations will have to learn, no matter how long it takes them to do so.

If, as I truly believe, Providence has enabled the people of the Netherlands to make some slight progress in this field, more so perhaps than many a far greater nation, then this very aptitude may well be an indication of the special qualification of our country to act as mediator between Western and Central Europe.

Two Wrestlers with the Angel[1]

It happens from time to time that a great thinker, looking back upon the variegated and often baleful course of the centuries, asks himself what may have been the *meaning* of it all, and tries to supply a single answer. Such men are seldom professional historians, for these are held back by the realization that their knowledge is inadequate to the task. Moreover they, who sample history as one might savour old wine, do not feel the same need for a definitive interpretation of the past—they are frequently content simply to correlate the bewildering diversity of factual data. So it is more often the philosophers who try to unravel the skein of world history or else those gifted dilettantes who seem irresistibly drawn to this learned discipline.

In recent years, two attempts to uncover the structure of history have attracted notice, so remarkable, so distinct from, and indeed opposed to, each other, and yet so characteristic of the national cultures that inspired them, that they seem positively to demand comparison.

In 1918, contemporaneously with the military and economic collapse of Germany, Oswald Spengler published the first part of his sombre *Decline of the West*.[2] This part, entitled *Form and Actuality*, consisted of 600 pages of clearly reasoned and brilliantly expressed historical exegesis. It made great demands on the reader's philosophical, mathematical, scientific, musical and artistic understanding. Nevertheless the book took Germany by storm. The very

[1]First published in *De Gids*, nos. 6 and 7, 1921.
[2]Oswald Spengler: *Der Untergang des Abendlandes*, C. H. Becksche Verlagsbuchhandlung, Munich, 1918.

title was bound to strike a chord in the 'Götterdämmerung' of late 1918, though Spengler was far from pandering to his public. In a short while, he found himself occupying the pedestal of the intellectual hero that he had himself erected. 53,000 copies were quickly sold, and publication of the second volume was eagerly awaited.

Yet trained thinkers were not slow to raise objections. Troeltsch, favourably disposed towards the work by his own passion for cultural syntheses, tempered moderate praise with sharp criticism.[1] Indignant refutations of the work came chiefly from classical philologers and art historians. In 1921, *Logos*, a journal that counted the foremost German thinkers among its contributors, devoted an entire issue to the refutation of Spengler's thesis,[2] denouncing it as a national danger, a poison paralysing the German spirit. How many authors have had the honour thus to become the personal target of an entire cultural élite?

In 1920, H. G. Wells rather casually launched his *Outline of History* in twenty-four instalments, afterwards revised in book form.[3] This was 'an attempt to tell, truly and clearly, in one continuous narrative, the whole story of life and mankind so far as it is known today. It is written plainly for the general reader'. The author did not for a moment pretend that he was an historian. He was an avowed amateur. He quite freely admitted that he had sought much of his information in the *Encyclopaedia Britannica*. But he also surrounded himself with a small corps of established scholars, who examined and revised everything he wrote, though he often put up a spirited and good-humoured resistance to their expert advice. This was the characteristic Wellsian independence of the powers that be. Spengler would doubtless be mortally offended at being bracketed with Wells.

[1]*Historische Zeitschrift*, 120, 1919, pp. 281-91.
[2]Vol. IX, 2 (*Spenglerheft*), Tübingen, Mohr, 1921.
[3]London, 1920.

But the fact is that, despite its popular character, Wells's *Outline*, like the *Decline*, is a serious attempt to determine the meaning, structure, true process and scope of world history. Moreover, it is a book that must be treated seriously, if only because its author's fame made it discussed wherever English is read or spoken, so that its readers were numbered by the hundred thousand. When Hilaire Belloc wrote deprecatingly of Wells's public as 'his million negligible provincials',[1] he was in fact merely parading his intellectual snobbery.

The reader who opens the *Decline of the West* for the first time, will surely be repelled by its author's conceit. Almost every page bristles with congratulation on the brilliant originality of his own ideas. I am giving you what no one else has ever had to give—that is the refrain he never wearies of intoning. This self-adulation culminates in such incomparable passages as those in which he claims that, unlike all the arbitrary and narrow schemes of others, his is the natural, the 'Copernican' interpretation which 'reveals itself only to an eye perfectly free of prepossessions'; that in his work, an act 'like the act of Copernicus' had to be accomplished once again,[2] in short, that his transformation of the humanities could be compared only with the Copernican transfiguration of natural science. Our smile is sceptical. And when, with triumphant cries, Spengler drives his docile flock of truths before him, a flock that he takes for the oxen of Helios, then we catch at least a glimpse of the ridiculous behind all his prodigious seriousness.

And yet he compels us to forget that we know better. He seizes us in a grip of iron, and forces us down upon our knees before his historical idols. He bewitches us with his fascinating imagination, and in the end we say: the whole

[1] *The London Mercury*, November 1920, vol. III, no. 13, p. 62.
[2] pp. 24, 136.

thing may be a horrible travesty of history, but it is so great a work of genius that perhaps, after all, we should respect it.

The general concept underlying Spengler's work is the antithesis between history and nature. 'The soul,' he says,[1] 'has two worlds in which it can realise and express itself . . . one of which is nature, formed by things-become and known and suffused with law, number, limit, logic, the world of system, mechanism, cause and effect; the other history, the immediate expression of becoming and life—this can be contemplated but never comprehended. History possesses a logic and necessity that cannot be put into words—the logic and necessity of Destiny. Nature and history confront each other as life and death, direction and extension, eternal future and eternal past.' Thus, to Spengler, historical interpretation consists in understanding the world in its process of becoming, in motion and direction. 'As soon as things-becoming have taken their place as things-become, the possible has become real, its destiny is fulfilled. The approaching future has become the static past. It has become Space and thus enthralled to the organic principle of causality'.[2] Clearly, Spengler has given the term history an entirely new meaning. How has a work of art or a political system fulfilled its destiny when it has been completed? Have they become 'dead' nature, and lost all dynamic contact with the future? Is history nothing but obsequies for the dead?

What drives Spengler to set nature and history poles apart is the deep awareness that measure, law and number do not exhaust our idea of the essence of things. 'Nature and history are extreme terms in man's ability to order the actualities about him as a picture of the world . . . An actuality is contemplated in its form . . . in that way there arises the world of Plato, Rembrandt, Goethe and Beethoven; or com-

[1] p. 506. [2] p. 230.

prehended in its element, as in the worlds of Parmenides and Descartes, Kant and Newton'.[1] This distinction Spengler carried to extreme lengths, and on it he based his book. To him the difference between things causal, scientific, exact and logical, and things aesthetic, intuitive and emotional was in fact the distinction between nature and history.

'Nature is what can be counted; history everything that has no relationship with mathematics.'[2] 'Becoming does not know finitude. Only the lifeless can be counted, measured, analysed. Pure becoming, life itself, is boundless in this respect. It lies beyond the realm of cause and effect, law and measure. Deep and pure historical research seeks for no causal laws; if it does it fails to understand its true essence.'[3] However, Spengler freely admits that these two world concepts are not mutually exclusive, in other words that history, too, is forced to work with the inert, with things-become. Nevertheless he holds fast to his main definition of history as the realisation, along a non-logical path, of a process of living, moving and becoming, as the contrast between process and law or between 'physiognomic' and 'systematic'. In so doing he denies causality to pure history, thus removing it from the realm of science. 'The desire to treat history scientifically is rooted in a fundamental misconception ... science may interpret Nature but poetry alone can understand history.'[4] 'An historical interpretation grows the more barren the more it imposes causal relations on its protean subject matter. The more profound our historical insight, the less use we have for so-called causal explanations.'[5]

There is much truth in this last statement. But Spengler's egregious error lies in supposing that he has discovered an entirely new approach. All he has done is to push to the extreme the differences between historical and scientific concepts as employed by his own compatriots during the preceding thirty years. It was in *his* mind, he claims, that there was 'at long last discovered the opposition through which

[1] p. 137; cf. p. 483. [2] p. 83. [3] p. 138. [4] p. 139. [5] p. 211.

alone the spirit of history can be grasped: the antithesis between history and nature'.[1] But it was in fact Dilthey, Windelband, Rickert and Simmel who sharpened—rather than
introduced—the already familiar contrast. It would take us
too far afield to explain how these men contrived to defend
history as a discipline in its own right at a time when it was
in grave danger of succumbing to the demand for scientific
accuracy and a scientific methodology. They proved that
history could continue to make valid contributions to human knowledge even if it refused to be remade in the image
of physics or biology. It was they who helped to restore the
intuitive element in historical research to its full value.

Now it is easy to understand why Spengler, who had
studied science, should have imagined that all historians
were busily worshipping nature. Simultaneously with the
demand that historians must subject themselves to the discipline of the natural sciences, historical materialism—
which was far more influential than the thought of the
philosophers we have just mentioned—was converting large
numbers, and not merely Marxists, to its crude dogmas of
'historical necessity'. 'The "exact" historian makes the
highly naïve assumption that successive historical phases
are a series of conditions of a mechanical type, that must
yield to reasonable analysis much like a physical experiment
or a chemical reaction.'[2] If the historian does indeed think
like that, then the sooner he changes his mind the better.
'Shibboleths resuscitated from Darwinism,' is what Spengler calls the principles of this economic 'explanation' of
history.[3] But all he himself does is betray his failure to grasp,
or refusal to recognise, the demands of modern historical
methodology. He cares for nothing but the incessant reiter-
ation of his mighty antitheses.

Spengler posits nothing less than two ways of apprehending reality: on the one hand, the inclusive way of be-
holding the world, common to primitive peoples, children

[1]p. 68.   [2]p. 212.   [3]p. 152.

and poets, a direct grasp of things as a whole, in all their complex inter-relatedness, that is in their special character and form, the apprehension of the full dynamic life of all things in their eternal motion and tragic destiny; on the other hand the exclusive way of regarding nature which only comes in a mature culture and involves the singling out of things by analysis, measurement, calculation, systematisation, the reduction of all mystery to the bare bones of causality. 'In civilised man, the tragic sense succumbs to the mechanising intellect.' It is the beginning of the petrification of a culture when this Medusa-look at the world—that of exact science and strict logic—prevails. Thus Plato the visionary was followed by Aristotle the reductive thinker; thus Kant, the exponent of 'the pure systematic cognised with the intellect of the eternally old' rose like an iceberg against Goethe, that champion of 'the pure physiognomic of the world perceived with the soul of the eternal child'.[1]

Persuasively and masterfully though Spengler embattles the semajestic counter-concepts throughout his work, the critical reader cannot help feeling that he is being driven up a perilous slope by a herdsman in whose eyes there is the fixed stare of the maniac. What, in fact, does he put in the place of causality, to which he denies any sort of sway over what he calls the historical? The answer is 'Destiny'. 'Destiny is an ineffable inner determinism. The essence of the causal can be defined by a physical or critical system, by number or conceptual analysis. The idea of destiny, however, can only be revealed by the artist, by a painting, a tragedy or music.' Magnificent stuff this—is is not? And Spengler continues: 'In the idea of Destiny the soul reveals its world-longing, its desire to rise up into the light, to accomplish and realise its vocation. It is not utterly alien to any man, and only in "late" man of the megalopolis with his love of facts and the supremacy of his mechanising intellect over his inner life has this vision been overpowered. But in some

[1] p. 218.

apocalyptic hour the vision will be restored to him with unmistakable clarity, shattering in a moment all superficial
"explanations" of the world. For the world as a system of
causal connections is not only a late but also a rare conception and only the declining intellects of high Cultures are
affected by it.'[1] Destiny is relevant to life, causality to death,
their relationship is that of space and time. 'We cannot
imagine the living process of world-becoming without the
intervention of Destiny, no matter whether we are contem-
plating a butterfly or a culture.'[2]

So far we have used the word 'Destiny' for Spengler's
Schicksal. But as Spengler himself points out, that word cannot really be translated. Its very essence seems intimately
related to the emotive overtones of the German tongue.
To *Schicksal* applies what is true of so many other German
words, for instance of *Geschick*, *Verhängnis*, *Zufall*, *Fügung*, or
Bestimmung—'no hypothesis and no science can ever hope
to impinge on what we feel when we immerse ourselves in
their sound. They are symbols, not concepts.'[3] It is completely in accordance with Spengler's general attitude that
so important a symbol as 'Western Culture' cannot be translated into Greek, Latin, Chinese or Egyptian, for it is
characteristic of, and hence comprehensible to, the spirit of
'the West', alone.[4] May we therefore assume that the
English and French are capable of understanding it? Well,
that is a thorny question. For though France and England
are geographically Western, we shall see that they do not
really have a full share in Spengler's Occident or *Abend-
land*.

Spengler presents his book not as a poetic flight of fancy,
but as *the* explanation of the 'morphology of world history'.
The vital question is: what does he *do* with his morphologi-

[1] p. 165   [2] p. 171.   [3] p. 164.
[4] Compare Spengler's remarks on the untranslatability of the terms
ἀρκη, ὑλη, and μορφη on p. 250.

cal principles, what does he achieve with his idea of
Schicksal or Destiny? Alas, the answer must be that he causes
trouble and confusion, that he deludes and blinds his fol-
lowers, and that the unbridled self-conceit with which he
tears aside the veil of history brings its own nemesis upon
him. While his own, loudly and forcefully proclaimed beliefs ought to have safeguarded him against all kinds of
systems, he himself fell victim to the most exaggerated
schematisation and misleading anthropomorphism (and
partly even phytomorphism) that have ever been imposed
upon historical processes.

To Spengler, the basic manifestations of historical phenomena are 'cultures', which have followed and will continue
to succeed one another in closely similar cycles of growth
and decline. He jeers at the idea of irreversible progress.
'There exists an infinitely banal optimism in respect of the
future of higher humanity.'[1] And here he is on safe ground,
for the feeling that so much in modern culture points towards decline and degeneration rather than to steady progress was expressed by many even before the appearance of
Spengler's work, and goes far to explain its fantastic success.
Moreover, rejection of the idea of progress is by no means as
recent as Spengler himself made out. It is completely untrue
to say that, ever since Petrarch, mankind has considered itself an irresistibly forward-looking and progressive force.[2]
Until the eighteenth century, the idea of the cyclical course
of cultural forms, each bearing the germ of its own decay,
as it was known since the Stoics, predominated over the idea
of an irresistible onward march towards an ever-higher
civilisation. For Macchiavelli, Bodin and Montaigne, history was cyclic. Vico expressed the idea of *ricorsi* in a form
much like Spengler's. Only with Herder was the idea of
progress, as pioneered by Bacon and Descartes, turned into
a dogma, even then to be questioned by thinkers of such
stature as Schopenhauer and Burckhardt.

[1] p. 28.   [2] p. 428.

The term 'culture' had a downright Neo-Platonic ring for Spengler. 'Cultures are the highest reality we can know.'[1] A culture is the 'phenomenon of a soul whose existence exhausts itself in the unceasing realisation of its inner possibilities, its idea.'[2] Having a soul and character, it must clearly have a 'destiny' as well. The fact that the 'idea' of a culture can be defined neither by its nature and composition nor yet by its scope and duration, does not worry Spengler in the least. Quite the contrary. For if cultures were indeed susceptible of circumscription and definition they would, *a fortiori*, be mere concepts from the dead realm of nature. That is why they can only be grasped intuitively and not comprehended. They can be grasped, moreover, in their destiny, which may be conceived through metaphors drawn from the organic life of plants or men. *Chassez la nature, elle revient au galop* . . . the proverb has been given a new twist by Spengler. The age-old imagery of youth, manhood, old age and death, of germinating, flowering, maturing and wilting, of spring, summer, autumn and winter are, for Spengler, no mere figures of speech but so many metaphysical truths. For him they intimate the real secret of historical events. Cultures, too, must undergo a wilting, a death in the fullest sense of the word.

Conceived in this way, cultures can naturally be described in the naïvely anthropomorphic ways common to myth and party politics. Arabian culture (we shall see later what precisely that is supposed to be) fettered as it was by ancient *mores* 'durst not move freely', 'prostrated itself humbly' before alien, antiquated forms, and 'tried to make do' with the Greek tongue. But once liberated by Islam, 'it flung itself with tremendous vehemence upon all the lands that had inwardly belonged to it for centuries'. To do so was the sign of 'a soul that feels it has no time to lose, that anxiously notes the first signs of old age even before it has enjoyed its youth'.[3] It could not have been put more strongly—

[1] p. 253. [2] p. 351. [3] pp. 288, 290.

Michelet was weak stuff in comparison. There has been a complete reversal of the normal rôles: while culture lives, feels and acts, man is dead and blindly obeys the 'force of entire epochs, which moves in a direction that nobody knows or desires and to which everyone must nonetheless submit'.[1]

This panorama of cultural life, too, is governed by two antitheses, namely 'culture' and 'civilisation.' Here Spengler follows Nietzsche. Every culture must turn into a civilisation, and when it does, it is the beginning of its end. Decline goes hand in hand with the victory of the great city over the countryside and the organic life of the small town. Not that 'hand in hand' is meant to suggest an illegitimate causal relationship. There can be no causation in Spengler's view of history, and nothing was further from his mind than the idea of causal chains of ghostly economic 'factors'. In the early period, cultural life is rooted in the soil; the world picture is the primitive, healthy and 'natural' outlook of the peasant or landowner. There follows the 'typical' battle between the 'soil-bound spirit of the countryman (nobility and priesthood) and the worldly, patrician spirit of the old, small and famous towns'.[2] The towns win but are conquered in turn by the world-city and its culture-destroying mechanism. That is how it all went in the fourth century and again in the nineteenth. Roman Empires are 'normal products, typical end phases'.[3] The advent of 'pure civilisation' is tantamount to a 'gradual decline'. 'World-city' man rules supreme—he is 'strong-willed, completely unmetaphysical' and cannot help being an imperialist 'with a profound aversion to the peasantry (and its highest expression, the county gentleman)' and with 'a total indifference to things traditional' and hence destructive of culture. The victory of 'civilisation' is a 'tremendous fall into the inorganic'. 'With the inception of civilisation, the moral factor becomes transformed from a natural product of the heart

[1] p. 297.   [2] pp. 44ff.   [3] p. 54.

into an intellectual principle, from something that is given unto man into a conscious means, an instrument that can be manipulated. It is no longer revealed by every breath of life, but has to be formulated and followed.' In place of humanity we now have the masses, and party leaders have stepped into the shoes of creative man. Values have been replaced with aims, symbols with programs, quality with quantity, greatness has dwindled to mere bigness.'[1]

Everyone who views the sterility of intellectual and social life as a modern symptom of decline, will find much warrant of this attitude in Spengler. Yet Spengler, not content with recognising general resemblances in the course of different cultures, must needs fit them into the Procrustean bed of his over-all interpretation. In accordance with his thesis of an unavoidable and organic cycle, each phenomenon is assigned its fixed place and corresponds precisely to a parallel phenomenon in every other culture. This homology of phenomena is basic and unspeakably significant. It is all rather reminiscent of the straining of evidence to harmonise the Old and the New Testaments in Christian apologetics. To the socialism of the 'West' there corresponds the Stoicism of the time of the Roman emperors and—if you please— Buddhism in Indian culture (Spengler knew or understood very little about ancient India). We must forever match event with event and person to person across the globe and through the centuries. 'As symbols of *identical*[2] phenomena then, the storming of the Bastille, Valmy, Austerlitz, Waterloo and the rise of Prussia correspond to such ancient happenings as the battles of Chaeronea and Gaugamela, Alexander's Indian campaign and the growth of Rome.'[3] Rembrandt corresponds to Polygnotus, Bach to Polycletus, Beethoven to Scopas, and Lysippus to Wagner.[4] Spengler shudders at 'historians' who 'never even dreamed that Protestanism had its counterpart in Dionysianism'.[5] Those armed with Spengler's 'physiognomic tact' can readily de-

[1] p. 502.   [2] My italics.   [3] p. 207.   [4] p. 312.   [5] p. 163.

duce 'the prevailing state form, for instance, from the details of the formal language of art'; indeed, it is possible to reconstruct 'forgotten and unknown epochs, even entire past cultures on the basis of morphological relationships'.[1] No doubt this task would keep one going for a very long time, especially when we remember that there is not merely an unshakable rhythm with periods of 50 and 300 years,[2] but that there are also 'fine threads from the person of Luther back to Henry the Lion and forward to Bismarck'. In other words, Henry somehow pre-figured the other two, which explains why the interval between 'the symbolic acts of Legnano, Worms and Königgrätz' was precisely 345 years.[3] Only astrology can come to our rescue here, and no doubt modern star-gazers must find Spengler's book entirely to their taste, albeit he himself would have nothing to do with them.

Is it really necessary to stress the absurdity of such hypostasisings of historical cultures as mystically alive beings? Must one insist that the 'organic conception of history is merely an offshoot of romanticism?' Or argue that Spengler has no eye for cultural tradition, and is blind to the fact that different modes of thought lie superimposed in every culture like so many geological layers? The very rashness with which he dismisses Roman history as the final act of Greek culture (as if Rome had no past of her own), simply because the two are commonly lumped together as 'classical antiquity', should be quite enough to explode his fantastic scheme of hermeneutics.

What is so provoking in Spengler's book is that he dismisses all 'merely' reasonable criticism because his own thinking comes down to us from loftier heights—and yet bases his whole exposition on a relationship between facts that can only be grasped with our 'mere' intellectual faculties. If we respond to his sweeping visions with our feelings

[1] p. 163.   [2] p. 158.   [3] p. 209.

alone, it is not merely hard, it is almost impossible to resist his strong persuasion. But if we feel duty bound to look at his work critically, to see whether or not the factual basis of his edifice is sound, then our admiration will turn into repugnance against what I cannot help calling the lack of simple honesty in the book. I shall try to qualify this criticism, by looking more closely at Spengler's distinction between cultures.

'Thus the notion of world history, in the strictly morphological sense,' he tells us at the beginning of the third section,[1] 'expands into the idea of an *all-embracing symbolism*. Historical research as such has merely to investigate the inner form of living reality, and to test its fugitive image . . . Here, however, we shall look at the ultimate questions of existence. Everything we are conscious of, in whatever form —soul and world, life and reality, history and nature, law, space, destiny, God, future and past, the present and eternity—has for us an even deeper meaning, namely that everything is as it is and not otherwise. And the one and only means of rendering the incomprehensible comprehensible . . . must be a kind of metaphysics that regards *everything whatsoever* as having the character of a symbol.' Do you hear the strains of Emerson, Whitman and a hundred other visionaries or poets? Seen from these heights, history lies so far beneath us that the individual signposts can no longer be recognised. You are in a realm beyond and above that of mere name and form.

But then Spengler comes along and tells us that it is from these awful heights that he will survey everything and give it a local habitation and a name. To each and every culture he awards an archetypal symbol (*Ursymbol*) defining it absolutely and in all its expressions. 'Symbols are sensible signs, final, indivisible and, above all, unsought impressions of fixed meaning.'[2] Thus the symbol of Egyptian culture is the Way, that of classical culture the Body, that of the West is

[1]p. 223.　　[2]p. 223.

Space. How these cultures originated and how they obtained their individualities are questions that do not concern him—after all, there is no causality in history. In actual fact, it is the opposition of Body and Space round which the whole paraphernalia revolves. For though Spengler managed to find a symbol for the Egyptian culture, no such symbol occurred to him for the Indian, Arabian or Chinese —their symbols remain nebulous and vague. This then is the basis of the whole system: whereas antiquity recognised in all things only the direct, strictly limited, body, Western culture sees in everything the principle of infinite space.[1] The opposition can also be expressed in a more suggestive way: the Apollonian soul of antiquity can be said to oppose the Faustian soul of the West. The conflict between these two phantoms runs right through the book.

The spirit of antiquity, it is alleged—for antiquity read Greece since, to Spengler, Rome represented only the period of 'civilisation' i.e. of the decline of ancient culture— grasped only what was at hand, at rest, and immediately given. It did not ask whence and whither. The Greeks, we are told, were completely unhistorical by inclination, in contrast to the Egyptians with their immemorial past and the tradition-conscious Westerners. Even the quite recent past was transformed into myth by the Greeks. They were suffused with the 'pure present'. The past 'dissolved into a timeless and changeless impression, polar rather than periodic in structure.' 'Classical culture had no memory.'[2] The Greeks identified reality with bodiliness. Plato could conceive of only three dimensions; four-dimensional space would have struck him as being nonsensical.[3] The Greeks had a fundamental aversion to incommensurable numbers. 'Their classical souls made them consider the irrational . . . a form of sacrilege.' In short, their spirit was 'Euclidean', and to Spengler this was the same in the realm of logical thought as 'Apollonian' was in the realm of culture

[1] pp. 243, 352.   [2] p. 509, 11, 12.   [3] pp. 96-7.

as a whole. The plastic, statuesque aspect of Greek religion was but another expression of the same restricting sense of finite bodiliness. The sense of the numinous withdraws anxiously into a multiplicity of clearly limned figures which, together, do not form a whole or fill the world. That is why the main art-form of the Greeks was sculpture, the pre-eminently physical and 'isolating' art, the 'counterpart to Euclidean mathematics. Both ignore pure space.'[1] So passionately does Spengler see Greek sculpture as limited and purely 'physical' that he calls it soulless.[2] Greek music, finally, is nothing but a 'plastic for the ear'. It is devoid of polyphony or harmony—which presuppose a tonal space— and 'hence lacks any deeper potentialities as an independent art form'.[3] Its main function was to serve as accompaniment to dance and drama.

Contrasted with this picture of classical culture and the Apollonian spirit is that of Western culture and the 'Faust-ian' spirit. We shall see below when this culture arose; here it suffices to state that it matured in the sixteenth and de-clined in the eighteenth century. Where the Greek, with his non-spatial view failed to see any world direction, aim or purpose, Faustian man, whose symbol is space, sees direc-tion, striving, aim and development in everything. He is man with a will—his thought is dynamic whereas that of antiquity was static. Everywhere he flouts limitation, and is determined to penetrate into the infinite. It is he who first experienced depth,[4] and who sees everything prospectively in time. The mere fixed relationship of independent magni-tudes and numbers is not for him, he looks for dynamic possibilities everywhere. It was he who discovered the in-finite principle; his mathematics completely transcends measurable quantities. His art, once the Faustian soul has reached its full maturity, is no longer sculpture but painting with its ability to evoke the distance between things and to explore depths, infinity, and the dissolving of all boundaries

[1] p. 311.   [2] p. 359.   [3] p. 314.   [4] p. 233.

in space. And more so even than by painting, his longing for the unlimited, the unknown, the inexpressible, is fulfilled by music. Music is the real Faustian art, and assumes the task of painting after Rembrandt. It culminates—for Spengler the Faustian character of music is bound to polyphony and counterpoint—in Bach. Beethoven signifies autumn and approaching decline.

The period of the Faustian soul embraces the Middle Ages and modern times—any distinction between these two is rejected by Spengler with uncalled for violence. The youth of Western culture lies in the Gothic period, a concept Spengler stretches to include the Baroque. Even in the Vikings and Crusaders, the Faustian soul yearned for the infinite.

Classical culture does not make way directly for Western culture—the two are separated by what Spengler chooses to call Arabian or Magian culture. He never tires of telling us that it was he who first hit upon its true nature and significance. The magical soul of Arabian culture 'was awakened at the time of Augustus in the land between the rivers Nile and Euphrates'.[1] To it belongs everything that has previously been called late-classical, early-Christian, Byzantine, Moslem, and early-medieval. Paul and Plotinus are no less 'Arabian men' than Mohammed; Christianity is of 'Arabian origin'; traces of 'Arabian-Gothic' are still found in Burgundy, Provence and Strassburg. The Gospel of St. John is a 'Young-Arabian speculation', the Basilica is 'Young-Arabian', and so is neo-Platonism. Diocletian 'completed the khalifate' and the Pantheon was the 'earliest of all Mosques'.[2] One wonders at first why Spengler, if he wished to lump all these things together under one heading, did not rather speak of a Semitic-Hellenic culture. The answer is obvious: had he done so he would have had to admit that the cultural period covering the first seven or

[1] p. 255.   [2] pp. 583, 230, 290, 104.

eight centuries of our era must be understood as a fusion of traditions of widely different origins. And this is precisely what he cannot afford to admit lest causality slip back into history and his miraculous cultural birth prove an abortion. Perhaps he would have done even better to speak of a Strzygowski culture. For this 'Magian culture' can only be the after-effects of getting drunk on strong potations of Strzygowski.[1]

They are truly marvellous, these dream-visions that Spengler sees in his inebriation. What joins the idea of monotheism to Mosaic and Arabesque art, algebra to the logos concept, golden backgrounds to the idea of revelation, Byzantinism to the view that history is a process of redemption? Why, the 'Magian world-sensation'. Those who realise that they are being led up the magical garden path of history by an inspired guide—let them follow Spengler into cloudcuckooland, couch in his Earthly Paradise and turn lotus eaters. Yet those who still feel some urge to know the past in the only way in which we can really come to know it, those who love things in their own singularity—albeit the singularities are inexplicable and irreducible—will hesitate before surrendering to the magician, and ask instead: was it really so?

Critics of Spengler's approach have placed special emphasis on his views of classical culture. He called this culture Apollonian, and this time he did acknowledge that the word was Nietzsche's and not his own. Yet Nietzsche himself contrasted Apollonian with Dionysian, whereas Spengler denies the Dionysian aspect in classical culture as alien and un-Greek. For him, the classical spirit had to be purely Apollonian, to be restricted to the body, the present, the immediately given. The Greek had to be burdened with a revulsion from the infinite, from flux, from the riddle of

[1] *Josef Strzygowski, Austrian art historian and author of a work on the origins of Christian church architecture. A.J.P.*

175

personality; he must be a creature of the day, his very soul a stranger to twilight and darkness.

It was in order to sustain this distorted view that Spengler had to strain the historical facts on which his misconstruction is ultimately based.[1] No one, before the appearance of Spengler's book could have supposed that the nation of Herodotus, Thucydides and Polybius, the nation that dramatised the *Persians* and the *Fall of Miletus* and remembered its colonial past so well, was totally devoid of any historical sense. Only by confusing legend which, far though it be from sober truth is not without foundation in historical fact, with myth, in the sense of pure fiction, was Spengler able to claim that for the Greeks the whole past dissolved into a timeless polarity. Only through prejudice could he, in an attempt to prove that the Greeks did not think in terms of process in time, deny the existence of a Greek chronology and claim that they knew nothing of clockwork.

By means of selected examples, Spengler suggests time and again that the Greeks had no conception of infinity. But all the examples are highly suspect. Indeed, the Greeks had a very good idea of infinite space, were familiar with the method of infinitesimals, tried to see things in perspective, and did not have an exclusively static conception of historical existence. 'Not with isolated perceptions was the Greek consciousness concerned but ... precisely with relationships.'[2] Spengler's claim that the Greeks were really averse to astonomy[3] rests on his misunderstanding of a simple fact. His opinion that they did not permit individual portraiture is due to an error: it is common knowledge that —however necessary it might be to Spengler's insistence on

[1] For a critique of Spengler's conception of classical culture, see particularly H. Nachod: *Bemerkungen zu Spenglers Untergang des Abendlandes*, in *Neue Jahrbücher für das klassische Altertum* ... 23, 1920, p. 324, and the articles of E. Schwartz, L. Curtius and E. Frank in *Logos*, ix, 2.
[2] E. Frank in *Logos*, ix, 2, p. 227.
[3] See Schwartz, Logos, ix, 2, p. 175.

the merely bodily, soul-less, non-personal aspect of their art—Greek portraits did not have blind eyes. When, to stress the purely 'physical' Greek conception of personality, he cites Oedipus' complaint that Creon harmed his 'body', and that the oracle applied to his 'body', we must reply that in the Middle Ages the 'Gothic-Faustian' Germans and French used the words *lip* and *corps* in precisely the same way. But Spengler's worst lapse is his appreciation, or rather depreciation, of Greek music. Thus Frank[1] has emphasised the exceptional significance of music in Greek culture and has stood Spengler's thesis on its head to show that, in fact, the Greeks enjoyed even their plastic arts in a 'musical' way.

At least as perverse as his interpretation of ancient culture are Spengler's tactics in arguing for the existence of his Magian and Faustian ones. He starts by taking medieval history—with its marked continuity, its inner consistency, its overall submission to the authority of the Christian church—and splitting it in halves. The break is said to have occurred in about 1000 A.D. All that went before belongs partly to Magian culture. What followed—the Gothic period (in a very extended sense)—is the spring of the Fausian soul, and hence the first phase of a cycle. Such a division can be accomplished only by systematic neglect of the real history of the first thousand years of our epoch. It is easy and tempting to combine gnosis and Christianity, Byzantium, cupolas, and algebra into one great and independent panorama and to call it Magian culture. Yet such a scheme ignores the plain fact that nearly all forms of philosophy, art and government through the ages have had links with their counterparts in preceding cultures. Spengler's method becomes most absurd when he keeps calling the Pantheon the first mosque, simply because it, too, had a cupola, and was allegedly built by a Syrian. The fact that the cupola was Italian is ignored and so is the fact that the type of mosque Spengler is concerned with is based on the Hagia

[1]*Logos*, 120, p. 222f.

Sophia, and was only built after the fall of Constantinople in 1453.

If only we are selective enough, we can construe history any way we please. Astonishingly wide though Spengler's reading must have been, it is a fact that his most 'incisive' and oft-repeated proofs are based on a very small number of examples taken from a few sources. Rembrandt represents all that was done in painting in the seventeenth century. To demonstrate the 'Faustian' character of music, i.e. to show how the impulse towards function and spatial conceptions, the striving for infinity, were embodied in polyphony and counterpoint, he neglects everything that contradicts this idea: opera, song, and the many reactions against contrapuntal music.[1]

Even more objectionable than the tendentious selection from limited material, is the fact that Spengler's heroic vision is distorted by certain extremely banal prejudices and preconceptions—his Germanic delusions. Is it really necessary to waste further space on the shallowness of that outdated Germanomania of which the best German writers had long since rid themselves? That the spirit of the German races was the fertilising element in all medieval and modern culture, that everything great in it was rooted in the depths and nobility of the German race—who outside Germany can still believe in this delusion of Breysig and Woltmann, this idolatry from the days of Romanticism? And yet this delusion is the very basis of Spengler's conception of the Faustian soul. In order to call the West Faustian, that is, in order to make German romanticism the quintessence of Western culture, he has to repeat all the old and empty boasts of his discredited predecessors. The poison may be hidden beneath his scintillating style, but it is there nonetheless. 'The love of the infinite slumbered deep in the northern landscape, long before the first Christian stepped upon it; and when the Faustian soul awakened, it trans-

[1] G. Becking in *Logos*, x, 2, pp. 292ff.

formed old Germanic paganism *and* Oriental Christianity alike in the sense of its prime symbol, precisely at a time when the physiognomically distinct units of the German, French, English and Italian nations emerged from the vague popular structures of the Goths, Franks, Longobards, and Saxons.'[1] In other words, the essence of all these people was Germanic, an extravagant claim that Spengler frequently reiterates. The Faustian soul was the first to conceive of time; 'among Western people it was the Germans who invented mechanical clocks', (the footnote tells us that the actual inventor was Abbot Gerbert of Aurillac (Pope Sylvester II), who happened to be—a Frenchman!²)[2]. Moreover it was 'the German spirit, the Faustian North' which created the Romanesque style out of the 'Magian' basilica, and turned that style itself into a precursor of the 'Gothic'.[3] This claim conveniently overlooks the Oriental element in the origins of the Romantic style. 'The Third Reich'—i.e. the longing for a perfect society—'is the German ideal . . .'[4] That is precisely why Joachim of Floris, though a Calabrian, was needs filled with the German spirit!

The Gothic style proper arose—according to Spengler— in Burgundy or in the Netherlands. Faustian music too is said to have originated in the Low Countries. This was the old idea of Ambros and Kiesewetter, based on an overestimate of the Dutch element in the musical history of the late Middle Ages, and long since corrected by Riemann and many others in favour of France, Italy and England. Seeing that Spengler also follows the old Van Eyck legend in attributing the rise of oil-painting to the Netherlands, our country, as it were, must have mothered a cultural triplet. 'This common geographical origin of the three great Faustian form-worlds is of the highest significance. Here we touch upon the last secret of all humanity: the bonds of the soul with its motherland from which all myths have it spring and to which they have it return.'[5]

[1] p. 256.   [2] p. 18.   [3] pp. 309, 310.   [4] pp. 508, 509.   [5] p. 316.

This deep bond also extends to the origins of modern, i.e. Faustian, mathematics. At the same time that the 'great Netherlander, Henry of Zeeland (of whom, alas, nothing is known—J.K.) raised the style of the fugue into a great art', Nicolas Oresme (1323–1382) introduced co-ordinates (thus, by the way, drawing on Greek learning, much as did Cusanus whom Spengler calls the pioneer of the differential calculus 'that contrapuntal method of numbers'). And if we should enquire whether Oresme, Bishop of Lisieux, was, in fact a good German, we may be gratified to learn that Paris, in about 1400, was 'part of the Flemish-Burgundian land' and that 'even as late as the fifteenth century, Flemish was as much spoken there as French (sic)'.[1] And this is the stuff of which Spengler spins his dreams!

Still, in view of the profound thoughts with which the *Decline of the West* is undoubtedly studded, one might be inclined to overlook many of his excesses, had not Spengler himself revealed the woolliness of his method in another work. His *Preussentum und Sozialismus* (The Prussian Spirit and Socialism, Munich, 1921)—he tells us—was based on 'notes that were meant for the *Decline of the West* and quite particularly for Volume II, and which were among the seeds from which my entire philosophy had developed'. This is an astonishing confession. For that little book already puts forward what is mentioned in the *Decline*[2] as the starting point of Spengler's entire work, namely a political doctrine based on an historico-ethnographic antithesis. Here the contrast is between the English and the Prussian characters and the whole thing reads very much like blatant Prussian imperialism. The method is precisely the same as that of the *Decline*—the author poses an antithesis, and uses everything he can lay his hands on to make it as striking as possible. But because it is stripped of everything that appears profound and wise in the *magnum opus*, his thinking in the lesser work is revealed as the shallow structure it really is.

[1] p. 324.   [2] p. 65.

The two images—they are no more than that—which are contrasted here in order to 'explain' the English and Prussian character, are the Viking and the German knight. The fact that the Viking was, strictly speaking, a Scandinavian does not perturb Spengler: the Englishman is the Viking in his 'fateful' metamorphosis from the earlier stages of the Faustian soul into decadent 'civilisation'. The English are 'pirates that have settled down'. Everything that is English springs from 'Viking instincts'. They see the world as 'prey' and the good life as 'success'. The Prussian, on the other hand, prefigured as he is by the knight (in its romantic connotation, of course) sees the world as 'state' and life as a 'vocation.' His task is to serve, organise and rule.

Nor does this exhaust the antithesis. Everything that is 'civilisation' rather than 'culture', including everything German that is opposed to the Prussian essence, is called English. Thus we get such ridiculous phrases as' Napoleon, when using French blood to spread the English idea across the Continent . . .' or: 'In Napoleon's victories and defeats was hidden the victory of England, a victory of civilisation over culture . . .' And those Germans who rose up against the Kaiser in November 1918 are 'the invisible English Army, which Napoleon left on German soil after Jena'.[1]

Is it surprising that this German schoolmaster refers to France much like *Simplizissimus*, the German satirical review, that he calls America a 'country without a future', or the Italians a people who have long since become 'an insignificant nation'?[2] Or that his English thesis has greatly caught on among his compatriots, even serving one, Paul Lensch, as a Marxist plank?[3]

The need to see in the whole course of Western culture

---

[1] *Preussentum und Sozialismus*, Munich, 1921, pp. 6, 7. *Unterg. d. Abendl.*, pp. 207, 205.
[2] *Preussentum und Sozialismus*, p. 32; *Unt. d. Abendl.*, p. 207, 205.
[3] *Am Ausgang der deutschen Sozialdemokratie*, 1919.

only the Faustian (read 'German') element as the essential, forces Spengler to neglect or disqualify all the manifestations we call Latin. There is no place in his view for St. Thomas Aquinas or for any of the Schoolmen. Still, with his exaggerated emphasis on the history of art, he could not ignore the Renaissance which, of course, could not be stamped as Faustian. With its serene mood, its stress on the rational and normative, its self-confident concern with noble forms, the Renaissance clearly runs counter to Spengler's conception of the soul of the West. He therefore dismisses it as an episode, a 'mere result of the all-too-conscious surface, not of the Faustian unconscious, the Western soul'. The Renaissance is no more than an act of defiance against the Faustian soul, one that delayed but could not basically affect the maturing of the Gothic into the Baroque.[1] How smoothly the Renaissance flowed out of the medieval culture, how consistently the Baroque stemmed from the Renaissance, indeed how 'Faustian' the Renaissance itself was in a number of respects—in science and philosophy for instance—to all this Spengler is completely blind. All he sees is 'a resistance of the soul against its fate, grasped at last in its full import'. 'Faust's second soul desirous of becoming separated from his first' tries desperately to alter the course of culture.[2] There are some fitting words in our language for this type of talk, but they would look somewhat startling in print. To call them to our mind is the risk anyone runs who thinks he can simply throw causality out of history.

Still, there is undoubtedly something in the Renaissance that represents a counter-current, albeit not nearly so fundamental a one as Spengler tried to make out. 'Gothic and Baroque exist, but Renaissance is merely an ideal postulate.'[3] True enough, but the *works* of the Renaissance are no ideal postulates; they are facts that cannot be overlooked. And then, like 'Renaissance' or even more so, 'Gothic' and 'Baroque' are also mere intellectual abstractions hardly

[1]pp. 345, 367ff, 320ff.   [2]p. 321.   [3]p. 369.

broad enough to embrace the full diversity of actual events.

Here we come to the fatal flaw in Spengler's approach—his disdain of facts. Where a mystic cycle of culture, whose meaning is unknown to its bearers, constitutes the content of history, real events and individual participants become irrelevant. Thus Spengler could argue that, had Columbus sailed from France and had Francis I become the master of America, the sixteenth century would have fallen under the French rather than Spanish influence, and instead of Calderón and Velasquez 'we should be talking of great Frenchmen who, in fact, . . . remained unborn'. (It strikes me that one or two were born nonetheless.) The Church would not have assumed the style given to it by the Spaniard Loyola and the Council of Trent. And so on. 'Chance chose the Spanish gesture for the late period of the West, but the *inward logic* of that age . . . remained intact.'[1] Elsewhere we read that German unity was a 'theme' that might easily have been 'worked out' in other ways as well, for instance by revolutions or diplomatic successes, though in either case what was needed were 'contrapuntally strong accents'.[2] Had Goethe died in early youth, '*Faust* and *Tasso* would never have been written but would nevertheless have "been" in a deeply mysterious sense'.[3] Even the lost tragedies of Aeschylus exist 'in a substantiality that is indestructible'.[4]

This is surely the most sterile nonsense anyone could write. And the whole book is studded with it. 'Goethe's life was one of fateful logic; Caesar's was one of mythical accident . . .' Diophantes cannot be part of ancient culture *because* he invented algebra. Spinoza was unable to grasp the Faustian force-concept because he was a Jew, and as such 'a representative of the Magian' and 'a stranger in the form-world of Faustian feeling'. The use of the boomerang by Australian aborigines betrays an 'emotional familiarity with

[1]pp. 202, 203.   [2]p. 198.   [3]p. 199.   [4]p. 299.

numerical categories which we must associate with higher geometrical analysis.'[1]

What true, living and fruitful knowledge is it possible to glean from all this straining of concepts and playing with contrasts? What is the sense of calling the German Centre Party 'Spanish', simply because of certain supposed similarities and traditional ties with sixteenth century Spanish policies, or of calling Bismarck 'the last statement in the Spanish spirit'?[2] And what is the good of distorting the concept of socialism, and calling Frederick William I of Prussia its real father and Karl Marx its stepfather? Is it anything more than that of which Eliphaz the Temanite asked: 'Should the wise man utter vain knowledge and fill his belly with the east wind?'

Let us return to the central antithesis on which Spengler's conception of the cycle of cultures is based: the opposition between the Apollonian and Faustian souls, between classical and Western culture, between the overruling concept of the bodiliness of all things and that of endless space, between the Euclidean, form-bound approach and that which seeks direction and infinity in everything—the Faustian, musical attitude. What does it all mean? It means that *we* can think of our relationship to the world as a dynamic relationship of function and space or a static relationship of number and body. Round these two attitudes we can group those cultures with which we are most familiar: the one, Western culture, known because we are involved in it, and hence known to be incomplete, vague and mysterious; the other, Classical culture, known to us through tradition and apparently completed. That is precisely what Spengler did. He made *our* Apollonian and *our* Faustian sides react by turns to well-chosen and suggestive light signals, leaving in obscurity everything that did not suit his purpose.

[1] pp. 200-1, 102, 590, 85. [2] *Preussentum und Sozialismus*, pp. 27, 64.

Does his playing with antithesis truly add to our knowledge? I doubt it very much. The favourable impression which any reader of Spengler is bound to gain, quickly disappears. On looking through my own notes, I find that I jotted down the comment 'excellent' on p. 303. It was one of the many passages in which Spengler developed the thesis that the true 'artistic feeling' of the Baroque (in Spengler's very wide sense) was musical rather than plastic or rather that the true classification of art has nothing to do with technical categories. 'Anyone who does not feel the drawings of Raphael, effected by outline, and of Titian, effected by flecks of light and shade, are dissimilar forms of art, that the art of Giotto or Mantegna—relief created by brush-strokes—and that of Vermeer or Van Goyen—music created on coloured canvas —are not alike in essence . . . will never grasp the deeper questions. In 1720, oil-painting and instrumental music were almost identical in inner form and feeling. Watteau belongs to Couperin and P. E. Bach, not to Raphael.' To call Watteau's art musical rather than pictorial—is not that a tempting idea? But when I re-read it all today, I find that I allowed myself to be blinded. It may be a suggestive metaphor to call oil-painting contrapuntal, or to contrast Van Dyck's *andante con moto* with Frans Hals's *allegro feroce*,[1] but that metaphor is no proper substitute for an historical criterion. And when Spengler keeps insisting more and more loudly that both the music of Bach and the art of Rembrandt have their real essence in the expression of the Faustian space-symbol, then I feel that this association of artistic appreciation with space is a dangerous denigration. My love of Rembrandt and Bach rebels against it—that love which delights in even their smallest drawing or simplest suite.

It hardly needs saying that Spengler was, at heart, a

[1] pp. 304, 343, 308 which calls iconoclasm a victory of music over painting! pp. 319, 311, 131.

Romantic, even though he wished to be the precise opposite. He, the proclaimer of approaching doom and of the
lesson that in this, the autumn of our Western culture, nothing remains but the deployment of our arid intellectual
powers, he, too, must needs march with the doomed battal-
ions. The only fitting theme for modern philosophy is the
'conception of the will to power in a civilised and intellectual form'[1]. Ours is a century lacking in great art or metaphysical fruitfulness, a time of decline. We may deplore it,
but we have not chosen our age.[2] All we can do is to co-
operate with the new spirit. 'Anyone who walks about with
the idealism of a provincial, hankering after the style of
by-gone ages, must renounce the desire to understand, experience or to make history.' And if the new generation
should be moved by his book to turn to technics instead of
lyrics, to the sea instead of painting, to politics instead of
epistemology—'they do precisely what I should want them
to do'.[3]

And yet his poor heart kept crying out for the beauty of
past ages, for the wisdom of the ancient statesman-philoso-
phers, for the healthy life based on the soil, for the noble
style of art at its highest. He is quite relentless in his judgment of modern art. It is a series of impotent lies, all varia-
tions on the same theme, and all mistaking mere versatility
for greatness. 'The supra-personal love of form, the appreciation of the religious significance of absolute form, is long
dead.' And the formless is characteristic of the 'waning
power of artistic expression'. Even the art of Wagner and
Manet is surrender to the barbarism of the great cities, the
beginning of dissolution as expressed in the sensuous, in a
mixture of brutality and refinement'.[4] And poetical Spengler, who loathes all these developments, leads us with great
emotion to those periods in which his heart lies: the Baroque above all, but the Romantic as well. He titillates our
artistic sense with his delightful game of transcending the

[1] p. 522.   [2] p. 62.   [3] pp. 54, 57.   [4] pp. 394-9, 49, 57, 472.

boundaries between painting, music and mathematics. He brings out the elegic qualities of late seventeenth-century art, or evokes the golden lustre of mosaics.[1] He says profound and fitting things on the subjects of 'world-fear' and 'world-longing' and how these two gave rise to the various forms of art and the various concepts of science.[2] To my mind, these moving, and always romantic, reflections on the functional aspect of art and on the deepest connections between philosophy and science, constitute the best part of Spengler's work.

If only he was not so prolix! If only he showed some reserve! If only he knew what it meant to be simple, modest, and above all reverent! If only he did not superimpose his cultural parallelism on the true course of history! How odd of one who grasps so well the unselective grasping of all things, for which he admired Goethe! Spengler, who stresses the importance of seeing things physiognomically, of seizing them in their 'irreducible' form, failed to realise that history too must examine historical facts without preconceived ideas. To him, 'no fragment of history can be fully elucidated until the secret of world history in general, or more precisely the history of higher humanity, has been revealed as an organic unit of regular structure'.[3] And this is his ultimate error, that is where he starts heaping Pelion upon Ossa.

No, it is not the relative importance of historical phenomena we must seek,[4] but their own significance, and that is why facts are dear to the historian, each one being what Henry James has called 'a quantity of significant truth, a handful of the fine substance of history'. Spengler, on the other hand, despises facts, and instead serves us with his mysteriously living cultures. He is not concerned with men as they live in history. For what he utterly lacks—and that is probably the basis of what I have just called his funda-

[1] pp. 341, 349, 383ff. [2] pp. 115ff, 263. [3] p. 66, cf. p. 223. [4] p. 63.

mental error—is love. 'We have to face the hard and cold facts of a *late* life . . .'[1] And throughout his book there is not a note of kindness, nothing of piety or devotion, nothing of the still heart, nothing of hope.

That is why Spengler with his 'cultures' reminds me so much of the giant in the *Edda*, Hrungnir by name, who had a stony head and a stony heart, and who went to battle against Thor in the company of a clay giant. Spengler is not the only one to wage war in the company of such clay figures. Yet they will not do in the long run—Hrungnir's collapsed before it had time to achieve fame.

If, after our first stupefaction with Spengler's seductive style (in this respect strongly reminiscent of Wagner's) has passed, we ask ourselves precisely *how* his system of opposites helps us to understand history better, then I am afraid the answer must be: in no way at all. Everyone truly interested in history would do well to banish Spengler's terms from his vocabulary, lest his joy in the past be marred by 'Magian', 'Faustian' and 'Apollonian' phantoms. Does that mean he will have wasted his time in reading Spengler? Certainly not, for the *Decline* remains a clarion call against shallow faith in progress. The denial that everything we experience is necessarily progressive has never been expressed more forcefully, and much of Spengler's thought is orderly and clearly-formulated and, as such, most refreshing in an age of shallow aphorisms.

There is something extremely tragic in Spengler's writing, and the tragedy may be called that of the German spirit. Here is a thinker, profound, clear, and wide-ranging as few others—a genius in the fullest sense of the word. But as Madame de Staël has put it, whereas thought soothes most people, it drives the Germans to distraction. And in fact, Spengler's own ideas went to his head, and his Dionysian— rather than Faustian—delusions become such that we have to take leave of him—with great admiration and regret but

[1] p. 63.

with little attachment or sympathy. We gain a sense of deliverance when we realise that all this is 'German business' and hence none of our own, a feeling that would be pharisaical were it not simple gratitude for our provincial ignorance. Lord deliver us from the Faustian, and give us simplicity and clarity instead.

Spengler failed because he endeavoured to join together two worlds of thought that can have no link except the rainbow. His spirit was most deeply rooted in the mystical, a sphere in which all events are *Schicksal*, fate, in which what has been continues to be, and in which number and measure do not exist. But in that sphere, historical facts lack a name. And it was in order to explain history in mystical terms that Spengler had to create an absurd historical logic—a world in which every event was simply the expression of inherent tendencies or prime symbols, and one that could never serve as a stepping-stone towards the future, a world, therefore, that kept breaking off. I, for one, am certain that I would not care to live in it.

Spengler's work has had a curative effect upon me—its absolute certainty that our civilisation is doomed has convinced me that we still have grounds for hope and that there is much we do not know. And whatever his faults, this at least no one would wish to deny—he was one who wrestled with the angel.

Those who turn from Spengler's *Decline of the West* to H. G. Wells's *Outline of History* will probably feel that they have exchanged portentous profundities for mere banality. The gulf between the authors of these two books, men who both offer to explain world history, no less, is so great that one can scarcely credit that they were contemporaries. What a falling off was there, we say, from the high-flown lucubrations of Spengler's *Götterdammerung* to the safely grazing sheep of Wells's plain man's progress. But where Spengler alienates us by incessant harping on his own genius and by suspicious silence about his sources, Wells, who has his limitations too, attracts us with his modesty and candour. He makes it quite clear that all his information is second-hand, and he carefully cites his sources—popular handbook, *Encyclopaedia Britannica*, or whatever. And how likeable is that humility which extends such liberal footnote hospitality to all and sundry, so much so that the notes not seldom contradict the text.[1] To dismiss Wells on that score as a mere amateur would be sheer pedantry. No one can help admiring the astounding versatility of a man, who, besides writing a host of literary works, had mind enough to gather and assimilate such wealth of historical material. Naturally, he makes mistakes—Dutch history, for instance, is not his strongest point[2]—but they are very few and in no way mar the tonic effect of the whole work.

The *Outline of History* must be called unsuccessful for a reason that goes deeper than the amateur status of its author. With all his gifts of clearsightedness and penetration, Wells does not really understand what history is about. When the author of *Joan and Peter* and *The Undying Fire* decided to write history, whose pedagogical importance he had stressed so convincingly in these two books, his decision was rash in the extreme.

Wells's idea of historical knowledge is guileless. He completely fails to comprehend the most peculiar mode of thinking, always changing, forever oscillating, that is the historian's. He believes that, if we only worked at it, the past must soon render up its secrets, that it is simply a collection of hard facts, and can be 'truly and clearly' understood by one and all. He detests specialists. 'All that can be thought and known is (to be) kept plainly, honestly and easily available to the ordinary men and women who are

[1]For instance on pp. 107, 315, 86, 424.
[2]See, for instance, pp. 429, 430, 479, 486.

the substance of mankind.'[1] Like so many others, he believes
that history, if not yet an exact science, is well on the way to
becoming one.[2] And, like so many others, he is caught in
the delusion that the essence of history is to grasp the past in
the form of laws—'as the outlook broadens, the clustering
multitude of details dissolves into general laws'.[3] It is as if
someone believed that a landscape is best understood by
shunning lime blossom and lark-song and surveying roads
and rivers from the air.

Wells believes that all the past was history. As motto for
his work, he chose a quotation from Friedrich Ratzel:
'A philosophy of history of the human race, worthy of its
name, must begin with the heavens and descend to the
earth, must be charted with the conviction that all existence
is one—a single conception sustained from beginning to
end upon one identical law'. But Ratzel, though a great
geographer, was a dangerous guide through the rapids of
history. All too often he uttered profound generalisations that
mean very little and merely impede the true understanding
of history. Faithful to Ratzel's unitarianism, Wells begins
with an account of the origin of our planetary system, followed by an outline of the origins of animal life, and so to
man; then on through the prehistoric ages of Palaeolithic
and Neolithic man to what he, too, calls the dawn of history.
Many have welcomed this retrospection into the steamy atmosphere of the oldest geological periods where life germin-
ates in the primeval mud. Happy thought! For this does
bring home to us (no doubt that was Wells's intention) how
brief a moment of geological time is spanned by the empires and civilisations to which historians usually confine
their attention. But this merging of history with geology and
palaeontology strikes me as a fundamental error. For it
overlooks the fact that all this knowledge, great and exciting
though it may be, cannot be grasped with our historical
'sense'. The concepts of geological and biological develop-

[1] p. 201. [2] p. 333[1], cf. p. 109. [3] p. v.

ment involved, though they too are events in time, have little or nothing to do with understanding history, which is concerned with human relationships and human thoughts. The historian tries to re-experience what was once experienced by men like ourselves, and stops short of saurians. Geological events cannot be turned into history simply by including them in our historic framework. The true study of history involves our imagination and conjures up conceptions, pictures, visions. Prehistory, on the other hand, calls for the scientific study of morphology, of the development and structure of forms and organs. Quasi-historical description of such phenomena, as Wells's readers will soon realise, is both tedious and barren. Attempts to enliven the story with word-pictures of the primeval scenery or the peculiar lineaments of Neanderthal man do not help—the whole remains a hopeless hybrid.

But it is not simply his predominantly biological orientation that prevents Wells from writing history. There is a further obstacle—his humour. Anyone at all familiar with his writings, even *The Food of the Gods* and such tales of imagination as are less demanding than the major novels, will realise how omnipresent is Wells's sparkling and refreshing sense of fun. Now the history of even the emptiest of human follies is never funny. A historian who cannot contro his sense of humour is in the wrong job. There are teachers of history who burlesque their subject. It is all too easy to gain a grateful audience and the reputation of a brilliant lecturer by doing so. But it kills all historical understanding. For the humorous treatment of history makes us see people of bygone days as they did not see themselves, it muddies the waters.

If this is true, Wells sins continuously, for he is nothing if not entertaining. Anyone who knows from experience how much self-control it takes not to turn the account of some historical situation into a comedy, will gain re-assurance from the failure of Wells's light-hearted approach. His farcical Charlemagne, for instance, is like a character in comic opera. After telling us that the emperor was responsible for introducing the words *filioque* into the Nicene Creed, an addition that finally split the Latin and Greek churches, Wells adds: 'But it is more than doubtful if he had any such separation in mind. He wanted to add a word or so to the creed, just as the Emperor William II wanted to write operas and paint pictures'.[1] And how ludicrously he sets historical judgment askew when he says of the Church in the late Middle Ages: 'It was hunting everywhere for heretics as timid old ladies are said to look under beds and in cupboards for burglars before retiring for the night'.[2] Sometimes, when he gives free rein to his ironical sense, we get the feeling that he could not stop if he wanted to, for instance in his treatment of Cato, Anthony and Cleopatra, or Mohammed. Only where strong emotion, such as his aversion to Napoleon, makes him feel that this is really no laughing matter, does his approach become truly effective. 'One reads in vain through the monstrous accumulations of Napoleonic literature for a single record of self-forgetfulness. Laughter is one great difference between man and the lower animals, one method of our brotherhood, and there is no evidence that Napoleon ever laughed. Nor can we imagine another of the most beautiful of human expressions upon the face of this saturnine egotist, that expression of disinterested interest that one sees in the face of an artist or artisan "lost", as we say, in his work. Out of his portraits he looks at us with a thin scorn upon his lips, the scorn of the criminal who believes that he can certainly cheat such fools as we are, and withal with a certain uneasiness in his eyes. That uneasiness haunts all his portraits. Are we really convinced he is quite right? Are his laurels straight?'[3]

Wells keeps reminding the reader that he wields the fountain pen or typewriter not the quill. And, in fact, an anachronistic strain runs through the entire work. Not a single

[1] p. 347.   [2] p. 362.   [3] p. 499.

person or event Wells describes gives us the 'there but for the grace of God . . .' sensation that history must and can elicit. Wells leads us into no Egyptian temple or medieval cathedral. I do not mean that it behoved him to describe these buildings, but that he ought to have written about Egypt and the Middle Ages so that we ourselves could feel what it was like to move among tall pillars and massive columns.

Here is a failing almost incomprehensible in the creative writer Wells undubitably was—his strange insensibility to art. Spengler may have exaggerated when he derived the deepest character of his cultures too exclusively from art, but Wells falls into the opposite error: 'Artistic productions, unlike philosophical thought and scientific discovery, are the ornaments and expressions rather than the creative substance of history'[1]. Wherever art flourished, it did so only because the conditions were ripe, because there was peace and prosperity. 'Unless we are to suppose that spontaneous outbreaks of super-men occurred in the past, it is reasonable to conclude that the Athens of Pericles, the Florence of the Medici, Elizabethan England . . . the Tang and Ming periods in art, are but samples of what a whole world of sustained security would yield continuously and cumulatively.'[2] From this environmental standpoint the pyramids can be dismissed as 'unmeaning sepulchral piles', Romanesque architecture praised as 'that pleasant Byzantine style that still . . . delights the tourist in the Rhineland', and Gothic as a 'lovely efflorescence'.

Closely connected with this disparagement of the significance of art is Wells's historical conception of religion. I say 'historical conception' advisedly. Readers of *First and Last Things*, *God the Invisible King*, and *The Undying Fire*, will know that Wells was a serious and original religious thinker, one who was deeply concerned with *how* modern life could be lived religiously. The more must they regret that the qualities of depth and piety which he showed there deserted

[1]p. 406.   [2]p. 605.

him when it came to history. Here, if anywhere, lies the proof that Wells did ill to turn historian.

According to him, all religions first burgeon with neighbourly love, unselfishness, peace and good works, only to wither into dogmatism, discipline, ritual and delusion. The culprit is, of course, the priest with all his hocus-pocus. In other words, Wells had no feeling, let alone respect, for the sacramental, the symbolic or ritual, for devotion, sanctity, mysticism, or ecstasy—in fact, for nine-tenths of what distinguishes religion from utilitarian ethics. It is hard indeed to draw a picture of religious life on these lines.

For the origins of religious conceptions, Wells went to Freud and Jung. 'Fear of the Old Man' as the motif of the oldest notions of supernatural awe lends itself very well to the levity with which, as we have pointed out, Wells continually spoilt his work.[1] Once men became aware of their personal need for protection, direction, absolution, and strength beyond their own power, the priest appeared. 'Confusedly, in response to that demand, bold men, wise men, shrewd and cunning men were arising to become magicians, priests, chiefs and kings.'[2] True, Wells hastens to add that these men were not to be thought of as charlatans, but his view has a certain Voltairian tint all the same—despite himself, I would say. The temple, the priest and the sacrifice are the clear signs that a religion has declined from its original simplicity and purity into a system of superstitious and perplexing practices. Every dogma smacks of decay.

The essence of Christianity, Wells thinks, lies exclusively in the moral and social revolution that he believes Jesus advocated. He is under the illusion that it is possible for him to keep 'closely to the facts' with respect to the life and message of Jesus.[3] These facts are, according to Wells, that the Kingdom of God proclaimed by Jesus simply meant unselfishness and the renunciation of private wealth. Repeat-

[1] p. 62.   [2] p. 66.   [3] pp. 283-90, 484.

edly he uses such expressions as 'that great revolutionist Jesus of Nazareth', 'the revolution collapsed utterly', and 'this abandoned leader'—all of them tinged with reprehensible anachronisms that can only confuse the reader. Paul was one of the first to spoil the Master's teaching, for it was because of him that 'the kingdom of God that Jesus of Nazareth preached was overlaid, as we have explained, almost from the beginning by the doctrines and ceremonial traditions of an earlier age, and of an intellectually inferior type. Christianity almost from its commencement ceased to be purely prophetic and creative. It entangled itself with archaic traditions of human sacrifice, with Mithraic blood-cleansing, with priestcraft as ancient as human society, and with elaborate doctrines about the structure of the divinity.'[1]

That all these things, no matter what we may think of them, once constituted the content of the greatest religions, and that historians must treat them as such—all this escapes Wells, who recognises as essential and valuable only what points in the direction he considers salutary for *our* age.

This completely unhistorical viewpoint appears with equal clarity in his treatment of Buddhism. 'The fundamental teaching of Gautama . . . is clear and simple and in the closest harmony with modern ideas.'[2] That, too, is nothing new. Even so great an expert as Rhys Davids felt free to chip away three-quarters of the Buddhist doctrine, the better to reveal the Buddha as an enlightened modern and Protestant reformer. For Wells, the Buddha was 'a good-looking, capable young man of fortune', who believed in the maxim *mens sana in corpore sano*, who drew up 'a plan of an emancipated life' into which everything pleasing Wells fitted wonderfully well. Primitive Buddhism aimed not at the destruction of desire, but at the change of desire; indeed 'devotion to science and art, or to the betterment of things,

[1] p. 361, cf. p. 390.   [2] p. 207f.

manifestly falls into harmony with the Buddhistic Right Aspirations'. There is no need to dwell at length on the doctrine of Karma 'because it belongs to a world of thought that is passing away' (*sic!*). And if Buddhism too became overgrown with weeds to turn into 'a wilderness of preposterous rubbish' then it was entirely the fault of its misguided disciples.

Or was it rather the fault of Wells's *bête noire* among the nations—the Egyptians? We begin to understand why he has so little sympathy for Egyptian art, when we learn that 'both Buddhism and Christianity wear garlands of ritual and formula that seem to be derived through Hellenistic channels from that land of temples and priestcraft, Egypt, and from the mentality of the brown Hamitic peoples.'[1] The doctrine of the Virgin, shorn and fasting priests, self-castigation and sacrifices—all these were 'things in the way of thought of the dark-white Mediterranean race; they were congenial to that type'.[2] Moreover, the 'dark-white race' had a 'superstitious temperament' and could do little to further culture, albeit it produced the greatest art known to mankind.

The back-dating of ideas of international co-operation and social harmony based on the possession of an enlightened intellect and altruistic ethics, which runs through Wells's entire work, becomes particularly ludicrous when it is applied to the Middle Ages. 'Sooner or later, mankind must come to one universal peace,'[3] Wells tells us, and that is why he sympathises in principle with the papacy's claim to world domination. He acclaims the first crusade as a practical result of international organisation, as the work of a 'new amphictyony of Christendom'. 'Here is a universal response of indignation at the story of a remote wrong, a swift understanding of a common cause for rich and poor alike.'[4] Here we feel the anachronism in his approach with particular force: in his mind's eye he saw not the barbarous

[1] p. 216, cf. p. 202. [2] p. 390. [3] p. 361. [4] p. 354.

attitudes of the eleventh century, but the benign outlook of a modern League of Nations.

Anyone who keeps reading modern ideas into the history of past ages, must find the story of mankind an even more absurd failure than those who do not. Time and again, the great principle of harmonious co-operation in the development of culture founders on the dark rocks of tradition and ignorance. Thus the actual course of the crusades could not but incite Wells's deepest revulsion. Why ever did the medieval Church have to be lumbered with all those concepts and practices that Wells would have liked it to forget? Why was it not more practical? Because of a mere trifle, we are told, for many of the difficulties could have been avoided by a better system of electing cardinals and by retiring them at the age of fifty. 'We have seen the Roman Republic wrecked, and here we see the church failing in its world mission very largely through ineffective electoral methods.'[1]

The reason why the church failed to take root in the great new Mongol Empire during the thirteenth century was that 'Christianity was in a phase of moral and intellectual insolvency, without any collective faith, energy or honour'.[2] And this in days when the Gothic style still flourished, in which St. Thomas Aquinas lived and worked, and Dante was born!

In conformity with Wells's views of the true nature of the Church and of Christianity, he holds the obsolete view, which historians have to contend with all too often, that all those who, in the Middle Ages, fought against the Church, were in fact enlightened precursors of the Reformation. His sympathies are with the Albigenses and Hussites no less than with Frederick II, all of whom were apparently so many modern democrats and men of independent thought. That the Albigenses drew the extreme conclusions from all those leanings towards renunciation and asceticism that Wells

[1] p. 366.   [2] p. 379.

finds so retrograde, seems to have bothered him as little as the fact that 'enlightened' Frederick was a tyrant who produced a model police state.

If we wished to be unkind, we might point out that the reason why Wells, despite all his efforts, arrived at a view that historians have long ago discarded, is that his book is based on the sort of liberal daydreams that are so often the *credo* of dilettantes. Alas, it is the sad task of scholars to point out that things are not really quite what the last but one historian would have had them be. This eternal fluctuation in historical views is in the very nature of historical knowledge, and we must not greatly blame the author of a popular synthesis if he lightly repeats outmoded opinions. Thus Wells sees fourteenth-century English economic history— the rebellion by Wat Tyler and the events leading up to and following it—through the eyes of Thorold Rogers; he holds views on Magna Carta that McKechnie destroyed much earlier, and puts forward ideas on American history that modern American historians have long since discarded.

What is much more serious is the fact that the basic concepts with which Wells tries to explain world history are false. Next to his inadequate conception of the value of ritual and culture, we must take him to task for his superficial race theories. Now racialism is one of the plagues of modern historical thought. It is astonishing with what blithe assurance and utter disregard for facts the most diverse historical phenomena are attributed to hypothetical racial characteristics. We have already seen how Wells traced the corruption of religion to the superstitious love of ritual and formulae of the Mediterranean race. Hand in hand with this aversion went a great predilection for the Nordic and Mongolian races.

In them he saw the culmination of a habit that he considers of the utmost importance in the growth of culture, namely the nomadic habit. The antithesis between nomadic and settled agricultural people, largely determines Wells's

ideas on the development of culture. 'From the very beginning of history,' he tells us, 'the nomad and the settled
people have been in reaction. We have told of the Semitic
and Elamite raids upon Sumeria; we have seen the Western
empire smashed by the nomads of the great plains, and
Persia conquered and Byzantium shaken by the nomads of
Arabia. Whenever civilisation seems to be choking amidst
its weeds of wealth and debt and servitude, when its faith
seems rotting into cynicism and its powers of further growth
are hopelessly entangled in effete formulae, the nomad
drives in like a plough to break up the festering stagnation
and release the world to new beginnings. The Mongol aggression, which began in the thirteenth century, was the
greatest, and so far it has been the last, of all these destructive reploughings of human association.'[1] Nomads and
settled people represent the two ideas of society that Wells
opposes as paramount principles, i.e. 'the idea of a *community of faith and obedience*, such as the earliest civilisations
undoubtedly were, and the idea of a *community of will*, such
as were the primitive political groupings of the Nordic and
Hunnish peoples.' 'For thousands of years,' he goes on to
say, 'the settled civilised peoples, who were originally in
most cases, dark-white Caucasians, or Dravidian, or Southern Mongolian peoples, seem to have developed their ideas
and habits along the line of worship and personal subjec-
tion, and the nomadic peoples theirs along the line of self-
reliance and self-assertion'. Civilisation is revitalised time
and again thanks to a 'refreshment by nomadic conquest'.
The spirit of the nomad, be he Germanic, Semitic or Mongolian, is 'more *willing* and more *erect* than that of the
settled folk'. Everything in history that is dynamic, renewing, creative and efficient is due to the nomadic way of life.
The sailor is a 'nomad turned go-between'. The longing to
discover and rule the world, revolutionary impulses—all
are but expressions of the 'lurking nomadism in our blood'.[2]

[1] p. 369.   [2] pp. 387, 388.

At the conclusion of his work, Wells sums up as follows: 'In this *Outline* we have thought to show two great systems of development interacting in the story of human society. We have seen . . . in the warmer alluvial parts of the world, the great primordial civilisations, fecund systems of subjugation and obedience, vast multiplications of industrious and subservient men. We have shown the necessary relationship of these early civilisations to the early temples and to king-gods and god-kings. At the same time we have traced the development . . . of the wanderer peoples, who became the nomadic peoples, in those great groups, the Aryans and the Hun-Mongol peoples . . . and the Semites of the Arabian desert. Our history has told of a repeated overrunning and refreshment of the originally brunet civilisations by these hardier, bolder, free-spirited peoples of the steppes and desert. We have pointed out how these constantly recurring nomadic injections have steadily altered the primordial civilisations both in blood and in spirit; and how the world religions of today, and what we now call democracy, the boldness of modern scientific enquiry and a universal restlessness, are due to the "nomadisation" of civilisation. The old civilisations created tradition, and lived by tradition. Today the power of tradition is destroyed. The body of our state is civilisation still, but its spirit is the spirit of the nomadic world. It is the spirit of the great plains and the high seas.'[1]

I have quoted at such length, for it is Wells's basic thought that is here expressed. His thesis is simple and attractive, it appeals to *modern* sentiments that we hold dear: our love of fresh air, of the sea and the wide plains, our courage and will-power. Is it equally attractive as an *historical* hypothesis? I do not think so. In the first place, Wells treats the term 'nomadic' in the vague and quite arbitrary sense by which any society that is predominantly concerned with stock-breeding can be called nomadic. Or rather, he as-

[1]p. 606.

sumes that if a people, in the course of its history, has moved on one or more occasions, he may call it nomadic, which simply will not do. To lead a nomadic existence, a people has to keep moving, sometimes every two weeks or so, within the boundaries of a very large territory, so that it often returns to one and the same place within a single year. Nomadism as such bears no relation to the large-scale migrations of people.

Now, whatever may apply to the Mongols of Northern Asia, as far as the Germanic people are concerned, most historians are now agreed that, apart from their large-scale migrations, they have been settled peoples since pre-historic times. Thus Wells would have had to attribute the culture-renewing influence to migration, invasion and conquest rather than to what does not follow at all from the fact of migration: the supposedly nomadic character of the invader. However, even were it granted that all migratory and conquering peoples had been nomadic, could we really prove the refreshing, revitalising and renewing effects of the conquests and invasions Wells had in mind? He speaks of 'the Western empire smashed by the nomads of the great plain' when, in actual fact, the Roman Empire as such was not shattered at all. True, its political unity was broken, but its several political organs continued their course of development or decay. The culture of the Empire became impoverished or dislocated, but more by violent internal convulsions than by the coming of Germanic tribes. Germanic penetration of the Empire, first as foreign armies and later as conquerors and rulers, was the symptom and consequence rather than the cause of Rome's decline and fall. After centuries of stagnation, the new, medieval civilisation gradually emerged. How much elements of ancient Roman culture contributed to it may be debatable, but to present the whole course of European history from the fourth to the eighth century as a revitalisation of culture by the positive forces of nomadic life is merely to misrepresent the facts.

The Huns, in any case, those true nomads who played some part in the fall of the Roman Empire, disappeared as quickly as they came, and may have had a destructive, but certainly not a constructive, effect on the development of Western culture.

This is true *a fortiori* of the Mongolian invasions and conquests since the thirteenth century. No one will begrudge Wells's sympathy for the Mongols under Genghis Khan. Without doubt, panic has painted them too black for far too long. His appreciation of the excellent strategy with which the invasion of Hungary and Poland in 1241 was successfully executed is perhaps not misplaced.[1] Yet where must we seek their positive influence on Western culture? 'For a time,' Wells tells us, 'all Asia and Western Europe enjoyed an open intercourse; all the roads were temporarily open, and representatives of every nation appeared at the court of Karakorum.'[2] Even if this claim were not exaggerated, yet the temporarily open road between East and West was more a potential than an actual advantage to culture. There was no forceful and durable penetration of European culture by Mongolian elements. But Wells thinks otherwise. 'That intercourse was to bring many revolutionary ideas and many revolutionary things to Europe, including a greatly extended use of paper and printing from blocks, the almost equally revolutionary use of gunpowder in warfare, and the mariner's compass which was to release European shipping from navigation by coasting.'[3] Yet leaving aside that it would have been the sedentary Chinese rather than the Mongolian nomads who bore these great gifts, in whose heads and hands did the gifts acquire their culture-invigorating powers? Surely in those of the European. Book-printing became the power it is not through Mongolian nomadism or independence but through forces that had grown up in

[1] p. 372. Wells took his opinion from Bury's notes to Gibbon's *Decline and Fall of the Roman Empire.*
[2] p. 374.   [3] p. 377.

medieval Europe itself. If, indeed, Western culture was rejuvenated after 1250, if a new will and a new sense of freedom (nomadic virtues according to Wells) rose up, then the Mongolians could at most have played the rôle of birds carrying the pollen, and even that I would deny. The Mongols turned back from Europe at Liegnitz, and in their Eastern empires there is little trace of spiritual or intellectual vigour.

Wells's conception of the nomad as a superior man of great decision and ability, is at root no more than a Romantic fantasy. It is the ideal of efficiency and practical sanity, the modern American ideal, I might say, applied to history. There is a certain relationship between Wells's nomads and Spengler's Faustian souls. For Wells attributes to his nomads all the qualities Spengler called Faustian: a roaming spirit, an active striving towards the highest ideals, towards the infinite.

The nomad, according to Wells, was the first to conceive of the higher and purer elements of religious thought. For whereas the agricultural settlers encouraged the rise of all the traditions, taboos, ascetic ideals, ceremonials, temples and magic that Wells abhors, the shepherds (who are not necessarily nomads) looked up to the stars and the sun.[1]

Most people see world history in terms of a struggle between good and evil, light and darkness. Modern men, who feel they can no longer speak of heaven and hell, now call it culture and civilisation, as Spengler did, or proletariat and bourgeoisie. Wells called it nomads and settled people, and this is certainly the most innocent way of them all.

It is odd that Wells should have thought so much of the Mongol conquerors, when he has such a strong dislike of power politics—his whole book is an indictment of political aggression. The statesman concerned with strengthening his own country's power abroad is an abomination to him. Un-

[1] p. 63.

fortunately, world history is full of such abominations. Whoever writes an *Outline of History*, no matter how he hankers after spiritual truths and the growth of happiness and cooperation, must needs recognise the struggle for power as the main drama on the stage of history at all times. This does not mean that the historian must simply write about battles or concentrate exclusively on diplomatic wrangling. But without some appreciation, albeit purely factual, of the political pressures involved, it is impossible to write world history.

So what does Wells do? He belittles the historical importance of political conflicts. He represents them as imaginary struggles, as phantoms, and delusions. Speaking of Rome and Carthage, he says: 'The history of the Second and Third Punic Wars . . . is not the history of perfectly sane peoples. It is nonsense for historians to write of the "political instincts" of the Romans and Carthaginians. Quite other instincts were loose. The red eyes of the ancestral ape had come back into the world. It was a time when reasonable men were howled down or murdered; the true spirit of the age is shown in the eager examination for signs and portents of the still quivering livers of those human victims who were sacrificed in Rome during the panic before the battle of Telamon. The western world was indeed black with homicidal monomania. Two great peoples, both very necessary to the world's development, fell foul of one another, and at last Rome succeeded in murdering Carthage.'[1]

Far be it from me to suggest that there is no truth in these remarks. As a picture of a struggle for national survival it is fitting enough. True, it may be rather cheap and not very significant to describe (as Wells does) the anti-cultural tendencies in history as so many atavisms, but no doubt it is right to attribute much in the course of events to passion and irrational factors. 'Not the history of perfectly sane peoples'. But have there ever been such? Measured by this

[1] p. 233.

standard, the whole of world history becomes a pandemon-
ium, and by no means only in respect of the great political
conflicts. For the moment I shall leave it at saying that here,
too, Wells's ineradicable modernism is involved—through
the window of Rome and Carthage he is really looking at
England and Germany,[1] just as he makes the whole of
Roman history digestible to the reader by speaking, in the
manner of Ferrero, of munition profiteers and American
presidents, and by comparing Virgil to Lord Tennyson.

Wells divides history into one part that does not matter,
because it does not 'work' in the 'proper' direction, and
another, independent, part of incomparable importance.
The unimportant part is roughly the whole of political history, with the possible exception of a refreshing Mongol
invasion or the occasional enlightened monarch who is
ahead of his time, for instance, Asoka, Tai-tsung, Frederick
II, and Akbar.[2]

In this way the whole of medieval and modern political
history becomes reduced to a mess of astonishing stupidity.
This is how he sees Europe's political condition since Charlemagne revived the notion of Roman Emperorship:
'Europe drifted towards a dreary imitation and revival of
the misconceived failures of the past. For eleven centuries
from Charlemagne onwards, "Emperors" and "Caesars" of
this line and that come and go in the history of Europe like
fancies in a disordered mind. We shall have to tell of a great
process of mental growth in Europe, of enlarged horizons
and accumulating power, but it was a process that went on
independently of, and in spite of, the political forms of the
time, until at last it shattered those forms altogether. Europe
during those eleven centuries of the imitation Caesars,
which began with Charlemagne, and which closed only in
the monstrous bloodshed of 1914–1918, has been like a busy
factory owned by a somnambulist, who is sometimes quite
unimportant and sometimes disastrously in the way. Or

[1]See p. 230.   [2]pp. 212, 318, 360, 383.

rather than a somnambulist, let us say a corpse that magically simulates a kind of life. The Roman Empire staggers, sprawls, its hrust off the stage, and reappears, and—if we may carry the image one step further—it is the Church of Rome which plays the part of the magician and keeps this corpse alive.'[1]

What an absurd picture! How the wonderful intricacy of history in all its parts, which we appreciate almost by instinct, is mistaken here! Does not everyone feel that all the expressions and phenomena of a given period have a certain inner consistency, and that Comte's 'solidarité' has rightly been made the basis of all great systems of historical exegesis —by Marx, Lamprecht and Spengler? Although we cannot prove it, we know full well that Molière would have been unthinkable without Richelieu. And yet Wells sees fit to saw the very substance of history in halves, as if it were the girl in the stage illusion! Seen in this way, the story of the development of political relationships between 1500 and 1800 must necessarily remain disjoined and vague. Wells completely washes his hands of political developments, which he dismisses as purely Macchiavellian. Sometimes he reminds us of Carlyle, who was wont to avoid logical argument by the repeated use of an ironic phrase. According to Wells, the European states in the seventeenth and eighteenth centuries were 'entirely fictitious unities'. 'These vast vague phantoms, the "Powers", crept insensibly into European political thought.' 'Europe . . . has given herself up altogether to the worship of this strange state mythology.'[2] No doubt there is a great deal of truth in this view, but it must nevertheless be admitted that they were mighty gods, the gods of this mythology. To dismiss them as vague phantoms —is not that the method of Christian Science which cures diseases by denying their very existence? Such an approach might do for the purposes of political journalism, or for combining John Bull, Britannia, Germania, France and

[1] p. 344.   [2] p. 437.

Cathleen ni Houlihan into a single illustration with the heading 'Tribal Gods of the Nineteenth Century',[1] but history is really something quite different. And when the author tells us that Crécy, Agincourt and Joan of Arc are no more than the 'ornamental tapestry of history, and no part of the building',[2] then our historical sense refuses to follow.

Here Wells earns the same reproach as Spengler: he too dismisses the facts of history as so many irrelevancies, he too falls short in respect for the dignity of the past.

Though I have spoken so ill of the *Outline of History*, I am nevertheless filled with the warmest and most sincere admiration for its author, a man who set to work, not in order to add historical to his well-earned literary laurels, but simply because he felt that his views might benefit all mankind. True, the work is a failure in historical terms—all the faults I have mentioned are so serious and complex that this judgment is not too harsh—but this failure is not due to incompetence, to dryness of spirit or lack of imagination, but to Wells's preoccupation with the here and now, with the great tides of modern life in his soul. His book may be called one great burst of sympathy and hope. 'This enormous prospect of the past . . . fills a modern mind with humility and illimitable hope.'[3] Wells had complete confidence that the coming generation would do far better than the present one —his deep sympathy with youth is movingly expressed in *Joan and Peter, the Story of an Education*.

He looked upon the world much as Oswald Sydenham, the guardian of Joan and Peter, looked upon Moscow in the evening: 'Did all those heavenward crosses now sinking into the dusk amount to no more than a glittering emanation out of the fen of life, an unmeaning *ignis fatuus* born of a morass of festering desire that had already forgotten it? Or

[1] p. 529; cf. the joint portrayal of Francis I, Henry VIII, and Charles V on p. 417.
[2] p. 404.   [3] p. 520.

were these crosses indeed an appeal and promise? Out of
these millions of men would Man at last arise? . . .'—'There
is going to be sense in it,'—that is the conclusion to which
man returns time and again, despite all the desperate mys-
teriousness and contradictions. 'But what is civilized life?'
'Oh . . .' (Peter answered quickly) 'Creative activities in an
atmosphere of helpful goodwill.'[1]

And it is on this simple formula that Wells himself constructed his programme for the future. The creation of an
atmosphere of goodwill is the paramount task facing this and
the coming generation. A true and pure spirit of internationalism, fostered by a broad education—that in brief
is Wells's path to salvation. It sounds almost naïve to speak
of internationalism in times like these, when a Great War
has been followed by a rampant nationalism that shouts
down any saner values. When Wells wrote his *Outline*, the
great disillusionments of the post-war era had already begun. He knew of Wilson's miserable failure, he saw all the
obstacles in the path of peace and goodwill, but he continued in hope and confidence all the same. 'In the writings
and talk of men about international affairs today, in the
current discussions of historians and political journalists,
there is an effect of drunken men growing sober . . . By
sea and land, men want no Powers ascendant, but only law
and service. That silent unavoidable challenge is in all our
minds like dawn breaking slowly, shining between the
shutters of a disordered room.'[2]

He is optimistic because he believes in education. 'The
essential factor in the organisation of a living state, the
world is coming to realise, is the organisation of an education.'[3] It was because they lacked a proper and universal
system of education that all previous attempts to unite the
world were doomed to failure. Rome's weakness and decline
as a cultural state were due to its lack of newspapers and
popular education. None of the great religious poets rea-

[1] *Joan and Peter*, pp. 485, 680, 720.   [2] p. 438.   [3] p. 384.

lised that the penetration of the new ideas and the new morality called for an educated public. Hellenism had to remain unfruitful because no one knew anything about the origins of culture, no one reflected on economic questions or solved any social problems.[1] Here we see once again the anachronistic tendency in Wells's mind, the tendency that debars him from seeing history historically. He assesses the results of the past with the standards of today.

And the basis of that anachronism is Wells's exaggerated faith in science. With all his heart and soul he believes that knowledge is power. 'The permanently effective task before mankind which had to be done before any new enduring social and political edifice was possible, the task upon which the human intelligence is, with many interruptions and amidst much anger and turmoil, still engaged, was, and is, the task of working out and applying a Science of Property as a basis for freedom and social justice, a Science of Currency to ensure and preserve an efficient economic medium, a Science of Government and Collective Operations whereby in every community men may learn to pursue their common interests in harmony, a Science of World Politics, through which the stark waste and cruelty of warfare between races, peoples, and nations may be brought to an end and the common interests of mankind brought under a common control, and, above all, a world-wide System of Education to sustain the will and interest of men in their common human adventure.'[2] What is this but Comte's positivism in new guise?

Wells believes very firmly that just as science has transformed production, so it can transform state and religion into what they can and ought to be.[3] He has so high an opinion of the importance of the diffusion of knowledge that he calls the invention of book-printing a watershed in the evolution of life. 'At last came a time in the history of Europe, when the door, at the push of the printer, began to

[1] pp. 240, 388, 332, 196. [2] p. 505. [3] p. 520.

open more rapidly. Knowledge flared up, and as it flared it ceased to be the privilege of a favoured minority. For us now that door swings wider, and the light behind grows brighter. Misty it is still, glowing through clouds of dust and reek. The door is not half open; the light is but a light new lit. Our world today is only in the beginnings of knowledge.'[1]

No wonder, therefore, that Wells devotes more space to Roger Bacon than to the Gothic and Scholastic periods put together. The conditions for a healthy development of culture as a whole are fulfilled only where a free group of intelligent leaders can, in safety and free from care, devote itself to the welfare of all. Good government, religious development, scientific advance and artistic greatness will then follow as a matter of course.[2] All this may strike us as old-fashioned liberalism, quite irrespective of whether or not the facts of history confirm it. In fact, Wells is far from being an old-fashioned liberal. But it is as if the muse of history wishes to be revenged on the bold man who entered her court uninvited, by forcing him to express ideas that more resemble the concepts of yesterday than Wells's own passionately prophetic spirit.

Is this also true of his conviction that man, guided by knowledge and understanding, is able to refashion the world in which he lives in such a way that it answers all his purposes and needs? That belief, too, is basic to Wells's conception, and is the reason why he sees the declaration of independence by the United States in 1776 as a turning point in history. Here, for the first time, a state was deliberately created in accordance with the wishes of those who wanted to live in it. 'Here were about four million people . . . setting out to do in reality on a huge scale such a feat of construction as the Athenian philosophers twenty-two centuries before had done in imagination and theory. This situation marks a definite stage in the release of man from

[1] pp. 113, 114.   [2] pp. 170, 313, 337.

precedent and usage, and a definite step forward towards the conscious and deliberate reconstruction of his circumstances to suit his needs and aims. It was a new method of becoming practical in human affairs. The modern states of Europe have been evolved, institution by institution, slowly and planlessly out of preceding things. The United States were planned and made.'[1]

But there was in truth no American parthenogenesis. In the establishment of the United States precedent and usage, old English judicial concepts and deep-rooted commercial customs played a major rôle. And what the Union was to become in fact, few of the men who fashioned her could have foreseen. Certainly not those of 1776, who built the tenuous structure of the loose Confederation, the 'rope of sand' that so soon and so very nearly parted; nor yet the men of 1787 who drew up the Constitution, whose singular principles had to be strictly fitted to the Procrustean bed of necessity and contingency.

It was the eighteenth-century idea of Enlightenment that Wells here put forward almost in spite of himself, the idea that man by his own will and wisdom could build and rebuild societies and hence determine his social fate. Wells thinks that in this the Americans fell short only through technical inexperience and by underestimating the difficulties of their task. 'They took too many things for granted that now we know need to be made the subject of the most exacting scientific study and the most careful adjustment.'[2] If all these conditions can be met, the ideal is within man's grasp: science and education are strong enough to help him elevate the world. To Wells, the existing laws seemed to be based upon 'a confused foundation of conventions, arbitrary assumptions, and working fictions about human relationship, and to be a very impracticable and antiquated system indeed.' However, he was persuaded that 'a time will come when the whole theory and practice of law will be recast in

[1] p. 461.   [2] p. 464.

the light of a well-developed science of social psychology, in accordance with a scientific conception of human society as one developing organisation and in definite relationship to a system of moral and intellectual education.'[1]

What matters, in other words, is 'educational government'. 'The modern citizen must be informed first and then consulted. Before he can vote he must hear the evidence; before he can decide he must know. It is not by setting up polling booths but by setting up schools and making literature and knowledge and news universally accessible that the way is opened from servitude and confusion to that willingly co-operative state which is the modern ideal . . . The ideal community towards which we move is not a community of will simply; it is *a community of knowledge and will*, replacing *a community of faith and obedience*.'[2]

Thus Wells believed that *unprejudiced* and pure knowledge is attainable, and that man, once he is given the correct data, will react with informed intellect rather than mere conditioned reflexes, that he will reason without passion, vanity or self-interest. Is there anything in the modern world to corroborate his views? What of the forces he himself so hates, those Great Powers with their 'internal political systems in a state of tension or convulsive change, with a creaking economic system of the most provisional sort, and with their religions far gone in decay'?[3] He well knows the culture-destructive tendencies of our world, 'a slipping off of ancient restraints; a real de-civilisation of men's minds.'[4] And yet he believes that everything will turn out well if only enough people will devote themselves to scientific study, and if only the educational system be perfected.

It is at this point that the works which Wells was writing at about the same time as the *Outline* complement and correct his historical approach. Historical writing forces him to formulate a strict thesis and to stick to it through thick and thin. But in *Joan and Peter* and *The Undying Fire* he can afford

[1] p. 303[2].   [2] p. 389.   [3] p. 542.   [4] p. 601.

to laugh at himself. Here, Wells, the great believer in education, freely acknowledges 'the external tragedy of the teacher, that sower of unseen harvests, that reaper of thistles and the wind, that serf of custom, that subjugated rebel, that feeble, persistent antagonist of the triumphant things that rule him. And behind that immediate tragedy Oswald was now apprehending for the first time something more universally tragic, an incessantly recurring story of high hopes and a grey ending; the story of boys and girls, clean and sweet-minded, growing up into life, and of the victory of world inertia, of custom, drift, and the tarnishing years.'[1] And does Wells really believe that all this can be changed in the foreseeable future?

No one knows better than Wells the novelist how much even the best part of our lives is steeped in folly. He treats our foibles humorously, yet also with warmth and understanding. He himself is very far from the kind of 'Bunnyism' he characterised so well. [2]Not for him the wish 'to assure the world and himself that at heart everything was quite right and magnificent fun, to laugh gaily at everything, seeing through its bristling hostilities into the depth of genial absurdity beneath'. Not for his own amusement or cheap acclaim does he castigate the weaknesses of his compatriots, much as Cobden did before him.

And it is not the strict moralising of his *Outline* but the more complex sensibility of his fiction that finds the seeds of better things even in our irrational extravagance. Everything—even the best, springs from impulse—from fixed ideas and blind enthusiasm. 'We're too little. These blind impulses—I suppose there's a sort of impulse to Beauty in it. Someday perhaps these forces will do something—drive man up the scale of being. But as far as we've got—!'[3]

'All history is one dramatic story, of *man blundering his way* from the lonely ape to the world commonwealth.'[4] There's

[1]*Joan and Peter*, p. 350. [2]*Joan and Peter*, pp. 591ff.
[3]*Joan and Peter*, p. 484. [4]*Joan and Peter*, p. 713.

the rub! 'Blundering our way' is the best any of us can do. But in that case, what of the polarity of fools and sages, blundering rulers and diplomats continually ruining the world and creative thinkers and scientists forever leavening the lump? What of the contrast between the thinkers and teachers, whom Wells calls 'the real makers of history in the nineteenth century', and ministers and politicians whom he dismisses as a mere troop of 'troublesome and occasionally incendiary schoolboys—and a few mental thieves—playing about and doing transitory mischief amidst the accumulating materials upon the site of a great building whose nature they did not understand'?[1] Surely even the politicians work at a task they consider their own, and perform it with the insight, honesty and self-denial that is given to them? And if they were all bunglers, must Wells not also concede that even the purest and noblest of the thinkers and builders, once drawn into the thankless tasks of leadership, are—and perhaps always will be—equally susceptible to every wind that blows, just as fatally responsive to the trumpets of Marengo and the idols of Genghis Khan?

How can anyone trust so absolutely in the glorious and precarious sovereignty of reason! But that is not the point, Wells would reply, what matters is the inextinguishable fire that burns within us, within every one of us, in the weak and confused as well as in the thinkers, teachers and creators. Let him say it in his own words, on a page in the *Outline*[2] I consider among the best, precisely because it is written more in the spirit of *Joan and Peter* and *The Undying Fire*:

'What a wonderful and moving spectacle is this of our kind today! Would that we could compress into one head and for the use of the right hand the power of ten thousand novelists and playwrights and biographers and the quintessence of a thousand histories, to render the endless variety, the incessant multitudinous adventure, and at the

[1] p. 505, cf. pp. 525, 536, 551, 497.   [2] p. 597.

same time the increasing unity of this display. Everywhere, with a mysterious individual difference, we see youth growing to adolescence and the interplay of love, desire, curiosities, passionate impulses, rivalries. As the earth spins from darkness into the light, the millions wake again to a new day in their life of toil, anxiety, little satisfactions, little chagrins, rivalries, spites, generosities. From tropic to the bleakest north, the cocks crow before the advancing margin of dawn. The early toiler hurries to his work, the fox and the thief slink home, the tramp stretches his stiff limbs under the haystack, and springs up alert before the farmer's man discovers him, the ploughman is already in the field with his horses, the fires are lit in the cottage and the kettle sings. The hours warm as the day advances; the crowded trains converge upon the city centres, the traffic thickens in the streets, the breakfast-table of the prosperous home is spread, the professor begins his lecture, the shop assistants greet their first customers . . . Outwardly it is very like the world before the war. And yet it is profoundly different. The sense of inevitable routines that held all the world in thrall six years ago has gone. And the habitual assurance of security has gone too. The world has been roused—for a time at least—to great dangers and great desires. These minds, this innumerable multitude of minds, are open to fresh ideas of association and duty and relationship as they were never open before. The old confused and divided world is condemned; it is going on provisionally under a sentence of great and as yet incalculable change.

Every one of these hundreds of millions of human beings is in some form seeking happiness, is driven by complex and conflicting motives, is guided by habits, is swayed by base cravings, by endless suggestions, by passions and affections, by vague exalted ideas. Every one of them is capable of cruelties and fine emotions, of despairs and devotions and self-forgetful effort. All of them forget; all of them become slack with fatigue and fearful or mean or incapable under a sufficient strain. The follies of vanity entrap them all into absurdities. Not one is altogether noble nor altogether consistent; and not one is altogether vile. Every one of them can be unhappy, every one can feel disappointment and remorse. Not a single one but has at some time wept. And in every one of them is a streak of divinity. Each one for all the obsessions of self is dimly aware of something in common, of something that could make a unity out of our infinite diversity . . . Through all the world grows the realisation that there can be no securely happy individual life without a righteous general life . . . An age is closing and an age begins.'

Very simple things, very simply put. Do you find this to be mere sermonising? I for my part do not. Only, I keep hearing the voice of Spengler as a kind of counterblast from afar:

'Life has no purpose. Humanity has no purpose . . . In its very aimlessness lies the greatness of the spectacle . . . But to live this life we have been given, to fill this reality round us into which fate has cast us, with the highest possible content, to live that we ourselves may be proud . . . that is the task.' And elsewhere: 'The true Internationale is imperialism, control of the Faustian civilisation, i.e. of the *whole earth*, by a single formative principle, not by compromise and concession, but by war and destruction.' 'War . . . Power . . . reign supreme . . .' 'We need hardness.'[1]

Such then are the views on the fate of modern humanity of two men who have reflected on the meaning of world history in our time. Spengler, by far the deeper thinker of the two, having savoured all the wisdom and beauty of the past, found for himself and his generation no better sustenance in history than hardness, defiance and pride. He found no solace for the heart and, as Wells put it, 'the cessation of respect and the cultivation of "superior" ideas are the

[1]*Preussentum und Sozialismus*, pp. 80, 84, 98, 52, 53.

cessation of civility and justice'.[1] We follow Spengler with admiration that never grows into sympathy. 'We need hardness.' Is that the greatest lesson history has to teach us? Perhaps—for him who thinks himself so wise that he can find in the history of his kind nothing but ultimate futility.

Wells had little appreciation of art or ritual. He failed to grasp the greatness of the past because he measured it with modern yardsticks. He fell victim to the exaggerated modern appraisal of exact science and technology. As a result he was not able to understand or evoke the past. To him it was for the most part sound and fury signifying nothing. He cast the enlightened few in his own mould. Yet what history taught him was a great gentleness, firm confidence and soaring hope. He may have expected far too much of human nature under rational control. Yet in this very faith he seems to me by far the wiser of the two.

[1]*Outline*, p. 555.

The Aesthetic Element in
Historical Thought[1]

If one is going to risk indulging in general reflections, it
might be more fitting to do so in a farewell lecture than in
an inaugural one. This is probably true of all learned disciplines, but at any rate, it is so of history. Maturity is, as it
were, a prerequisite. As Ranke once put it in a letter to
Bismarck: 'I have always thought that the historian must
first grow old; he must gather a great deal of experience and
witness the overall course of a prolonged period before he
can be deemed competent to judge other ages.'[2] And if a
just perspective on the turbulent scenes of history is only
granted to those who can look back on a long and not pain-
less journey, what shall he say who is just setting out and
sees, as through a morning haze, the first trees of the wood?
If he accepts the responsibility of guiding others he must
look to his provisions and ponder well the choice of path.
It is in some such mood as this that I shall try to point out
the way that I hope to follow in the responsible rôle I am
now undertaking. At least I may claim that this choice has
been long and anxiously considered. My preludium might
just as well be called a confession of faith, or of one article of
faith. And this article I may best and briefly define as faith
in the importance of the aesthetic element in historical
thinking.

Those who venture into the theory of history already find

---

[1]Inaugural Lecture as Professor of History at Groningen University on
4 November 1905.
[2]Quoted by Dove: *Ranke und Sybel in ihrem Verhältnis zu König Max*,
1895, p. 15.

themselves upon a battlefield. Every step is perilous, and to none more so than the neutral who wanders into No Man's Land. So before plunging into the fray I must sound a preliminary warning. The study of history long kept the even tenor of its way, undistracted by the clamour of challenge and criticism. But in the last century, it has been sternly called to account. What is its proper field, it has been demanded, and what the title to its domain? Whence came these challenges, and how is it that they found the champions of historical studies in such disarray? The main answer is that, among both historians and their critics, the traditional ideas of what constitutes knowledge has changed almost out of all recognition under the impact of the astonishing development of natural science. Serious students of history could not but ask themselves whether a discipline that differed so radically from physics—in method, in the structure of its concepts and in the certainty of its results— could hope to arrive at assured truths. And once the criteria of physics were applied, there was nothing for it but to admit that history was not a science, or else to make it one by drastic changes in its methodology. The general voice was for the second alternative. What else was to be expected in the age of Comte and Spencer? This view was reinforced by the emergence of a new discipline that shared its systematic character with the exact sciences, and many of its interests with history, namely sociology. And sociology was in fact making concerted efforts to claim the entire historical field for its own, and to monopolise the name of historical science.

But to earn itself the dignity of a science, does historical research, in fact, have to adduce generally valid historical laws comparable to those of natural science? This question was eloquently dealt with last year by the outgoing Rector Magnificus of this university, who answered it with an emphatic NO.

With respect to the relationship between history and

sociology, we must ask: should true history confine itself to the investigation of historical events as such, or must it rather endeavour to uncover the laws whereby these events can be inter-related and explained? Closely connected with this question is another: is it individuals or crowds with whom the historian must primarily concern himself? And that raises the thorny problem of whether the course of history is determined by the actions of great men or whether great men are rather moulded by their environment and circumstances. But such a choice is purely philosophical and hence outside the sphere of historical research.

The demands of the scientific school could be answered in two ways. We might challenge the champions of exact historical laws to produce propositions that are invulnerable to the detailed criticism of the tried historical method. It would, however, be most unfair to throw down that challenge at the present stage. The principles of the new approach might be correct even if their applications cannot yet stand up to every test. To condemn Lamprecht's method on the basis of a critical assessment of his *Deutsche Geschichte* would be precipitate and unjust. But it would be quite another matter if the basic principles themselves could be shown to be logically invalid. In that case the so-called new direction would be in a bad way indeed. And it must be admitted that the method has suffered blow after blow in the past few years. In fact, the use of positivism in historical research which is advocated by those who call themselves the younger historians has become thoroughly discredited.[1] An independent theory of the humanities has been newly established on firm foundations by Dilthey, Simmel, Windelband, Rickert and Spranger, to mention only the more recent of such thinkers in this field.

From the critical appraisal of the claims of scientific method to supersede all other approaches to history, two

[1]H. Rickert: *Die Grenzen der naturwissenschaftlichen Begriffsbildung*, 1902, pp. 331, 406; F. Gottl: *Die Grenzen der Geschichte*, 1904, p. 64.

conclusions make themselves strongly felt. One is that real life can never be entirely reduced to general concepts, and that the recognition of a certain uniqueness in each and every event must always remain the main task of historical research, which is not to say that historians have no sense of what is generally valid. The other is simply the converse of the first: the conviction that the impartial character of historical research suffers grievously from regimentation by submission to a preconceived systematic rule, even though impartiality is precisely what the latter purports to offer.

This does not mean that historical writing may not sometimes be legitimately drawn upon to support special disciplines with systematic norms—for instance, to support theology, economics or anthropology. In that case the method becomes openly selective. One takes out of the total historical context only such things as are seen to have a bearing on the special concern and ignores the rest. Consequently, such operations can never take the place of history, although the re-ordering and evaluation of selected data may contribute to history. To the historian, it is always a totality of psychological and sociological phenomena—indivisible, interdependent and irreducible—that has to be examined, and as far as possible without 'explanatory' preconceptions or delimitations of 'significant' factors.[1]

The claim of theology to hold the key to history is an old story. Nowadays we hear much more of the similar claims of economics, sociology and anthropology. Each of them has tried time and again to foist its own concerns upon history as the most important of all, and indeed to introduce new historical methods. And it must be admitted that all of them have immeasurably enriched history with new material and new points of view. The economic interpretation of history

[1] E. Spranger: *Die Grundlagen der Geschichtswissenschaft,* 1905, pp. 112, 96; W. Wundt: *Logik,* ii, p. 11. —According to S. Simmel (*Die Probleme der Geschichtsphilosophie,* 1095, p. 46) historical research without a limited viewpoint is impossible in principle.

has left its mark on all of us, so much so that its pertinent questions spring to our lips during every investigation, and we delve deeply into sources of historical causation that we have neglected for far too long. And yet the pure historical approach remains independent of this and all other special viewpoints; it must be universal and unprejudiced.

If the most orthodox Protestant and the most doctrinaire Marxist were to investigate, say, the influence of agrarian conditions on the Reformation, without allowing their judgments to be affected by their respective dogmas, and if both had equal talent, diligence and critical ability, they would have to arrive at the same conclusion. But, in fact, we should hardly expect them to do so, because their dogmas are never kept out. The result is that their historical 'laws' reflect their doctrinal bias rather than the historical relationships.

No one would maintain even for a moment that the rules, types and categories established by such systematic disciplines as ethnology, economics and jurisprudence, have no value for history as such, and Von Below goes too far when he alleges that it is the proper task of historians to oppose all systematic constructions.[1] Why should we not use them for what they are worth, i.e. as guides for determining and classifying facts and relationships? When a group of historical phenomena can be better understood after they have been combined under one formula, as for instance in Bucher's *Wirtschaftsstufen* (economic stages) and *Betriebssysteme* (industrial systems), why not use the formula? As Spranger very rightly points out in his *Die Grundlagen der Geschichtswissenschaft* (the basis of historical science): 'That Burckhardt's discovery of individualism should have attracted so much attention clearly proves the historian's urgent need for an increase in the number of scientific, and particularly of psychological, tools.'[2] Provided, that is, one resists the temptation to treat these unavoidable expedients as

[1] *Die neue historische Methode* in *Hist. Zeitschrift*, vol. 81, 1898, p. 243.
[2] *Die Grundlagen der Geschichtswissenschaft*, p. 95.

definitive 'explanations',[1] and remembers that they owe what life they have to the totality of life itself and not *vice versa*. For it is life itself that is bodied forth in an historical event, and not merely some particular 'law' or formula.[2]

No attempted classification of historical phenomena has been so much discussed in recent times as Lamprecht's famous series of cultural epochs (*Kulturzeitalter*). It is now usually rejected *in toto*, quite wrongly in my view, for there is no reason why the setting up of such a series should be considered wrong in principle. By no means, for even when the terms in the series are inadequate and one-sided, the series itself may prove useful. I, for one, have not found the characterisation of the Germanic Middle Ages as conformist and conventional devoid of interest. The danger comes not when such an hypothesis—made to formulate what may turn out to be a valuable insight—is cautiously tested, but when it is elevated to the rank of doctrine (and this Lamprecht expressly does[3]).

What a long preamble! But such is the current clash of theories that it was necessary to declare at the outset that, albeit one fully appreciates the importance of the systematic principles of historical science, one nevertheless believes that the primary task of historical research is the investigation of separate events, not as types or special cases of a general category, but for their own sake. We cannot follow Lamprecht when he tries to clear the field for his 'socio-psychological' analysis by banishing all historical studies concerned with isolated events into the realm of art.[4]

[1] E. Spranger, *op. cit.*, p. 124.
[2] Cf. E. Meyer: *Zur Theorie und Methodik der Geschichte*, 1902, p. 27.
[3] K. Lamprecht: *Die kulturhistorische Methode*, 1900, p. 26; cf. *Moderne Geschichtswissenschaft*, 1905, pp. 22ff, 77ff. The fragility of Lamprecht's system is particularly apparent in his chapters on modern art in the first supplement to his *Deutsche Geschichte*, 1902.
[4] *Die historische Methode des Herrn von Below*, 1899, pp. 15, 49; *Die kulturhistorische Methode*, pp. 5f, 25, 29, 35.

'The singular and individual,' he declares, 'can only be grasped artistically. Its study can therefore be given no more than secondary importance in historical science.'

This was a highly strategic pronouncement by this indefatigable pioneer. For serious historians fear nothing more than seeing their labours counted amongst the arts. Lamprecht was by no means the first to object to that. But does the fact that history does not in all respects answer to the norms of science and has unmistakable connection with the arts stamp her as one of these? The question has often been posed and answered. Some have said one thing and some the other. A third possibility was generally overlooked, namely that the definitions of science and art might be rather arbitrary and that the alternatives were not so mutually exclusive as they seemed to be.

In my opinion, even Bernheim has adopted too narrow a definition of art.[1] As a result the distinction between history and art seems to him much simpler and easier than it really is.

Bernheim calls the inclusion of history among the arts the height of conceptual confusion, and attacks this view in various ways. Fully aware that imagination is essential in both history and art, he sees a characteristic distinction between the vision of the historian and that of the artist in that the latter is completely free to invent while the former is bound to his material, to critical standards and to real facts. One might object that this is at most a matter of degree and that, if the boundaries are to be drawn here, more than one branch of art will fall on the wrong side of the frontier, e.g. architecture, where imagination is set limits by the recalcitrance of the material and the needs of rigidity and inhabitability, and naturalistic portraiture, which must reflect the true proportions of the model.[2]

[1]*Lehrbuch der historischen Methode*, 1903, pp. 126-38, 571-89.
[2]See A. Jolles: *Zur Deutung des Begriffes Naturwahrheit in der bildenden Kunst*, 1905, pp. 6ff.

As against Lamprecht's apodictic position, Bernheim argues that the historian, even when he investigates the supposedly unique event, invariably looks for links, causal factors, evolution—call it what you will—while the artist grasps the moment as it flies, leaving it to God, perhaps, to look before and after. Whether this distinction is justified I shall not enquire; what I do question is Bernheim's view of art, which strikes me as being far too academic and formal. To him all art is the conscious striving for beauty, the wish to produce aesthetic forms, to conjure up an elegant unity from an unpromising diversity. For him the artistic factor in history is only introduced once the historian, having assembled and ordered his material, indulges in the luxury of inscribing a few cameos or miniatures in the margin of more weighty narrative. Bernheim does not banish the artistic factor entirely from historical studies, but as he wants to draw the boundary between history and art as sharply as possible, he is constantly tempted to depreciate the *writing* of history—in which the artistic element is unavoidable—and to emphasise the importance of historical *research*.

It strikes me that the relationship between art and history goes much deeper than Bernheim's argument might suggest; he far too easily dismisses the essential point—the rôle of the imagination. I certainly do not wish to identify history with art, whether as generally understood or in Lamprecht's rather derogatory sense. But if we may not marry art and history, we must not forbid them to meet, or we shall deny to history the very quality of spiritual insight which is most essential to it.

What the study of history and artistic creation have in common is a mode of forming images.[1] Does that compromise the scientific character of history—and does it matter? As Eduard Spranger put it,[2] if history itself could speak she

[1] See G. Simmel, *op. cit.*, p. 54.
[2] *Zur Theorie und Methodik der Geschichte*, p. 23.

would not insist on being called scientific. 'History is fully content that she exists, such as she now is, and that she should satisfy an undeniable human need.'

This is not the last time that I shall quote these German authorities for I am concerned to show that my own preference of the aesthetic point of view is borne out by the results of epistemological studies.

Perhaps it is not necessary to define art more broadly than I have suggested, for the philosophers have met us half-way by extending their definition of science. It is not really surprising that the connection between history and art has been more fully appreciated by philosophers than it has by historians. In the first place, epistemology has made it possible to probe more deeply into the workings of the human mind. In the second place, historians have—perhaps unwittingly—been more reluctant to admit the connection than was strictly necessary. They were afraid of opening the flood-gates to a torrent of dilettantish products, of which there were too many already, and which do not so much spring from the depth of the soul as from superficial fancies based on slight evidence. It was their bounden duty, even *vis-à-vis* such a genius as Carlyle, who did not so much relive history as remake it in his own fiery image, to demand a more disciplined procedure. The philosophers, on the other hand, were faced with no such dangers.

No wonder, therefore, that purely philosophical treatments of the subject show a much deeper understanding than Bernheim's. In them the concept of *Darstellung*—representation—is extended to cover far more than mere description; it becomes the very root of all truly historical interpretation. Rickert[1] uses the word *Darstellung* for the finished work as well as for the psychological work that is demanded of author and reader of historical works alike. That this kind of activity is not simply the joining together of critically established data or facts is so clear, he says, that

[1] *Die Grenzen der naturwissenschaftlichen Begriffsbildung*, p. 313.

we do not have to enter into the question.[1] Nor is there the slightest doubt but that everything connected with the function of the historian's brain cannot be fitted into logical formulae. However, this fact can never serve to rob his activity of the veridical character it has in common with science or saddle it with the allegedly fictitious character of art.[2] For when all perception of reality is 'transformation and simplification rather than reflection'[3], then the process may be more radical in historical research than in other sciences, but its essence is the same. In the preface to his *Probleme der Geschichtsphilosophie*[4], Georg Simmel calls the subject of his book a critique of historical realism, according to which history is a 'mirroring' of the past, although, of course, on a much smaller stage. As against this view, he argues that the 'transformation' of present experiences which enables us to construct the theoretical picture that we call history is a much more radical process than the realists assume.

Umbildung—transformation—is also the term that Lazarus[5] uses to describe the psychological activity of the historian. 'It is a metamorphosis of the given conceptual data, not a mere recapitulation or simple classification, nor yet a simple sifting and re-arrangement of the material under investigation, but the free creation of other conceptual sequences that have the same weight as the data which constitute their content.' What history makes of the past, Lazarus is saying, is never photography and always involves intellectual re-interpretation.

Now there is no *a priori* reason why the reconstruction of historical material with the help of logically defined and

[1]Rickert, *op. cit.*, pp. 305, 314.
[2]Rickert, *op. cit.*, p. 389; *Kulturwissenschaft und Naturwissenschaft*, p. 43.
[3]Rickert: *Kulturwissenschaft und Naturwissenschaft*, p. 30.
[4]Second edition, 1905, p. v; cf. W. Dilthey: *Studien zur Grundlegung der Geisteswissenschaften*, Proc. Roy. Pruss. Acad., 1905, p. 322.
[5]*Ueber die Ideen in der Geschichte* in *Zeitschrift für Völkerpsychologie und Sprachwissenschaft*, vol. 3, 1865, p. 402.

simple concepts should be impossible, why historical reconstruction should not be a purely rational function. But do such simple concepts exist? As general logical abstractions, they do not. For we can arrive at them only after analysis and comparison. Now, historical analysis and comparison are greatly impeded by the fact that the whole of history is an irreducible complex—comparison because it is impossible ever to find any kind of elementary similarity between the objects compared; analysis, because the final historical unit to which it must apply itself is itself a complex problem *par excellence*: man and his actions.

Hence there can be no question of the existence of historical concepts *qua* logically defined generalisations. What we can do is to speak of historical concepts as ideas expressing an essential ingredient of reality, one aspect of the unsurveyable complexity of events. All historians can hope to do is to form the clearest possible ideas of the past.[1] Now all ideas have a subjective element, they involve imagination, historical insight, historical sense—words that speak of a more than simply logical activity.

When we speak of historical reflection, we quickly think of intense intellectual work and easily forget that even in the simplest historical construction, the rational function works hand in hand with intuition.[2] Only on superficial examination can an historical interpretation be considered a purely rational 'explanation'; rather is it the 'complete focusing of our emotional forces on the subject'. 'The actual process,' Spranger wrote, 'cannot be analysed. The anticipation, interpretations and flair of the historian are comparable to the mysterious intuitions of the artist.'[3]

Only in this way, it seems to me, can we come closer to

[1]Rickert: *Grenzen . . .*, pp. 328, 384; *Kulturwissenschaft und Naturwissenschaft*, pp. 44, 47.
[2]A good example is found in Bernheim: *Lehrbuch der hist. Meth.*, p. 572.
[3]*Die Grundlagen der Geschichteswissenschaft*, pp. 80, 89, 19, 82, 125. Cf. Simmel: *Probleme der Geschichtsphilosophie*, pp. 21, 38; E. Meyer: *Zur Theorie und Methodik*, p. 2.

the nature of the relationship between history and art. Whether or not history, like art, strives from time to time to create beautiful forms is quite immaterial. Long before the historian starts making suppositions, long before the poet puts his spirit into metre and rhyme, the imaginative activity they have in common has begun to operate; it does not lie in the particular form of presentation but in the nature of the original response and the emotion that accompanies it. Only when the stage of actual composition is reached, does the differentiation between, say, poetry and history begin to emerge. But even then the means—the evocative use of language—remain much the same. 'The historian,' Windelband wrote, 'has the task of reviving a picture or pictures from the past. He must fashion what once existed in reality much as the artist fashions what exists in his present imagination. Here lies the relationship between historic and aesthetic creation.'[1] Thus in history, no less than in poetry for instance, the intention is to help the reader's imagination conjure up a vision that goes far beyond the precise meaning of the written words. It is, however, the duty of the historian to use his words in such a way that the reader's imagination cannot stray into the realms of private fantasy.[2]

Those who accept what I have said about the formation of historical concepts, will not be unduly disturbed to find that they involve a subjective factor. For if Wundt, Simmel, Windelband, Rickert and Münsterberg are right to think that the essence of historical knowledge—unlike that of natural-scientific explanation—is the psychologically plausible demonstration of a connection between critically established historical facts,[3] and hence more a matter of 'comprehending' than of 'expounding'; if, moreover, this

[1] *Geschichte und Naturwissenschaft*, p. 30.
[2] Cf. Rickert: *Kulturwissenschaft und Naturwissenschaft*, p. 39; Münsterberg: *Grundzüge der Psychologie*, vol. I, 1900, p. 129.
[3] Wundt: *Logik* III, p. 539.

comprehension is a way of reliving the past (*Nacherleben, Nachempfinden*)[1], then our own psyche is, indeed, the only constant standard of comparison.

But then the question arises: what precisely is it that we can relive? What other than the life of men, and moreover of individual men rather than of groups and classes? Thus we come back along a different path to the question I touched upon at the beginning: the significance of personality. Here, we are not so much concerned with the metaphysical as with the methodological problem—not with the question of whether individuals make history or merely go with the stream, but the question of whether or not understanding historical connections involves understanding individuals. Now it strikes me that even those historians who deny freedom of decision, cannot leave historical personalities entirely out of account.

For even if individuals did not determine history, we cannot hope to grasp special phenomena without them. How can we understand human action except by observing people? What sort of idea can we form of an age, if we see no people in it? If we may only give generalised accounts we do but make a desert and call it history. Truly, he who wishes to see real history come alive, should not miss the trees for the wood, the individuals for the mass.[2]

Can we transform 'the great theatre of the world' into an automatically operated puppet show?[3] Only a biassed and short-sighted generalisation of the natural-scientific principle can lead us to mistake unique persons and events for automata that must dance to the same tune in the same way. To history, if we take her as she is, with a wardrobe not limited to a logical strait-jacket, every figure is individual.

[1]Windelband: *op. cit.*, p. 30: Rickert: *Kulturw. und Naturw.*, p. 39; Münsterberg: *Grundzüge der Psychologie*, 1, pp. 123, 129; Simmel: *Probleme . . .*, pp. 20ff.
[2]Von Below: *Die neue historische Methode* in *Historische Zeitschrift*, 81, p. 239.
[3]Lamprecht: *Die hist. Meth. des Herrn von Below*, p. 25.

Not empty processes but human actions excite our interest. What matters is not the levelling of objects into more or less amorphous though intelligible entities, but the understanding of subjects—men and their actions—in their individual aspect.[1]

The dogma that only human societies, groups and associations form the subject of history, leads straight to absurdity. For in that case I would be allowed to take an interest in monasticism—in the Benedictines, the order of Friars Minor, or even of the Franciscan Spirituals—but not in St. Francis himself, either as a representative of his order or as a man.

The scope of history is wider than that of, say, physical science because, behind the smallest historical unit that can be investigated, there always lies a man, no less problematic than each one of us knows himself to be.

It is very true to say that our historical knowledge consists, in much greater measure than heretofore, in the identification of trends, movements and developments. The need to fit all special knowledge into one great edifice is more urgent for us than it was for historians in the past. We do not so much see people as types. But are we to be satisfied with that? If a man's type has been conclusively established by one's predecessors, as something as definitive as a category in natural science, does that mean that there is no more to find out about him? Everyone knows that the historian's task is not as simple as that. He has to grapple with something that transcends all categorisation.

When I study the great catastrophes of circa 1300 A.D., I immediately think of such things as apostolic power, the concepts of apostolic poverty, or of the constitutional state.[2] And it is my pleasure to follow these threads back and forth, to see the idea of Papal power grow from Innocent to

[1] Cf. Windelband, *op. cit.*, p. 35.
[2] Quite irrespective of whether I happen to take an idealistic or materialistic view of the matter.

Boniface and then collapse; to see the tragic victory of the idea of poverty in Celestine V and then its corruption in the *Defensor pacis*. But what good are these mighty ideas if I do not see the men behind them: Boniface VIII, Jacopone da Todi and Nogaret? I know that my ideas are merely *my* ways of comprehending, and hence so many relative points of view.

For that reason, too, biography is so important—it keeps reminding us of the dangers of rationalisation. I remember an anecdote of Michelet's about Robespierre. Years after the Revolution, a young man asked the old Merlin of Thionville why he helped to condemn Robespierre. The old man kept silent, but seemed to be groping for words. Suddenly he rose up and said with a violent gesture: 'Robespierre ... Robespierre! If only you had seen his green eyes, you, too, would surely have condemned him.'[1] His green eyes! What better way of teaching us about true historical motives, of warning us to beware of reducing man, with all his hate, fury and delusion, to a bundle of political or economic drives! The little anecdote emphatically shows us that we may never know what strange quirks of human nature might in any given case have been decisive.

We must also beware of assuming that great thinkers were of greater historical importance than kings, warriors and diplomats. 'What are Pericles or Augustus today,' Lamprecht exclaimed, 'but mere names; labels of a great age?'[2] What presumptuous exaggeration of the importance of literature! Have art and literature then so lifted us into the clouds that we can afford to be bored with mere courage and determination?

However, since we have just mentioned Robespierre, that greatest of psychological enigmas, we may ask if we can ever

[1]Michelet: *Histoire de la révolution française*, VI, 1897, p. 97.
[2]*Ueber den Begriff der Geschichte* . . . in *Annalen der Naturphilosophie*, II, 1903, p. 267.

really probe into the human mystery? And even if we could, is that a proper activity of historical interpretation? Is it not rather the task of psychology? And since psychology is still a young science, must we wait until it has learnt to handle its tools with complete assurance and meanwhile abstain from wondering why some people in the past acted as they did?

Let us see what the psychologists themselves have to say, for there is no doubt that they can help us in many ways. Thus we believe them when they tell us that men have a tendency to exaggerate so that all evidence as to quantity, size, strength, number and duration grows in the telling.[1] We also learn that it is only human to make a good story out of indifferent facts,[2] to lend an air of verisimilitude to an otherwise bald and unconvincing narrative. To say nothing of the power of suggestion that makes us remember things only as we, or someone else, wants us to remember them. How many great obsessions have not been caused that way!

But all that hardly answers the question I have just raised. When it comes to entering into the psychological condition of historical personages, so as to gain a better understanding of their doings and nature, psychology is very poorly thought of by philosophers of history, especially Rickert, according to whom the application of the customary psychological methods to historical studies is bound to produce misleading results and has already done so.[3] The concepts of general psychology are too barren to render the historian any service.[4] Historical research, like art, wants to grasp psychological processes not in general terms but in their individual manifestations, and the intuitive ability to do that requires no experience in scientific psychology.[5] The psychological insight needed by both artist and historian

[1] *Beiträge zur Psychologie der Aussage*, I, p. 39; cf. Ramsay: *Historical Review*, 1903, p. 625.
[2] *Beitr, zur Psych. d. Auss.*, I, p. 248.   [3] *Kulturw. und Naturw.*, p. 16.
[4] *Grenzen . . .*, p. 536.   [5] *Kulturw.*, p. 41.

is not one of preconceived concepts;[1] it is a skill that may be improved by scientific psychology but can never be replaced by it. For even if a psychological theory could explain psychological processes in general terms, it would not greatly help us to understand a particular historical case.[2] There is an historical psychology, Rickert admits, but it is not and cannot be a science. All that matters is 'reliving', that manner of understanding which eludes classification into a system of general concepts. It is precisely in the lack of systematic concepts that the power of historical psychology resides.[3]

Windelband says much the same: the fact that it has not so far been possible to formulate a perfect set of psychological laws has not prevented any historian blessed with intuition, tact and some understanding of human nature, from getting to know some of his heroes and their actions. Windelband doubts strongly whether a mathematical formulation of elementary psychological activities would yield a significant result for the understanding of real human life.[4]

A slightly different point of view is adopted by Spranger, following Dilthey and Simmel. He, too, recognises the necessity of distinguishing between scientific psychology and historical insight, and says that the kind of unsystematic psychology used by the historian—based on experience and imagination—does not so much involve psychological elements as such as very complex processes. Historical analysis stops short at 'vital processes'. In these, the historian admittedly sees relationships and connections, but he is not concerned with isolating the abstract factors of psychological processes.[5] Spranger, however, does not despair of the

---

[1]*Grenzen . . .*, p. 543.   [2]*Kulturw.*, p. 41.   [3]*Grenzen . . .*, p. 536, 188.
[4]*Gesch. und Naturw.*, p. 37: cf. Münsterberg: *Grundzüge der Psychologie*, I, p. 131.
[5]*Die Grundlagen der Geschichtswissenschaft*, pp. 25, 54, 72, 19; cf. 21, 48, 82

possibility (which I report here merely for the sake of completeness) of providing historical psychology with a systematic mainstay in the form of empirically determined psychological types. Whether such types can in fact be established remains to be seen.

What concerns us here is that the historian—at every stage of his activity, in the formation of his concepts, and the interpretation of his data—has constantly to rely on something in himself that is much deeper and more impenetrable than the purely logical association of ideas. Historical knowledge is never the mere sum of chronological and political ideas; the chain of visual memories is never a mere summation. It is pure delusion to suppose that the non-rational elements of historical understanding can be banished from that discipline and confined to the category of art. Let the term 'art' be revised just as 'science' has been. Why call the historical sense an artistic emotion simply because it involves a non-rational faculty? Only the confusion of the concepts 'artistic' and 'aesthetic'—two ugly words for two beautiful things—can lead us to mistake the activity of the historian for that of the artist.

Yet if historical feeling has its own hold on truth, that is certainly not to the exclusion of aesthetic pleasure. They cannot be separated. Even when an historian has no intention of stimulating the free imagination, a responsive reader may nevertheless discover unsuspected and unintended connections. A real event may have many meanings, one no less true than another. This multiform reality may show through the very language that seems to limit it. Hence the imaginative response of different people to one and the same description will vary very greatly, depending on their prior knowledge, general attitudes, training and particular bias. 'While there is only one true factual picture of nature, every deviation from which is an error, it is possible to have a host of quantitively similar but qualitatively different ways of interpreting one and the same series of historical events, all of which are true, albeit from different points of view.'[1]

Hence there is, strictly speaking, no history of jurisprudence, economics and philosophy, but only legal, economic and philosophical glimpses of history. But we may still ask whether, among the different viewpoints, there is one that is more suited than any of the others to being considered the historical viewpoint in general? Is there, for instance, one that stimulates the kind of historical imagination which, as we saw, is so important? Surely there is—and it is, of course, the aesthetic one. Is not Ranke's 'universal sympathy'—which caused him to delight in every human faculty—closely related to an aesthetic attitude?[2] Is that vital characteristic of our culture, rightly called a sense of history, anything but a very general, highly developed aesthetic sensibility? I am thinking of the mood that—in contrast to the highly selective attitude of previous generations—enables us to enjoy Van Eyck as well as Rembrandt, the Rococo as well as Millet, to be rationalists with Diderot and Calvinists with the Sea Beggars. It is something quite other than general interest—it combines the highest attainable objectivity with a highly subjective feeling.

My theme leads me to ask one further question: how can the aesthetic approach with all its evocative powers, heighten our appreciation of history?

It does so by helping us to conjure up living pictures in the private theatre of the mind. In natural science, as Windelband has pointed out, the tendency is towards abstraction, in historical imagination it is towards visualisation. Again, whereas in natural science all knowledge must be translated into strict concepts, to whose sobriety all imagery appears bacchanal, history has quite a different task. If it wishes to fulfil its mission—the evocation of the past—then it must deliberately step across the boundaries of the purely

[1] Wundt: *Logik*, II, p. 540.
[2] Cf. Spranger: *Grundlagen* . . . , p. 117.

conceptual[1] and vivify an intuitive response. In other words, it must evoke dynamic images.

Let us now try to see how historical intuition affects our view first of persons who lived long ago and, second, of social behaviour and human relations in general.

In order to create an historical picture, one must be able to select and assemble from the mass of data only what is relevant to its essential nature, only what explains its origins.[2] Now where the mass of data relates to only one man, the question of what historical elements are essential for understanding him will be answered differently by different investigators. He whose dull vision does not look beyond mere diplomatic activity or practical common sense will be blind to a great many qualities that history could reveal to him. The greater his experience of men, the broader and more many-sided his own spirit, the more subtle the discoveries he will make in the field of psychological relationships,[3] and the more discriminating will be his choice of illustrative material.

But in general we may say that he searches always for the unique person behind every word and deed. The more penetrating his gaze, the more surely the real man will stir again to life, and so will all his complex, conflicting and irrational passions. 'L'histoire,' said Taine, 'c'est à peu près voir les hommes d'autrefois.' And Michelet added resoundingly: 'L'histoire, c'est une résurrection'. The strength of the vision is not reducible to the sum of notions about the conditions and qualities of the person. Only his intuitive powers decide how many facts the historian will need in order to resurrect an historical personage.

Not that the historian can 'pluck out the heart of the mystery' of what was once a man, or even of his own. The further we try to explore our own ways of understanding

[1]Rickert: *Grenzen* . . ., pp. 382ff, 142.
[2]Bernheim: *Lehrbuch der hist. Methode*, p. 148.
[3]Spranger: *Grundlagen* . . ., p. 112.

men and their actions, the more we realise how inexplicable and mysterious this being called man really is.[1] Can the probing of this mystery ever lead to valid conclusions? It is only when we realise how simply and spontaneously we reach out to others and how psychological intuition has been the great strength of all truly 'scientific' historians, that the doubt disappears. No one has mastered the art of reconstructing historical characters from only a few traits and presenting them in sharp personal outlines so well as Ranke; we only have to open his books to be struck by this fact.[2] Now it is clear that the need for intuition is the greater the more unusual is the character one is trying to understand. A psychological enigma such as Robespierre, who does not at all lend himself to analysis, can yet be brought to life by a good writer. What matters here is the echoes that are awakened in our own hearts. Italian accounts of the *cinquecento* often give us the feeling that we have become too soft and humane to understand such times. If we Netherlanders find it hard to share in the feelings of some other nations of today, how can we possibly relive those of long ago: the tribal feeling of the Barbarians, respect for divine right, the feudal concept of service and loyalty? Let us then go to the poets, let Shakespeare show us the true essence of majesty.

Any historian who despises the evocative powers of intuition as not scientifically respectable, will lose in depth and scope of vision. Will he be the more the scientist for that?

Let us pass on to the importance of aesthetic intuition for the understanding of general historic processes. According to Lamprecht, historical imagination is quite out of place here. Lamprecht banishing imagination, his own most

[1] See Simmel: *Probleme . . .*, pp. 20ff, 50ff.
[2] Good examples are also found in Lambeck: *Wie schildert der Historiker die Persönlichkeit* in *Preussische Jahrbücher*, 1903, p. 282.

precious gift! It is Satan rebuking sin indeed. If an individual can only be 'artistically apprehended', so only can men in general. Indeed, the share of aesthetic intuition in the formation of a general historical picture is particularly important. Take your own general picture of Egyptian culture. Is it not almost entirely made up of notions based on Egyptian art? And how strongly is the general picture of the Middle Ages dominated by Gothic art! Or reverse the question and say: how much do we know about the thirteenth century when we have read all the Papal bulls but do not know the *Dies irae*?

Suppose you have a somewhat vague idea of the fall of the ancient world. You may do something to clarify it by careful reading. But how much better to visit Ravenna and see the mosaics there! Then, whenever you think of those times, you will always see their actual splendour as it survives in the flecks of green and gold in the San Vitale and the hue of nocturnal blue in the mausoleum of Galla Placidia. The true image of the era is now indelibly fixed in your imagination. Is not that something finer than the most elaborate structures of thought? Do logical mosaics give you a better appreciation of what it was to live there long ago? Nor are the logical connections in historical knowledge nearly as pellucid as they may seem; the association of ideas is always more or less arbitrary.

I do not mean that general history and the history of art are synonymous. We must not derive our picture of the past from art as a separate phenomenon, or make art the only key to an understanding of the mental climate of an age, but see everything else we know about that age reflected in or illuminated by it. The historian, while investigating the past in all its forms, must heighten his intuitive powers with paintings and books. But he must also become familiar with the natural settings, walk across meadows and hills, until he feels that the sun that shines upon him illuminates again the life of old.

But I can hear the objection that in heightened aesthetic receptivity lies a great danger for serious historical research. It leads to reading things into history, creating false pictures. All objects look different by moonlight, the figures among the ruins may be phantoms of the mind.

Are we, in fact, in greater danger from the aesthetic conception than we are from logically constructed historical hypotheses? I, for one, do not think so. The aesthetic insights of different men may be vastly different, but what of that? What different artists see in the same model are so many aspects of the same person: they complement and do not contradict one another. Who would be without such sentences as this of Herodotus: 'And when he saw the Hellespont hidden by ships, and all the coasts and plains of Abydus teeming with people, Xerxes thought himself fortunate indeed, but then he cried.'[1] We are there: we see the sun on the white sails, the milling crowds, the blaze of arms and the crimson costumes. We can hear the murmur of the voices, the splashing of the sea, and feel the salt sting of the wind upon our faces. And we see *through the eyes of the king* and feel his pride and his passion. If now we follow our imagination, we shall find that the details that have sprung unbidden to our minds can either be verified or else do not affect our logical understanding of the whole. Only when we deliberately encourage our imagination to transcend the bounds of historical imagination and to soar into the realms of sheer fantasy, do we risk falsifying the true past.

Now look at the dangers of making historical hypotheses. Whenever a false hypothesis is temporarily adopted (which must necessarily happen now and then) it fathers a kind of proliferating confusion. Take, for instance, the questionable theory that all property was once held in common. It caught on everywhere—in economics no less than in cultural history. If it is wrong, much historical writing will need radical revision. Now this happens to every science, and

[1] *History*, VII, 45.

science is none the worse for having to revise its hypotheses from time to time. On the contrary, this is what keeps it alive and growing. By the constant correction of error human knowledge advances.

But should the great insights into history gained by aesthetic intuition be counted no gain simply because they cannot be fitted into pigeon-holes? Who has grasped and described the truly *classical* essence of the thirteenth century more lucidly than Viollet-le-Duc? Often, by penetrating deep into history, aesthetic intuition blazed the way for rational explanation. No one was more affected by aesthetic influences than the Grimms and their contemporaries. Our picture of the Middle Ages may differ vastly from that of the Romantics; but there is no doubt that their aesthetic enthusiasm helped to clarify our view of medieval history.

Perhaps it will always be so. How recently were our eyes opened to the breath-taking beauty of the work of Breughel the Elder? Why do we now admire him so? With astonishment we now realise that it is something more than bawdry he has to offer—that his work ranks with the greatest and most profound. This deeper understanding has not sprung from a systematic study of sixteenth century cultural history. Yet it will lead us into seeing sixteenth-century Dutch history more lucidly, more sharply and more colourfully—in short, more historically.

Must we then, in the interest of strict science, be apprehensive about our aesthetic pre-occupations? No need. For the historian there is one ethical demand that predominates over all others: to present the truth, or what he understands by the truth. What I have tried to say here about the theory of historical research impinges on only one facet of this vast problem. I have held my rushlight near one crevice in a huge mountain wall and tried to focus all its light upon that spot. But had it been a lighthouse it would not have reached to the unscalable heights.

The contemplation of beauty is not the historian's daily

task. Soon we shall have to bend our heads from the panorama of theory to the humble spadework of critical research. But let us always remember how vast and beautiful the world around us really is. From time to time we must look up from the constraint of diligent work, in order to feel anew that while our strength is limited, history is not, and to know again the deep responsibility of the historian who, the more he knows that he can only walk by the light that is in him, the more firmly he fixes his mind's eye on the ideal of the objective truth.

[Professor Huizinga concluded his address with expressions of his sense of the responsibility of his new position and a tribute to his new colleagues and former teachers. *A.J.P.*]

My Path to History[1]

I have never had the wish to write an autobiography, nor have I even kept a diary—the daily entries I made during my visit to the United States in 1926 do not deserve that name, and during my trip to Java, Bali and Hong Kong in the winter of 1930–31, I suffered from an injury to my right eye and was consequently forced to rely on my memory. Only once, at Woudschoten on 17 March 1936, did I address students on my own life. Even then my intention was not so much to tell them about myself as to illustrate the nature of historical interest, and I felt I could do that far better by personal example than by philosophical speculation. If I return to the subject now at some greater length, it is because I have come to feel that my historical development has been unusual enough to merit the reader's brief attention.

My first contact with history was rather occasional and has left me with keen memories, some of which I have been able to check against my elder brother's recollections. It was during the autumn of 1879. I had just finished my first year at primary school and must have been seven years old. The Groningen Student-Corps was holding ,its quinquennial celebrations, and the theme of the carnival was the entry, in 1506, of Edzard, Count of East Friesland, into the city of Groningen. I doubt whether the costumes were historically accurate, even though a lot of research had gone into the procession. The heart and soul of the organising committee was J. A. Feith, later State Archivist and unsurpassed historian of Groningen. With some of his fellow committee

[1]First published by H. Tjeenk Willink & Zoon, Haarlem, 1947.

members, he had called on the Count of In- and Knyp-
huizen, at Lutetsborg Castle near Vorden—the castle
burned down on Christmas night 1909—where they were
most warmly received, the daughters dressing up specially
in the costumes of the Mannings family. Feith told me all
this much later, when we had become close friends or, to
be more precise, between 1905 and his all too early death in
1913.

The carnival was the most magnificent spectacle I had
ever witnessed. I remember the procession leaving Markt-
straat, close to our own house at the corner of Ossenmarkt
and Lopende Diep, that it blew hard that day and that a
flagpole was snapped off nearby, the flag enveloping a rider,
and many other details which I shall spare you. The princi-
pal character was Willem Alberda van Ekenstein, later
Judge van Ekenstein, who made a magnificent Count
Edzard, armoured from top to toe in glittering metal. When
the main spectacle was over, it was the schoolboys' turn.
Our mothers had dressed us all up in beautiful costumes,
but since the burgomaster would not have another street
procession, we had to content ourselves with the old theatre
in Nieuwe Kijk in 't Jatstraat. Then life resumed its normal
course, not, however, before I had become fascinated by
our colourful past.

During 1881–82, when I was in my fourth year at school
(there were seven primary grades altogether) we began to
learn Dutch History. Our teacher was Miss J. Nuiver, the
niece of Mr. A. Nuiver, our headmaster, a man whose tall
hat, black whiskers and strict yet gentle face I have never
forgotten. Miss Nuiver later taught in a teachers' training
college and, I believe, died a few years ago. She must have
been an exceptionally good teacher of history. Frisians,
Franks and Saxons came to life for me, I felt a great kinship
to the Counts of Holland, and I warmly embraced the
cause of the Noble Confederates who signed the Compromise in 1565. I have always been certain that what his-

torical knowledge I have acquired since, is firmly based on Miss Nuiver's teachings. As time went by, I naturally made extra-curricular contact with history as well. Our reading-matter included a large number of school and children's books from the collection of Grandfather Huizinga, pastor emeritus since 1879, many still with those old, long s-s which we found utterly ridiculous, and full of old-fashioned ideas on pedagogy. If only I could look at that collection now! Jules Verne, whom my friends devoured so greedily, gave me but little pleasure; in fact, I left most of his books unread. My greatest favourites were Andersen's Fairy Tales. My friends called them childish, but I paid no attention to their jibes, and enjoyed the tales then as I continue to love them now, particularly the simplest of them, for instance, *The Old House* and *The Goblin at the Grocer's*. Later, in Form 2 of High School, when I was awarded a prize and was asked to choose a book, I asked for Andersen's Fairy Tales—to the astonishment of teachers and governors alike—and was given a fine German edition on which I hope to lay my hands again one day.

Before 1885, when I entered High School, my interest in history was kept alive in a number of ways. There were first of all two hobbies which I shared with my older brother Jacob, born in 1870 and now a retired doctor. Jacob, who was keenly interested in history but was driven to medicine by the vicissitudes of his school career, has retained a strong love for the past and for literature. For a time, we were very keen on heraldry, knew everything there was to know about helmets, coats of arms, shields, chiefs, quarterings, common charges and what have you. I cannot tell whether this hobby was partly responsible for a secret vice that I have never been able to shake off altogether: a hankering for patrician origins and names, and a certain scorn for my own, all too obviously plebeian, descent from Baptist pastors and provincial farmers.

Our other hobby was of rarer quality: we became enthusiastic coin collectors. I do not remember how it all started, but our collection included old shillings and silver riders, together with pieces dated 1500 and even earlier. We also had a Sea-Beggar's penny made of lead and bearing the inscription 'Sooner Turks than Papists', notes issued during the siege of Groningen in 1672, and an 1814 penny commemorating the bicentenary of Groningen University and bearing the legend: *dummodo monumentum adsit*. Our greatest treasure, hower, was a Louis the Pious denarius, which we acquired in the autumn of 1884, on the occasion of yet another quinquennial celebration. This time the subject of the pageant was the life of the Stadholder Frederick Henry. Pieter Jelles Troelstra in a simple black suit was Gysbert Japicx, and I think that Gerrit de Jongh, later Judge de Jongh, took the part of d'Estrades. As far as I can remember De Marees van Swinderen, who later became Dutch Ambassador to London, also played some part. Some ten days later, when Jacob and I were alone at home, our Uncle Sam, who was in fact our half-cousin Dr. Samuel Meihuizen, called and pretended to be very cross with us for not watching the procession from the steps of his house in Boteringestraat. It had all been agreed, he had gone to a lot of trouble, etc., etc.; in short, Uncle Sam put on a great act, as only he knew how. We felt terribly ashamed and foolish about it all, and when he saw that, he grinned and presented us with the denarius, dug up from a mound in Hunsingo. I think that our friend Piet Hofstede de Groot, later director of the Amsterdamsche Bank, must also have had some share in our collection. His father, Professor C. P. Hofstede de Groot who died in 1884, presented us with two beautiful mahogany coin cases, divided into a number of compartments, which he had bought at the auction of Jonkheer Mello Backer's effects. My chronological sense is also bound up with a large seventeenth or eighteenth century silver wedding penny. On the reverse, a festooned column or pillar bore the—to me then quite mysterious—inscription

Charitas omnia suffert, which made me wonder what an old dotard (Dutch: *sufferd*) was doing at a wedding. In other words, I must have acquired this penny before I started Latin, i.e. before the end of 1885.

What happened to our collection? Years later, when I was approaching the end of my school life, my brother was very short of money and took my good nature for granted. I had not been taking any interest in our coins for quite some time, so that I was taken completely by surprise when, one fine day, he told me with his characteristic and disarming smile, that he had disposed of the entire collection piece by piece.

Despite all these incidental contacts with historical events, my intellectual curiosity between the ages of twelve and eighteen was not at all bound up with things historical—new interests helped to push these into the background. I can still remember how it all started. Dr. Jan te Winkel, our Dutch master at High School, was not a particularly good teacher of his subject—only during one of my last years at school did he manage to arouse my interest with a dictation on Middle-Dutch literature. In the lower classes, he taught us Dutch from Van Helten's impossibly erudite textbook, which was full of such helpful grammatical terms as syncope, metathesis and synalœpha, and from Cosijn's even more absurd but at least more amusing *Cacographie*. It did not escape us that the thoughts of our good teacher were elsewhere. He was forever sucking at the stub of his cigar and rattling keys in his trouser pockets. He completely spoiled our taste for Vondel by making us read *Roskam* in our second and *Lucifer* in our third year.

Even so, I owe Mr. Te Winkel a great debt. I was still in my first form, and we had just started on Latin verbs, when I asked him if our 'hebben'—to have—was not related to the Latin *habeo*, and this set him off on a general dissertation on phonetic changes: how *pater* becomes vader (father) and *caput* hovet or hoofd (head), etc. I found all this extremely fascinating, so much so that I decided there and then to become a philologist. Oddly enough, although I was fairly good at Greek and Latin, the thought of studying classical literature never even entered my head. My heart and imagination were in the Middle Ages, about which I knew precious little beyond the fact that they were full of chivalrous knights in plumed helmets. Also I remember making a large drawing of a Hanseatic town. What books it was based on I can no longer tell.

Mr. Hermans, our history teacher, knew a number of Oriental languages and was rightly thought to be a very learned man. He taught us much, even if he failed to give us a sound historical background. Hermans was not a good disciplinarian, but he was so well-liked that we never played him up. He would generally spend the lesson by chatting about this and that. If necessary, we would set him off with such leading questions as: 'Please, sir, what is the precise meaning of *mésalliance*?' 'Do you mean to tell me you do not know?' he would chuckle. 'Well, take the case of so and so,' and he would mention a recent Groningen society engagement. Hermans' historical sense was often a little piquant, to say the least. Thus, in our fifth year, he gave us a full list of Catherine II's lovers, which was probably far less dubious than the decision of our Dutch history master, one year later, to tell us the story of Onno Zwier van Haren in all its gory detail.

However, I am greatly indebted to Hermans for one thing if for nothing else: he also taught Hebrew and when, in the fifth year, the prospective theologians began to study that language, I decided to join them. We had not yet gone very far when Hermans said: 'Look, boys, Arabic is really a much better language, wouldn't you like to learn that as well?' The good theologians and I all agreed to take the extra lessons, but whereas they quickly tired of the difficult script, I greatly enjoyed it. In fact, I utterly neglected my Hebrew for the sake of Socin's Arabic Grammar in the

Porta linguarum orientalium which I devoured with such enthusiasm that within a fairly short time I could read Logmân's *Fables* and the story of King Solomon and the Hoopoe. When I entered university, I had made enough progress to take private lessons in Arabic with Mr. Van den Ham, and to read all sorts of Arabic authors, alas, without making the acquaintance of Islamic science.

My father opened up yet another important avenue of study. Being exceptionally intelligent and sensitive, he must have guessed what was needed to stimulate my youthful thirst for knowledge. One day, he brought me a book by Friedrich Max Müller from the University Library. It contained two separate dissertations entitled *Biographies of Words* and *The Home of the Aryans*. I read them, took them for the very embodiment of wisdom, and made copious notes. Next he brought me a number of books on mythology, including Fiske's *Myth and Myth Makers* and on ethnology, including one by Andrew Lang that cast some doubt on Max Müller's infallibility. E. B. Tylor's *Primitive Culture*, finally—which I must have read during the winter of 1888–89—opened up perspectives that, in a sense, have inspired me ever since, though Tylor's central thesis that animism is the basis of intellectual life has been discarded long since.

When the final examination was within sight, I decided to read Semitic literature, so keen was my interest in Arabic. However, my father was told that there was no future in it —purely materially speaking, of course—and he would, in any case, have found it financially embarrassing to send me to Leyden, a town that, moreover, did not attract me nearly as much as my native Groningen. That is why, in September 1891, I joined Groningen University as a student of 'Dutch letters', a term covering almost everything that could not be called classical or Oriental. The intellectual luggage I brought to University was, to say the least peculiar. My Latin and Greek were simple school stuff, taught without great depth or feeling. Greek, alas, I quickly neglected and never took up again, and classical Latin, too, never again attracted or inspired me—my Latin came to rest between St. Augustine and Erasmus (neither of whom I read until much later).

A great factor influencing my strong feelings for post-classical Latin and also my general literary development was Rémy de Gourmont's *Le Latin Mystique*, which I read during one of my first years at university, at about the same time that I also came across J. K. Huysman's *Là-Bas*.

My literary repertoire was, however, somewhat sparse. I had read a modicum of Shakespeare, a few German writers but nothing beyond the most familiar—Schiller, a little Goethe, Heine, a few snatches of poetry—and knew next to nothing of French literature. In fact, I was no great book-worm, nor have I since become one. What astonishes me when I look back on those years now, is my almost complete absence of interest not only in mathematics and philosophy but also in science, when so many of my friends were full of Haeckel and Büchner, Lorentz and Maxwell, and my father was as interested in biophysics as he was in letters and history. These gaps have never been filled, and I must confess that I have never felt particularly uneasy about them; nor have my children shown any greater interest in scientific matters. Perhaps I should call it an hereditary myopia of the intellect. But if I cared little for natural science as a child, I was already very susceptible to nature itself. Even before adolescence, I was prone to lyrical and sentimental moods.

When one read Dutch letters, the main subjects were history (exclusive of ancient history) and Dutch (including Germanic) studies under W. L. van Helten. A favourite ancillary subject was Comparative Philology. It was taught by B. Sijmons, whose outstanding course of introductory lectures made a very great impression on most of us. Sijmons described philology in such clear and glowing terms that I would dearly love to attend his lectures again. He gave me exactly the kind of impetus I needed in my studies. However, van Helten's detailed historical treatment of Dutch grammar based on profound Germanic studies, quickly aroused my interest, as well. In fact, what I know of the structure of our language I owe entirely to these lessons. Subsequently, Van Helten also introduced me to his favourite subject: Old Frisian. I also listened to P. J. Blok's broad and stimulating surveys of long periods of Dutch and world history with great enjoyment, without, however, being really moved or permanently enriched.

It goes without saying that, interested though I was in academic subjects, they did not occupy me to the exclusion of everything else. Thus—though this sort of thing was frowned on at Groningen as disloyal to the *esprit de corps*, which was actually not all it was made out to be—soon after we enrolled, ten of us from the class of 1891 formed a club, of which six members are still alive. Within the club itself, Willem de Sitter, then still a devotee of mathematics, C. T. van Valkenburg, the neuro-psychiatrist, and I formed a kind of inner circle. We were all enthusiastic supporters of the *Tachtigers*, a literary movement round the journal *De Nieuwe Gids* (1885), and consequently rated literature far higher than science, sought the meaning of life within ourselves (which was a great blessing) and completely ignored politics and allied topics (which was a grave fault)— throughout my student years, I never took a newspaper. We looked up to Van Deijssel, Kloos, Gorter *et al.* as to so many demigods. In the comfortable reading-room of *Mutua Fides*, we not only followed the Kloos crisis in *De Nieuwe Gids* month by month, and dutifully denounced Van Eeden, but also devoured the *Mercure de France*, watched Pierre Louÿs's star rise by the side of Rémy de Gourmont's, and finally hailed Alfred Jarry's *succès de scandale*—in short, we took a most one-sided view of what was happening in literature, even though Edgar Allan Poe, Robert Louis Stevenson,

Dante Gabriel Rossetti and many other authors made a great impression upon us as well. In later years, our enthusiasm for the *Tachtigers* was jolted by the appearance of P. L. Tak's *De Kroniek*, in which our own contemporaries, among them Jan Kalf and the talented and precocious André Jolles, put forward their views. At the time, literary ideas had begun to have a profound effect on me. Until late into my twenties I remained an incorrigible daydreamer. In the afternoons, when my medical friends would attend their practicals, I would often stroll out of town and remain in the country until it was time to meet again over drinks. On these walks I would enter into a kind of trance, to which I cannot really give a name today, let alone describe it clearly. All I remember is that I allowed my mind to roam freely outside the confines of daily life into a sort of ethereal state of bliss, perhaps akin to nature worship—a state that quickly subsided again in the sober light of reality.

To this kind of reverie and the normal pleasures of student life, there was now joined an influence that was both fortifying and sublime—the love of music. At home, no one played a musical instrument and, alas, I have remained a musical illiterate throughout my life. I owed my introduction to the new pleasure to the sister of my friend Van Valkenburg, later the wife of Johan Wagenaar. In their large house at Winschoten, she would, whenever we asked her, regale us with Grieg and Brahms, sung in her warm and natural mezzo-soprano voice.

I graduated towards the end of October 1893, which entitled me to teach Dutch language, history and geography. True, we still had to do practical work, involving research into original documents, but to all intents and purposes, we had done with history. The academic regulations of 1877 were singularly liberal when it came to handing out teaching diplomas, but sticklers for detail when it came to post-graduate research. For in order to get your master's degree, you were forced to read Sanskrit, even if all you wanted was to be an archivist. I was by no means averse to this requirement, although I preferred comparative philology and Arabic to Sanskrit. In any case, Groningen was fortunate in counting among its teachers the great Sanskritist, J. S. Speyer, who later succeeded Kern at Leyden. In 1913, I spoke at his graveside and declared with no exaggeration that I never knew a better teacher. It did not take him long to inspire me, and within a year all of us had progressed far enough to read the *Jātaka* stories in class. These Buddhist texts were doubly welcome to me because I had become interested in Indian religion and Indian mysticism—*inter alia*, I greatly enjoyed pitting my wits against the Upanishads. As a major subject, we could choose between Dutch literature, Middle High German or Anglo-Saxon. I would much rather have taken Old Norse, but Sijmons, who would no doubt have been an excellent teacher, was not very keen, and moreover, left the subject to R. C. Boer, who had only just begun to teach at Groningen. Hence I chose Middle High German, in which my interest was rather lukewarm. For a while, I also attended Boer's Old Norse lectures which went far more deeply into the finer points of phonetics than I cared to follow. Dutch literature, alas, was taught by Van Helten whose heart and soul were in philology. He ridiculed Vondel, attacked poetic symbolism, and tried in vain to infuse us with his rapturous admiration of 'divine Staring'. I, for my part, failed to put as much effort as I should into working for my M.A.; I lacked a firm plan and was preoccupied with a host of emotional problems. Luckily I had the reputation of being an early riser and of working far harder than I did, so that I was not even asked to sit the preliminaries. I passed the finals in 1895, though not *cum laude*, for which failure my mother blamed the faculty rather than me. Still, I had finished my studies in less than the normal time, and it was decided that I should go abroad for a while, before submitting my thesis. My own wish was to study comparative philology, and that meant Leipzig and the 'Young Grammarians'. Accordingly I went there in October 1895 but, because the Kaiser was to open the new High Court, the term, that year, did not begin until November.

Studying in Leipzig was not an unqualified success. The man from whom I expected most and received least was Karl Brugmann, the leading Indo-Germanist of the day. I intended to read Slavonic languages under August Leskien, and Sanskrit as well as Old Irish under Ernst Windisch, the great expert in both. That, of course, was much more than I could swallow. Then, as chance would have it, I arrived in Leipzig on the very same day as H. G. Cannegieter, a classicist from Utrecht unknown to me at the time. We soon became friends, and because we met frequently and spoke Dutch, I missed a great chance of improving my German. Finally, I failed to realise that, in Germany, advanced students attended seminars rather than lectures. As a preparation for comparative linguistics, Sijmons had advised me to make a brief study of Lithuanian, which was in great vogue at the time on account of its archaic forms, and I had, in fact, made so much progress in it during the last summer in Groningen that, in Leskien's lectures, I was able to follow the Lithuanian reader far better than could the few Bulgarians and other Slav students in my class. Leskien had also just begun a course of lectures on Slavonic dialectology, to be held on Wednesday mornings at 10 a.m., but I heard that at precisely that day and hour the Gewandhaus Orchestra held its weekly rehearsals, at which you could get far better seats for one mark than you could for many times that price at the expensive gala performances on Thursday evenings. Leskien kindly excused me from Slavonic dialectology, and I became a faithful follower of the orchestra under Nikisch, who had succeeded Reinecke only a short time before. It goes without saying that I rarely missed the so-called Motets of the St. Thomas Choir on Saturday afternoons, while an entirely biassed and misplaced enthusiasm caused me to go to the Opera only for performances of Wagner.

I quickly realised that the formal grammatical approach in favour at Leipzig neither attracted nor really satisfied me. Windisch, under whom Cannegieter and I studied Sanskrit and Old Irish, was not nearly as good a teacher as Speyer, and Old Irish was, in any case, much too difficult for a mere subsidiary subject. I never mastered it, and regretfully dropped it once I left Leipzig. The vague magic of the Celtic world, originally fanned by my reading of Hersart Viscomte de la Villemarqué's romantic *Barzaz breiz*, the first collection of Breton folksong, has haunted me ever since.

As I have said, my head was full of dreams, fantasies and confused emotions. Yet I was not without diligence. Leskien, that serious and somewhat melancholic North German, always treated me with great kindness. When I told him that I would like to study Russian, not so much for philological as for literary reasons, he brought me an excellent textbook, and gave me a few hints on pronunciation.

I had taken rooms in the Kurprinzstrasse, up a great many stairs. My landlady, Frau Wunderlich, was always covered in face-powder and could perhaps have been a little tidier than she was. Following the silly Dutch custom of using the word *doctorandus*, i.e. candidate for a doctor's degree, as if it were of great importance, I had had the words *litt. docts.* printed on my visiting card, with the result that Frau Wunderlich insisted on calling me Herr Doktor, no matter how often I protested.

I used to lunch at 1 p.m. in the Panorama Restaurant on the Augustusplatz with Cannegieter and Callenbach (a student of chemistry who later went to America) and we shared a table with a number of English and American students of chemistry. One of them was F. G. Donnan who became a Member of the Royal Dutch Academy of Science in 1927; but when I met him again in Leyden, he could not recall our meeting thirty years before. Not surprisingly, I thought, for our acquaintance was very slight, and most of their student slang was lost on us, anyway.

At the beginning of 1896, I found a suitable subject for the thesis I meant to write after my return to Groningen at the end of the term. It was to be purely philological and I intended to call it *The expression of light and sound sensations in the Indo-Germanic languages.* I think I based it more on my knowledge of literature (since 1894 I had been studying English writers, particularly Shakespeare and his contemporaries, though much too cursorily) than on philological research. The only advice I was offered was to read one F. Bechtel, who did not, however, take me beyond the purely formal and etymological approach of the 'Young Grammarians'. In my search for help, I even succeeded in approaching the great Wundt himself, but he could only refer me to his own contributions, which had but little bearing on my subject.

The term finished in early March, and I returned home via Dresden and Berlin, with less direct profit to my intellectual progress than I might have hoped. I quickly threw myself into my thesis, making a systematic search in the dictionaries of the various languages I had studied for expressions of sensations of light and sound and setting them up side by side.

This is perhaps the place to refer to a subject which, though it was not directly connected with my studies, yet had considerable impact on them and was, moreover, of some considerable personal consequence, namely the art exhibitions I helped to organise in Groningen in 1895–97. In 1895, Willem Leuring, a medical student from Leyden, transferred to Groningen. He and his friends were enthusiastic supporters of the latest trends in art and, what was more, knew a number of modern artists personally. Thanks to Leuring, it became possible to arrange a series of exhibitions, and a group of older students played a leading

part in organising this. We never became a club or committee, but merely came together to discuss and arrange
exhibitions, only to disperse again when our particular job
was done. The chief members, apart from Leuring, who
later became a dermatologist at The Hague, retired early
in life and died in his country house at Mook, were Albert
Schilthuis, now Meester Albert Schilthuis of Santpoort-
Station, the late Dr. R. Rijkens, of Amsterdam, Jacob
Huizinga, my brother, now a retired physician at Hilver-
sum, C. T. van Valkenburg, now Dr. C. T. van Valkenburg,
the Amsterdam neurologist, and myself. The first exhibition,
in the autumn of 1895, was devoted to the lithographical
work of T. H. van Hoytema. On that occasion, as on that
of the Van Gogh exhibition which followed, I was away at
Leipzig. The Van Gogh exhibition must have been a great
event in Groningen. Most of his canvases were still in the
possession of Mev. Bonger van Gogh, who kept them un-
framed or partly framed in a loft in Bussum. But, as I have
said, I did not see the exhibition.

All of us were very anxious for a Toorop exhibition and,
thanks to Leuring, we succeeded in assembling a truly representative collection of that master's work. We had the use
of a large hall in the Museum of Antiquities, now the
Groningen Museum. As a background, we purchased a
great quantity of somewhat overpowering green satin and
covered the walls ourselves. The material ended up in my
possession and for many years I used it to cover the walls of
my room in 4, Dreef, Haarlem. Our collection of Toorops
included works from his Katwijk period, among them *Les
Rôdeurs*, *The Three Brides*, *The Garden of Sorrows*, *La nouvelle
Génération*, *Le Passeur d'eau* (after the poem by Verhaeren)
and many others. To crown it all, the master visited us in
person. It was June 1896, the weather was glorious, and he
stayed with us for a week or even longer. Toorop was then
36 years old, and looked like an Eastern prince. He had a
soft, bewitching voice and a somewhat halting manner when

it came to expounding his work. He would vaguely point to the line of dunes that so often formed his horizon and begin to mumble: 'the dunes . . . mystery.' In the long bright summer evenings, we would drive with him to the Appelbergen, that charming region of hillocks interspersed with smallholdings, long since levelled and forgotten.

As the winter of 1896 approached, we made fresh plans. In the autumn I had invited André Jolles to give an illustrated lecture, based on the collection of photographs of Italian art he had brought back from his travels. It is hard to imagine today how hard it was to get good reproductions of old masterpieces. For a number of reasons, the lecture had to be put off time and again, with the result that it came at the conclusion of our entire series of exhibitions, in the spring of 1897. In the interval, we arranged an exhibition of the work of Johan Thorn Prikker who enjoyed a great reputation but whose work was completely unknown to us, and of three other up and coming Belgian artists, namely Frantz Melchers, William Degouwe de Nuncques, and Karel Doudelet. Doudelet forgot the whole business and fobbed us off with a few prints at the last moment. The exhibition, which opened in December 1896, was to include a lecture by H. P. Bremmer as an added attraction. Bremmer was then only just beginning to make his name as an art critic, and all we knew of him was that he was a strange ascetic, a man who had just discovered how to live on twopence a day. His lecture was entitled: The origin and essence of modern art. I drew up a small notice, a shoddy piece of work if the truth be told, which we distributed far and wide. Of the lecture itself, all I can remember is that the speaker kept using the phrase 'by degrees' over and over again, and that he made light of the art of earlier centuries. I also remembered that we were all greatly taken with the work of Degouwe de Nuncques.

An unimportant detail has stuck in my mind. At the time, exhibitions and museums used to keep open on Sunday afternoons. On Sunday, 1st January 1897, the weather was balmy and at about 2 p.m. R. Rijkens, my brother and I were standing on the museum steps looking out for visitors to our exhibition. When not a soul turned up, we fetched an 1830 fireman's bugle and helmet from the museum, donned the helmet and blew the bugle as hard as we could. But all to no avail.

And so this episode in the artistic life of Groningen came to an end. Barely a month later, my brother left for South Africa, as doctor to the Nederlandsch South African Railway Company, where he was soon afterwards joined by his friend Rijkens. In May, I graduated and began to prepare for my teaching career in Haarlem. Our whole group dispersed as quietly as it had formed. Meanwhile, our last exhibition had brought us a final surprise in the form of public derision. It must have been in January of 1897, that the *Kroniek* published a cartoon with an ironical caption on the subject of provincial art. On it appeared Bremmer together with a few anonymous faces (our names were not known to the public). What particularly annoyed us was that the cartoonist had placed us all under the wing of Professor A. G. van Hamel, the well-known Romanist, who had nothing to do with us, and whom we did not even like. Only towards the end of his life, when I had the honour of being his colleague in Amsterdam, did I come to appreciate the true value of this man, who was far too often an easy butt of cheap jibes.

The problem I had to deal with before I could write my thesis could not be solved with what philological knowledge I possessed. In particular, I could not tell why different languages used the same set of words for different sense impressions—why it was that such concepts from the realm of touch and weight as heavy, light, sharp and blunt could also be applied to sounds, colours and light intensities. In fact, I have never been able to discover the answer. Thus when, after a few months of study, I drew up a plan of work and submitted it to Sijmons, he quite rightly rejected it as being completely inadequate and, just as rightly, advised me to desist from what was far too difficult a task for a mere beginner. I took this advice and accordingly went to Speyer in the hope that he might find me a subject from Ancient Indian literature that was neither too broad nor too forbidding. Speyer suggested a study of the *vidūshaka*, the court jester in Sanskrit drama. An excellent introduction to the subject had been available for a few years in the form of Sylvain Lévy's *Le théatre indien*; I also read a number of the most important Sanskrit plays, including the *Çakuntalā*, *Mrcchakatika* (The Little Clay Cart), *Vikramorvaçī*, the strange *Mudrārākshasa* (The Minister's Signet Ring) the *Nāgānanda* (Joy of Serpents) with its Buddhist leanings, and others. This led me to the Indian view of the comic as such, and hence to the subject of the eight emotions or flavours in poetics called *rasas* in Sanskrit, among which *hasya* is not really the same as our mirth, although it is generally identified with it. Thus it came about that the short thesis which helped me to become a Doctor of Letters in 1897 was, in fact, a contribution to Ancient Indian dramatic theory. In brief, the course of my studies had pushed history further and further into the background and it was only by pure chance that I ever returned to it.

I had never been particularly worried about a career, vaguely hoping that I would find something to my liking when the time came. But when nothing of the sort happened, I was forced to look round for a teaching post— something that I would far rather not have done. One evening in February, my father and I read in *Het Schoolblad* that applications for a history post at the Haarlem High School closed that very day. Now, for a number of reasons, I had been drawn to Haarlem for many years, and teaching history was much more to my taste than teaching Dutch. My father wired his old friend and fellow student, Mr. H.

D. Tjeenk Willink for permission to apply at this late stage, and his request was granted. The headmaster, Dr. H. Brongersma, with his white moustache, looked terribly old to me (in fact, he must have been in his late fifties) but received me most cordially. Later, I had to call personally on all the members of the city council. For that purpose, I ordered a special coach that looked particularly choice, though not nearly so distinguished as the clean-shaven coachman in his dark blue uniform. We had hardly started out when he asked me whether I would allow his fellow to ride with us, because, as he said, the horse was nervous. I was too diffident to argue, and in a jiffy a second resplendent figure in livery had joined the first on the box. And there was I, a poor applicant for a job, riding through the town like a great gentleman, while the two coachmen kept discussing the governors, most of whom were luckily out, in terms that struck me as rather unseemly in the circumstances. In any case, I came second in the list of candidates to Dr. J. Prinsen who, as Mr. Tjeenk Willink pointed out, had to be given precedence *propter annos et barbam*. That I nevertheless got the job was due to the good offices of P. J. Blok, who was to use his influence on my behalf on more than one occasion. Appointed in April, I took my doctorate in May, so that I could use the whole summer to prepare my lessons. And that was, in fact, sorely needed, for no one at University had breathed a word about the practical problems of teaching. Had I been able to consult someone on the matter, I should no doubt have been spared a great deal of bother and unnecessary work, but in my blindness I did not even look for advice and decided to find out for myself. I did, however, take elocution lessons for six weeks, and learned how to use my voice and breath. This ability has stood me in excellent stead throughout a teaching career that came to an untimely conclusion after 43 years—with the closure of the University of Leyden.

I was now a teacher of history, but not at all a sound

historian. Ever since my departure for Leipzig I had sorely neglected my historical studies. I considered myself a linguist and Sanskritist, and all I wanted to do was to progress in these directions. However, history had not entirely lost its old hold on me, and though I did not look upon it as solid intellectual fare, it continued to haunt me as it had in childhood.

Dr. Brongersma realised that I was rather young and inexperienced, and wisely entrusted me with no more than the two lower forms—altogether seven streams of boys between the ages of 12 and 14 together with a sprinkling of girls. For the first time in my life I was forced to form some sort of overall picture of general history. My concern was not so much with depth as with being able to tell an exciting story. I rarely bothered with textbooks; instead, I would dictate short passages for subsequent verbal discussion and elaboration, with the result that I was talking most of the time—an extremely tiring task. I devoted a great deal of time to Egypt and the Ancient East, and also to Greece and Rome. In the second form, I tackled the Middle Ages, in which I have always felt very much at home. Unfortunately, my complete lack of pedagogical training made itself felt almost daily. With a 'good' class I could let myself go, enjoying the living contact and rich humour that falls to the lot of every teacher, but with 'bad' classes, my authority fell far short of the desirable minimum, particularly late in the afternoon. I reserved my trump card for the last lesson before the end of term: a series of blackboard drawings that always proved a great success. A few years later, when I was given the higher classes as well, I was faced with a new challenge. To teach history in the atmosphere of a school in which science is considered far superior to the arts is no simple task at the best of times. To make things worse, Haarlem was a great sports centre at the time and all the boys cared about was football. Many of my pupils were completely deaf to any kind of historical information, and I had little pleasure in teaching them. Worst of all, I myself had neglected Dutch history, so that I was unable to inspire my charges with glowing accounts of our own past.

In the fourth form however, everything changed for the better. The pupils were older and more receptive to my disquisition—at far too great a length—on the French Revolution, based chiefly on Aulard's article in Lavisse and Rambaud's *Histoire de France*, with bits of Michelet and Carlyle to fill in the gaps. These were most enjoyable lessons, even though they fell far short of excellence.

In the fifth form, the approaching finals began to overshadow everything else; still, we would occasionally get down to discussions of socialism or of what little I knew about philosophy, with the keen participation of Meijer Ranneft, Kloeke, Corry Stoop and many others whose names I can still remember.

It is difficult to imagine today how free and easy life was under van Brongersma's tolerant leadership. In September 1899, I was granted two weeks' extra leave, immediately after the beginning of term, to attend the Congress of Orientalists in Rome. I went there with J. P. Vogel, who intended to go on to India, and with André Jolles with whom I had started a close friendship in the autumn of 1896. This friendship was to play a large part in my life for more than 35 years, until 9th October 1933 when it was abruptly cut short—and not by me. I could write a whole book on my relationship with Jolles, so full is my mind of him and—despite all that has happened—my heart as well.

In the years before 1900, I moved further and further away from historical research. Instead, I developed one of the ideas in my thesis and sent the result to Brugmann for publication in the *Indogermanische Forschungen*. His reply was unequivocal: You have much to learn before you can begin to teach others. He was right in many respects, though he might have been a little more polite about it. In 1890, I began a study of Old Indian medicine, my interest in the

subject having been aroused by my friend Van Valkenburg. I wrote for information to Julius Jolly[1] whom I had
met in Rome, read the two great Indian classics on the
subject, i.e. the *Caraka* and the *Suśruta*, and made a great
many notes and strange observations on the subject of the
doshas, the Indian equivalent of the Greek humours.

Apart from cycling with friends, my life during those
years was very much that of a hermit. I had recurring
phases of excited and slightly manic moods which dominated, and irregular fits of depressions lasting a few weeks
and manifesting themselves chiefly in greater taciturnity.
Though I found this phase oppressive, I never completely
succumbed to it and carried on with my normal life.

All this changed radically in March 1902, when I married
Mary Vincentia Schorer, of whom, alas, death robbed me
in July 1914. In the happy interval, during which five
children were born to us, I also delighted in the music of
Bach and Schubert and sometimes of Mozart, Beethoven
and Brahms, and in all the paintings on which I could
feast my eyes. Academic studies, too, occupied me greatly.
From Indian medicine I had passed on to the subject of
theology. My brief *On the bird Charadrius*[2] was inspired by an
illustration in Émile Mâle's *Art religieux du treizième siècle
en France*; I found even greater satisfaction in making a
detailed study of the snares of Varuna, the Vedic god. To
that end I threw myself into the *Atharva Veda* and various
Brāhmanas and wrote a German draft for an article, which
must still be among my papers. In the spring of 1903, I
became unsalaried lecturer in the history of Ancient Indian
Culture and Literature at the University of Amsterdam.
Though I fully appreciated how scant was my knowledge
of these two vast fields, I had the strong feeling that I

[1]Author of Part III of *Grundriss der altindischen Philologie und Altertums-
kunde* (Outline of Ancient Indian Philology and Archaeology).
[2]Proceedings of the Royal Dutch Academy of Science. Literary Section,
1904.

nevertheless had something important to offer to my students. Still, it was not until October 1903 that I gave my first public lecture—on the study and true appreciation of Buddhism.[1] The words 'true appreciation' were meant as a reprimand to the then fairly popular theosophical ideas of Mme. Blavatsky, that prophetess of hierophantic dimensions, as F. W. Thomas so scornfully called her.

During my first year as lecturer, i.e. in 1903–1904, I gave a series of regular lectures on the Vedic-Brahman religion, and my class, which met on Thursdays from 4 to 5 p.m. in the Oudemanshuispoort, consisted originally of some 60 students, but naturally dropped off after a while. I took some of my best ideas from Paul Deussen's *General History of Philosophy*, even though I myself was critical of many of his opinions. During the next academic year, i.e. in 1904–1905, I lectured on Buddhism, this time on Wednesday evenings, to a small but select and extremely faithful audience, including Mevrouw C. Boxman-Winkler, Mevrouw A. Veth-Dirks, Mej. M. Strumphler (now Mev. J. P. Vogel), Mr. R. de Block and a young student by the name of van Brakel.

However, my heart and soul were not altogether in the East. Deep down my interest had gradually been shifting from philology and Oriental studies towards history in the narrower sense of the word, and I fully realised this. Even while I had still been deeply immersed in the *Atharva Veda* and in Buddhist doctrines, I had felt something of a stranger in the world of the East. For instance, I was never filled with a desire to visit the rivers Indus and Ganges, unlike my friend Vogel who did so with great enthusiasm. It became increasingly clear to me that the treasures I sought were closer at hand—in the medieval West, which had never completely relinquished its hold on me. However, that hold had not yet begun to engage my academic interest; rather was it in the nature of a vague longing, a longing fed mainly

[1] Tjeenk Willink, Haarlem, 1903.

on artistic notions and greatly re-inforced by the Bruges exhibition of Old Dutch paintings in the summer of 1902.

Moreover, my intellectual transition went hand in hand with purely practical considerations. Though I liked the work, I found the prospect of remaining a teacher for years to come extremely oppressive, and I began to look around for an escape. When Kern jnr. gave up his post as foreign editor to the *Nieuwe Rotterdamsche Courant* to take up a lectureship in English at Groningen, the job was offered to me. That must have been in 1900. At the time, I still looked upon myself as an orientalist and linguist, and since journalism held no attractions for me at all, I declined the offer. Sometime during the next few years, I applied for the post of Keeper of Manuscripts at the Royal Library, although I knew that Brugman was among the candidates. Subsequently I began to feel so keen an attachment to Zeeland, Middelburg, and above all to our beloved Toornvliet that I decided to work for the Zeeland Public Record Office, and I should have been given a job there had I not withdrawn my application in the nick of time. I even called on Professor A. E. J. Holwerda, with a view to obtaining a post in the National Museum of Antiquities, but he quickly convinced me of my utter unsuitability by discoursing at length on a Greek shard.

During my search for a new job, I invariably consulted Professor P. J. Blok, who had taught me history during my first years at University, who had always shown me the greatest kindness and consideration even when I had deserted history, and who was most sympathetic when I expressed the wish to return to the fold. Quite naturally he expected some proof of my historical prowess, and he himself suggested that I test my mettle on the early history of Haarlem. From the moment I entered the new field, consulting the Public Records of Holland and Zeeland and what few other sources were available, I was completely carried away. Though the relevant documents were few and far between, they yielded many new glimpses into the life of our oldest towns. Thus, while I could not expect to discover anything new, save for a few unimportant details, I also knew that my endeavours would not be entirely in vain. Luckily I was allowed to devote most of my day to the new task, for throughout the academic year of 1904–1905, Dr. Brongersma was kind enough to let me work half-time for half-pay, which meant giving no more than 10 lessons a week, and to someone like me, who has always been used to a few hours of intensive work during the day and relaxation at night, this proved a very great boon, indeed. At the beginning of 1905, I published the first, introductory, part of my study, entitled *The Origins of Haarlem* in the *Contributions to Dutch History and Archaeology* (Third series, Part IV). At about the same time, I was lucky enough to make a discovery that was to lend far greater weight to the second part: I discovered the sources of Haarlem municipal law, and hence of all the municipal laws derived from it via Leuven and 's Hertogenbosch. When the conclusion of my study finally appeared in the *Contributions* (Third series, Part V) I had somersaulted along the road to history into a University chair.

Despite my flirtations with the Orient and linguistics, Blok had always maintained that a chair of history was where I truly belonged. When P. L. Muller died in 1904, the professorship of general history at Leyden was given to Bussemaker, whose own chair at Groningen thus fell vacant. With my single and not yet fully published contribution to history I was anything but a qualified candidate. Those who knew my work thought of me primarily as a Sanskritist. Yet despite it all, Blok was determined to get me the appointment, and in this he succeeded despite opposition by the faculty and most of the curators. My appointment on 1 August 1905 must have been one of the last documents to bear Kuyper's signature.

My path to history was thus completed. What else I have to say is chiefly concerned with Blok. Of his many friends and colleagues, most have passed away—now that Kernkamp is dead, J. W. Muller, W. A. F. Bannier, Colenbrander, Martin and myself are about the only ones left. From 1915–1925, I was Blok's closest colleague at Leyden. He was a man who, though exceedingly friendly and generous, nevertheless fell out with a great many of his colleagues. Yet he suffered in silence and tried to forget his differences as soon as possible. My own understanding with him remained quite intact until 1925, when we disagreed so violently on the question of his successor that we avoided each other for some time. However, our estrangement did not last for long.

Blok died in late October 1929. My conscience is often plagued by the feeling that I did not make him fair return for his untiring and unstinting support and warm affection —that the gratitude I showed him was not nearly deep enough.

I can no longer remember when precisely I hit upon the idea that historical understanding is like a vision, or rather like an evocation of images, a term I shall not attempt to define here. What I do know is that I held this view for quite some time before I decided to commit it to paper or to elaborate it. My mind was not generally given to the turning over of theoretical problems. Direct access to the colourful details of the past, no matter how acquired, was enough for me. It was only when I was faced with the task of preparing an inaugural academic address that I returned to the problem of historical understanding. Dutch historians had previously paid little heed to theoretical and methodological questions. The long controversy, in which the hollow schematism and fragile concepts of Karl Lamprecht were attacked by Windelband, Rickert, Simmel, Eduard Meyer and others, had gone almost unnoticed in this country. And yet this attack meant nothing less than freeing the arts from the shackles of scientific determinism, a restoration of the humanities to their proper rôle and worth, and thus a rejection of naïve historical realism. With the advice and help of Heymans, I quickly came to grips with the subject and I was surprised by the novel vistas that were opening up to me. The inaugural lecture, with which I accepted my appointment at Groningen on 4 November 1905[1], turned out to be a rather long and difficult affair that bored most of my audience prodigiously.

It was not my purpose then or later, to probe too deeply into epistemological problems, and whenever I did deal with them[2] it was always more or less incidentally. I would tell my students, many of whom were keenly interested in these questions that, while they ought to learn something about them, they should not become too deeply involved, lest they were deflected from the historian's true path.

At Groningen, I spent my first few years preparing lectures, and hence published very little. Bussemaker, my predecessor, had remained partly true to the system also used by Blok, that of covering all the main periods of history in succession. I quickly broke with that tradition, consciously implementing a lesson I had learned from Dr. J. H. Gunning, the great pedagogue: all academic teaching, to be worthy of that name, must pay scrupulous attention to detail. And, in fact, the cursory has a deadening effect on the mature or maturing mind. I accordingly made full use of the enviable freedom enjoyed by Dutch teachers in the choice and treatment of their material: for each academic year, I picked special subjects of limited scope, which I, nevertheless, failed to 'do' completely—but then what historical subject can ever be 'done'? I also took care not to return to the same subject except after long intervals. Work-

[1] *The aesthetic element in historical thought*, Tjeenk Willink, Haarlem, 1905. English version in this collection; see p. 219 ff.
[2] *Socio-historical Research*, 1929. *History as science*, 1937.

ing as I did in Groningen, I concentrated chiefly on the regional history of our North, in which field I also published a number of studies.

I never became a full-blooded historical research worker. There are no weighty and critical source books in my name, for my *Sources of Haarlem Law*[1] does not deserve that title. I began this last study at the request of Meester Samuel Muller, not without reservations, for I knew that I should discover nothing new or unknown—few of the statute books have been preserved. Nevertheless I worked at this task with great enjoyment. It was one of the few occasions on which my research took me to the archives, and work with handwritten material has an attraction that can become an obsession, almost incomprehensible to the uninitiated. Precisely in the apparently dull and dry work of examining ancient documents, you very often have the overpowering feeling that you are in contact with the living past—hence the craving to catch further glimpses of it.

Two of my books were based entirely on unpublished and untapped sources. Both are among my least known publications, though I myself consider them part of my best work. One is a history of Groningen University during the third century of its existence, i.e. in 1814–1914, and appeared in the memorial volume, *Academia Groningana MDCXV–MCMXIV*, published on the occasion of the centenary celebrations—probably the last truly international gathering before the war which broke out a month afterwards. Though I began the work without great enthusiasm, it quickly absorbed my full attention. Apart from the odd assortment of Groningana that the University Library had to offer, my main sources were the Curator's records. My friend, J. A. Feith, the State Archivist, allowed me to consult the neat stacks in the vaults of the Public Record Office, a privilege granted to few. Finally, I drew on living sources, on the

[1]Published by the Association for the Publication of the Sources of Old Dutch Law, 1911.

memories of old students, some of whom had entered the University as early as 1845, among them A. F. de Savornin Lohman, Professor J. Oppenheim, Governor Tonckens and many others. But when the festive volume finally appeared, I had long lost all my own festive feelings—the wasting disease that, before the month was out, was to rob me of my young wife, was nearing its end.

The other original study was my *Life and Work of Jan Veth*. More than twenty-five years of solid friendship had bound me to this man, and his house in Bussum had been my second home, though I never did succeed in getting to Parklaan 33, through the labyrinthine Het Gooi without losing my way. Our interests complemented each other remarkably well, and his conversation was always a delight and great benefit. When he died in June 1925, I felt that writing his obituary for the Royal Academy of Science, to belong to which was one of Veth's last great satisfactions, was not enough. The very fact that, after his election, Veth should have been scorned by those who, still steeped in the ideas of the *Tachtigers*, set the aesthetic tone in our country, endeared him to me all the more. Mevrouw Veth placed his entire correspondence, carefully arranged in chronological order, at my disposal, and Mevrouw Moes-Veth, too, gave me every possible assistance. I seldom worked so hard as I did in the winter of 1926. In July, 1927, I read the manuscript to André Jolles who praised it greatly. Others concurred when it was eventually published, but the public at large took little notice of it.

Though the subject of this essay is 'My Path to History', I may perhaps be allowed to say a few words on the origins of what is probably the best-known of all my writings: *The Waning of the Middle Ages*. I still remember how the idea suddenly hit me out of the blue, though I can no longer fix the precise date. It must have been between 1906 and 1909, probably in 1907. In the afternoons, when my wife was fully occupied with our small children, I used to stroll out of the town into the spacious Groningen countryside. On one such walk along the Damsterdiep—I think it was on a Sunday—the thought suddenly struck me that the late Middle Ages were not so much a prelude to the future as an epoch of fading and decay. This thought, if indeed it may be called a thought, hinged chiefly on the art of the brothers Van Eyck and their contemporaries, in all of whom I had been keenly interested for some time. It was just becoming fashionable, following Courajod, Fierens-Gevaert and Karl Voll, to speak of the Old Dutch Masters as initiators of a Northern Renaissance.

My ideas were radically different, but it was some years before I began to develop them more fully. In the autumn of 1909, W. Martin and myself were invited to Noordwijk to celebrate Blok's twenty-fifth teaching anniversary. Blok told me that it was high time I published something of real importance, and it must have been then that I mentioned my vague ideas on the Middle Ages to him and decided to work on them. During that year I delivered a series of lectures on Burgundian Culture. My own views of the subject kept changing, and I thought it best to read as many Burgundian and French historians of the period as I could, and Chastellain in particular. I still remember poring over 25 parts of Froissart in the Kervijn de Lettenhove and Luce and Reynaud editions in my Toornvliet attic during the warm summer of 1911. Then I had to forsake these labours for the history of Groningen University, and it was 1915 before I could resume them under very different circumstances at Leyden. For the rest, the book must speak for itself.

Ever since history became my life's work, my relationship to this, the strictest of all muses, has been rather flighty—which is peculiar in view of the fact that my personal inclinations and physical constitution are sedentary, to say the least. I have already pointed out that I never took to historical research—that I never specialised in a particular field, period, country or subject. Hence it was that I never kept subjects in reserve—either for myself or for my students. Instead, I kept tumbling from one topic to the next, without plan or forethought. Every time a student asked me to suggest a subject for his thesis, I would become highly embarrassed and remember the answer of Wildeboer, one of my colleagues at Groningen, to all such requests: 'You might as well ask me to find you a wife'. Still, find them the subjects I did—some yielding the desired degree, others, alas, not. The fact that only a relatively small number of students graduated under me is, by the way, not entirely my fault: in our country arts graduates find it exceedingly difficult to obtain their doctor's degree at an early stage in their academic life.

The scope of my bibliography is not likely to be awe-inspiring. I have never been a fountain of knowledge, nor have I laboured prodigiously in the cause of learning. I have always proceeded in brief spurts, usually in the morning, though quickly and systematically. Apart from the work in hand, I read very little, much too little, as I have been telling myself ever since I realized what disgraceful gaps there were in my literary education. I have always enjoyed my enviable freedom. Luckily I was spared the honour of sitting on examination boards, and I was always careful not to be landed with the job of secretary, let alone that of treasurer, to any committee on which I served. If I have any merit which may help to explain the success of my work, then it is the twin gift of happy invention and imagination. It is not false modesty when I say that, though I have been known as an early riser since childhood, I never rose quite as early as people believed.

Many of my writings have been based on lecture notes or on ideas that occurred to me in connection with them. Thus the thought of writing about Erasmus—of whom I knew next to nothing before 1920—sprang directly from a lecture on the problem of the Renaissance. Soon afterwards, Edward Bok urged me to make Erasmus the subject of a contribution to his series *Great Hollanders*, and my work eventually appeared directly after Barnouw's excellent *Vondel*. The speed with which I tackled the subject and selected information from the ten volumes of J. le Clerc's standard edition is something I cannot recommend to any serious historian. The best thing about this whole study was the close friendship it brought me with P. S. and H. M. Allen.

Regarding my biography of Erasmus, many people have expressed the view that here was a man after my own heart. As far as I can tell, nothing could be farther from the truth for, much though I admire Erasmus, he inspires me with little sympathy and, as soon as the work was done, I did my best to put him out of my mind. I remember a conversation in January 1932 with a German colleague who contended that *Erasmus* was much more my line of country than the *Waning of the Middle Ages* with which, he claimed, I must have struggled manfully. I thought about the matter for a moment and then I had to smile. In fact, my historical and literary studies never struck me as partaking of the nature of struggle in any way, nor any of my work as a great challenge. Indeed, the whole idea of having to overcome enormous obstacles was as alien to me as that of having to compete in a race, as alien as the spirit of competition whose importance in cultural life I myself have emphasised in my *Homo ludens*.

No, the work I have done for better or for worse and which must soon come to an end, struck me rather as a brief sojourn in a garden, touching a flower here and there and then moving on. I barely know the meaning of excessive mental exertion. I have spoken of my complete lack of talent for, and even considerable indifference to, natural science, mathematics, technology and philosophy. This failing undoubtedly explains some of the shortcomings of my historical work as well. I have never felt at home in the closed circle of philologists and historians, in which rules are rigidly obeyed and regulations slavishly observed. To use the language of our old Windesheim monks, I was endowed with a small spark that I endeavoured to fan into brighter flame from time to time.

De Steeg, 27 December 1943

INDEX

Index